Jane Kroll

D0903995

ENGLISH SENTENCES

PAUL ROBERTS

Professor of English
San Jose State College
San Jose, California

HARCOURT, BRACE & WORLD, INC.

New York

Chicago

Atlanta

Dallas

Burlingame

© 1962, by Harcourt, Brace & World, Inc.

All rights reserved. No part of this book may be reproduced in any form, by mimeograph or any other means, without permission in writing from the publisher.

PRINTED IN THE UNITED STATES OF AMERICA

CONTENTS

vi

PREFACE

That which is new in this book derives mainly from the work of Professor Noam Chomsky and his collaborators at the Massachusetts Institute of Technology. Chomsky's transformational, or generative, grammar is certainly one of the major developments in linguistics in recent years. It is a development particularly interesting for students and teachers of English, since it goes a long way toward reconciling highly divergent views about English teaching — the linguistic and the traditional. Without losing sight of the valuable advances in linguistic science, Chomsky has been able to rehabilitate, and provide a theory for, many features of earlier language teaching. Though *English Sentences* contradicts very little of what is said in such books as my *Patterns of English*, it will, I believe, seem much more familiar than that book did to teachers and students used to more conventional books.

English Sentences is meant for, and addressed to, high school students. If other people find it useful and interesting, I shall be delighted, but it was not written for other people. In particular, it should not be taken as establishing the details of transformational grammar. I am most grateful to Professor Chomsky and also to Professor Robert Stockwell of the University of California for helping me understand transformation theory. But neither has read the manuscript, and neither has any responsibility for the contents. I have tried to be faithful to the material as I understand it, but I have no doubt made many mistakes, and I have made no attempt at a rigorous treatment.

I want to express my gratitude to Professor Archibald Hill of the University of Texas, who introduced me to transformational grammar by inviting me to the Texas Conference on Syntax in 1959 at Austin. I am grateful, as always, to Professor Donald H. Alden of San Jose State College, who read the manuscript and taught the material and made useful suggestions, to Professor Frederick B. Agard of Cornell University for valuable conversations on the subject, and to the members of the 1960 Seminar in Linguistics at San Jose State College for working out many of the details.

My greatest debt is to my wife for untiring aid and interest and encouragement and comfort.

PAUL ROBERTS

Rome, 1961

1

WHAT IS GRAMMAR?

There are many ways of thinking about grammar, many senses in which the term is used. One way is this: grammar is something that produces the sentences of a language. This is what we shall mean by *grammar* in this book.

We may then ask, what do we mean by "something"? What sort of something? Well, the grammar might be a book or a series of books containing the rules for making the sentences of a language. An English grammar would be a set of rules for making English sentences. Or we might think of the "something" as a machine with the rules built into it. It is possible to conceive — it might even be possible to build — an electronic machine that, by following its rules, would come out with an English sentence every time it went through its operation and that never would produce a non-English sentence.

But there is another, and a more interesting, meaning that we can give to the "something" that produces English sentences. We can mean simply a speaker of English. If you speak English natively, you have built into you the rules of English grammar. In a sense, you *are* an English grammar. You possess, as an essential part of your being, a very complicated apparatus which enables you to produce infinitely many sentences, all English ones, including many that you have never specifically learned. Furthermore, by applying your rules, you can easily tell whether a sentence that you hear is a grammatical English sentence or not.

This may strike you as absurd. You may protest that you have never studied English grammar or that you have studied it without profit or understanding — in any case, that you know nothing about it. But it is perfectly easy to demonstrate that, if you speak

English natively, you know virtually all about Eng'ish grammar, all its essential rules. For example, which of the following are grammatical English sentences and which are not?

1. Henry bought his mother some flowers.
2. Henry some flowers bought his mother.
3. He isn't very nice to me.
4. He are not to me very nice.
5. Those things don't trouble me at all.
6. Those thing to me are not of a troublesome.

Obviously, 1, 3, and 5 are grammatical English sentences, and 2, 4, and 6 are not.

Now, how do you know? You don't know because somebody told you. Nobody ever gave you the words "Those thing to me are not of a troublesome" and informed you that it was not an English sentence. You don't know by intuition. If it were intuition, it would presumably work just as well on Chinese as on English, but in fact whatever is working for you works only on English.

GRAMMATICALITY

What is working is your grammar. You reject sentences 2, 4, and 6 because they do not conform to the rules of English grammar as you know them. You know that *those* modifies plural nouns, not singulars, that an adjective like *troublesome* does not occur after *of a*, that such a prepositional phrase as *to me* comes more commonly after the verb than before it. What you may not know is how to talk about such matters. You may have a foggy understanding or none at all of such terms as *plural, adjective, prepositional phrase,* so that if someone asked you why sentence 6 is ungrammatical, you might not be able to explain very well. Nevertheless, you readily reject 6 as wrong, because it doesn't accord with the rules of English. You know the rules, whether you can describe them or not. Knowing them is what makes you a speaker of English. Now what about this sentence?

Horses that think for themselves smoke filter cigarettes.

Is that grammatical or not? Of course it is grammatical. It is also nonsensical: horses don't smoke cigarettes, filter-tipped or otherwise, and don't think for themselves either. But it is grammatical, conforming perfectly to the rules of English sentence structure. We see then that by *grammatical* we don't necessarily mean "meaningful" or "true." We can talk nonsense grammatically or lie grammatically and often do. Though the following are all nonsensical or untrue, they are all grammatical English sentences:

Dick Tracy is the President of the United States.
All Boy Scouts can swim six miles under water.
Nobody seems to have chorkled these crambons.
The earth is oblong.

Yet the following, though much more sensible, are ungrammatical:

Dick Tracy very brave character of comic strip.
Every Boy Scouts easy hike six miles.
Nobody seem this plants to have watering.
The earth almost round is.

THE STUDY OF GRAMMAR

We have said that all of us who speak English know English grammar, and you may ask, if that is so, why you are required to study it. What we are after now, of course, is not the knowledge that permits us to distinguish grammatical sentences from ungrammatical ones, but rather a conscious understanding of the system and the way it operates. Such an understanding has certain practical uses in the study of writing and other forms of communication. It permits, for example, more efficient discussion of punctuation and of the structures of written English. The sentences that we write are often more intricate and more bound by convention than those we speak. We have a greater chance in writing than in speech of losing our way and blundering, and the blunders of writing are preserved, whereas those of speech disappear on the echo.

To be sure, learning to describe the grammatical system is not the same thing as learning to write. Some people who have never studied grammar write very well, and some who have studied grammar intensively write poorly. We learn to write largely by reading and writing, by imitation and practice. Nevertheless, a conscious understanding of the grammatical system can be a help in the process of learning to write and for some students a considerable help.

However, the author of this book would not wish to recommend the study of grammar on practical grounds alone. Grammar is the heart of language, and language is the foremost of the features that make human beings human. We said earlier that every speaker of English *is* an English grammar. When you study English grammar, you inquire most intimately into yourself and the way you work. You will surely get most out of the study if you undertake it objectively, with a simple wish to understand what it is like, accepting any practical application as a kind of bonus.

We are sometimes told that grammar is dull but useful, a disagreeable medicine we take to cure our writing ills. It is better to look at it differently: properly approached, grammar is an absorbingly interesting study, and it may even do us some practical good.

EXERCISE 1

Some of the following sentences are grammatical and some are not. Number from 1 to 30 on a separate sheet of paper and write a **G** beside the number of a grammatical sentence and a **U** beside the number of an ungrammatical one. Some of the grammatical sentences are nonsense.

These are all reasonably clear-cut cases, and you shouldn't have much trouble in sorting them out. If the sentence is ungrammatical, you might consider to what extent you can explain what is wrong with it. Your teacher may wish to ask you to explain in order to determine your present knowledge of grammatical terms and categories.

1. There wasn't anybody in the room.
2. These young child to whom I spoke answered me insolently.
3. Nobody in his right mind are willing to do such a thing.
4. Frowning slightly, he went on stoking the furnace.
5. Margery seemed paying no attention to us.
6. She refused indignantly accompany him to the Junior Ball.
7. It was a very good example of what can happen when someone pours glue into a radiator.
8. He had bringed me a large glass of milk.
9. The next speaker, a writer of Western stories, humorously explain to us some of the problems he have to solve.
10. We had never in our lives known a Siamese cat that could speak more than three languages.
11. My Aunt Edith a very talented performer on the banjo.
12. Knowing perfectly well that Bradbury would never emerge from the swamp.
13. It was interesting to observe how quickly the children responded to humane treatment.
14. I have not understand exactly what you meant by that remark.
15. Square tennis rackets do not drink milk.
16. The machine we called David was an electronic device that could produce all the grammatical sentences of English and only those.
17. Never John speaks the simple truth.
18. John never speaks the simple truth.
19. John speaks the simple truth never.
20. Never does John speak the simple truth.
21. Only television producers have wings.
22. To whom you gave the map that shows where the money is buried?
23. Walks he to school every morning?
24. You should try to remember that even politicians have feelings.
25. It didn't seem to me to occur these events.
26. He picked up it and carefully put it away.
27. It just happens that he does be the best friend a boy ever had.
28. Fortune often smiles on those most indifferent to her.
29. Cleaning out his desk drawer, Lloyd came upon an old snowball that he had put there the previous winter.
30. We elected president of the senior class Al.

2 DIALECT DIFFERENCES

The sentences examined in Chapter 1 were clear examples of grammaticality or ungrammaticality. Virtually any speaker of English would call the grammatical ones grammatical and the others ungrammatical. But the line between grammaticality and ungrammaticality does not always appear so sharp. There are several borderline areas where we will not all agree which is which. What, for example, shall we say about the following sentences? Are they grammatical or are they not?

> Henry brung his mother some flowers.
> Seems like he don't like nobody.
> Me and Eddie grabbed him and throwed him out.
> I like mine better than yourn.

Certainly there is some sense in which these are grammatical. They are produced by native speakers of English according to a built-in set of rules of English grammar. They are certainly more grammatical than the non-English sentences of Chapter 1. Compare these:

1. Henry brought his mother some flowers.
2. Henry brung his mother some flowers.
3. Henry some flowers his mother brought.

Sentence 3 is wrong absolutely. No native speaker of English, no matter how uneducated, would ever say it. Sentence 3 would be used only by a foreigner in the process of learning English and not yet acquainted with some of its essential rules.

But what we have said about 3 does not apply to 2. Both 1 and 2 are produced normally by speakers of English, according to their systems. They are not non-English, as 3 is. Yet there is a difference.

Most of us, including many of us who customarily say 2, have a feeling that 1 is more correct, more grammatical. But we must ask, if 2 is not non-English, in what sense it is ungrammatical. If 1 is better, why is it better?

First, we must perceive that it is not a question of clarity. Sentences 1 and 2 are about equally clear and both are clearer than 3. If someone says either 1 or 2, you grasp the meaning in about the same amount of time. Second, there is nothing in the *sound* of the words *brought* and *brung* that makes one better than the other. There is no rule in English that all verbs, or all verbs of a certain class should end in *–ought* rather than *–ung* or that they should never end in *–ung*. For if there were, we should have to reject not only "He brung her a book" but also "She clung to her book." In short, there is nothing in the nature of language which leads us to prefer sentence 1 to sentence 2. The two sentences differ simply in that they represent separate *dialects*, or varieties, of English.

GRAMMAR 1 AND GRAMMAR 2

If we prefer sentence 1 to sentence 2, we do so simply because in some sense we prefer the people who say sentence 1 to those who say sentence 2. We associate sentence 1 with educated people and sentence 2 with uneducated people. Hearing sentence 2, we infer that the speaker is uneducated. Hearing sentence 1, we do not make this inference. But mark this well: educated people do not say sentence 1, "Henry brought his mother some flowers," because it is better than 2. Educated people say it, *and that makes it better*. That's all there is to it.

So we see that the sentences we listed at the beginning of this chapter are all, in a certain important sense, grammatical. They are all part of the grammar of a great many native speakers of English. But these people are for the most part not well educated and therefore not very influential. The grammar of the educated and influential differs in certain important respects, particularly in verb forms and pronouns, and the position of its users gives this

English grammar a prestige that the other one does not have.

Any speaker of Grammar 2 must decide whether he should not expend the effort necessary to become automatic in the forms of Grammar 1. People planning to enter the business or professional world almost certainly must master Grammar 1. If they do not, they are headed for certain embarrassment and probable failure.

SOCIAL IMPLICATIONS

We have said, and we repeat, that Grammar 2, so far as language characteristics go, is every bit as good as Grammar 1 — capable of just as much clarity, complexity, power, and tenderness. Nevertheless, it is true that speakers of Grammar 1 commonly have a certain measure of scorn and contempt for speakers of Grammar 2. This is not sensible, let alone charitable, but it is the way it goes. Even the high school student who does not plan to go to college cannot afford to assume that this is an unimportant matter. One who cannot manage the language forms of the educated will find closed to him many doors that he may want open.

Have we been perfectly clear? There is nothing shameful or illegal about saying "Henry brung his mother some flowers." Don't go home and sit about despising your parents if they happen to say it. The best speaker of English is not necessarily a person who uses Grammar 1 only and always. Even better is he who can use them both, and all the shades between, varying his speech according to the occasion and the company he is with. Not everyone can do this. The child who learns Grammar 1 in the home as his first language would rarely find it useful to learn Grammar 2; his use of it, indeed, would probably seem artificial and be resented. But the child whose first language is Grammar 2 is in a different position. He might well look on his acquisition of Grammar 1 as an addition rather than a replacement. Acquiring it, he becomes in a sense bilingual.

We must make one other, somewhat more subtle, point before leaving this topic. What about the following sentences? Grammatical or not? Grammar 1 or Grammar 2?

1. Who were you talking to?
2. He wanted to really understand it.
3. I will see him tonight.

Sentence 1 ends with a preposition and uses *who* instead of *whom*; 2 splits an infinitive; 3 uses *will* instead of *shall* after *I*. Some books on usage warn against such sentences, recommending instead:

1. To whom were you talking?
2. He wanted really to understand it.
3. I shall see him tonight.

But it must be pointed out that the original sentences are not only (obviously) English, but also are quite consistent with the system of Grammar 1 as well as with that of Grammar 2. They are normal forms for educated speakers as well as for uneducated. Certainly "Who were you talking to?" is not on all fours with "Henry brung his mother some books." If you say the latter, people will think you uneducated, but nobody would make such an inference if you say, "Who were you talking to?" This could hardly even be called colloquial, if we mean by that something less than top drawer.

It is no doubt true that certain styles of writing — perhaps certain occasions of speech as well — would call for the second set of sentences rather than the first. One may achieve a certain formality by using the second set; he may also sound a bit standoffish and forbidding. But neither one is ungrammatical except in the most trivial sense. Certainly there are other, far more serious, matters to worry about first.

EXERCISE 2

The sentences that follow fall into three groups, like the set of examples on page 6:

1. Henry brought his mother some flowers.
2. Henry brung his mother some flowers.
3. Henry his mother some flowers brought.

Number from 1 to 30. Write 1 beside the numbers of those sentences that are grammatical for all speakers of English or for educated speakers; write 2 for those that are grammatical for uneducated speakers only; write 3 for those that are ungrammatical for all speakers of English. All cases are fairly clear-cut. You should have no trouble distinguishing the 3's. If you have trouble distinguishing 1's from 2's, use your dictionary.

1. No one had seen him for ten months.
2. Nobody seen him yesterday.
3. Why you not tell me you were busy?
4. Apparently someone had been snooping around while we were gone.
5. This much is known, that no one at headquarters ordered the attack.
6. It just ain't none of his business.
7. We customarily at eight have dinner.
8. Several valuable papers had from his hotel room been stolen.
9. He should have tended to it hisself.
10. Shall we go into the garden, Maud?
11. Anyone wishing to sell merchandise or services from door to door must apply at city hall for a license.
12. There was simply no one else to whom we could turn.
13. According to the papers, a truck run him down.
14. Chauncey didn't get very good grades in English, but he always done real good in math.
15. He was somewhat uncertain about to use the verbs correctly.
16. Feeling he was in the right, Elvin refused apologizing.
17. He slung the pack over his shoulder and set out for Paris.
18. It seemed to me that he spoke pretty sensible.
19. She won't take the warning seriously, because she don't believe in ghosts.
20. We were surprised to see him, because we thought he had fell in somewhere.
21. Your father speak to me like he no like me.
22. It is sometimes very hard understand foreign policy.
23. I can't quite figure out why you and him quarrel all the time.
24. He was always accompanied by several gentlemen who wore slouch hats and kept their hands in their overcoat pockets.

25. Sally had her heart set on going to the party, but she didn't get an invite.
26. All the mothers whose children had received grades lower than B resigned from the PTA.
27. He stamped his feet and blowed on his hands to try and keep warm.
28. Stanley seems very happily lately.
29. All we ask is that everyone do his best at all times.
30. He just come into the living room and laid down on the sofa and didn't say nothing.

3 WORD CLASSES

Suppose we write each word of the English language on a separate slip of paper and put all the slips into a large bin. Then suppose we try to make five-word sentences by having someone reach into the bin and draw out a word and write it down, then another word and another and so on. Most of the sentences made this way will of course be ungrammatical. We might, for example, draw such combinations as these:

X	X	X	X	X
House	a	of	go	plenty.
To	sunny	dream	picnic	around.
Reduce	tiger	from	absent	eat.

Once in a great while, mathematical chance will produce a grammatical English sentence:

The	man	shot	a	wolf.

Now suppose we take all the verbs of English (*go, dream, reduce, shot, sent, eat,* etc.) out of the big bin and put them in a separate bin, using only their past tense forms. Now we draw words for slots

1, 2, 4, and 5 from the big bin, but we draw words for slot 3 from the verb bin only. Our chances of drawing an English sentence, though still very small, are now greatly improved, because we will always have a verb in the third slot, a position where a verb is likely to be in an English five-word sentence:

X	X	V	X	X
Picture	Sam	sent	from	the.
Because	with	reduced	the	flabby.
The	man	shot	a	wolf.

Let us now make a further refinement. We take out of the big bin all the nouns of English (*house, picture, Sam, resentment, wolf, man,* etc.) and put them in a noun bin. And we take out the articles (*a, an,* and *the*) and put them in an article bin. Then we draw articles for slots 1 and 4, nouns for 2 and 5, and verbs for 3. Our chances of getting grammatical sentences are much better:

Article	N	V	Article	N
The	resentment	hurried	an	house.
An	onion	occurred	the	dog.
An	picture	studied	a	uncle.
The	man	shot	a	wolf.

Not only do we come out with more grammatical sentences, but all the sentences we draw are more nearly grammatical than most of those we got when we chose at random. "The resentment hurried an house" is not grammatical, but it is much closer to being grammatical than "House a of go plenty" or "To sunny dream picnic around." The fact is that a common English sentence pattern has the form "Article noun verb article noun." The sentence "The resentment hurried an house" has this general form, and it is therefore nearly grammatical. It is not fully grammatical, because the nouns and articles and verb that occur are not precisely the right kinds of noun, article, and verb. *House* is not the sort of noun that can be object of a verb like *hurry. An* is not the form that goes with *house. Hurry* is not the kind of verb that has a noun like *resentment* as its subject. The sentence is right in general but not in particular.

HOW WORD CLASSES OPERATE

If we keep on refining our classifications, we can eventually get to the point where all the sentences we draw will be grammatical. They may not be sensible, but they will be grammatical. Suppose we divide nouns into such subclasses as human (*man, boy, lawyer, chairman*), animate (*man, boy, dog, beetle*), abstract (*courage, resentment, hope, sadness*), some nouns occurring in more than one subclass. We divide verbs into transitive (those that take objects) and intransitive (those that don't). We further divide transitive verbs into those that have human subjects (*hope, see, dine, love*), those that have animate subjects (*live, eat, die, breathe*), those that have any kind of subject, and so on. Then we make a rule that we choose the article *a* only before consonants and the article *an* only before vowels. Now we can easily set up patterns in such a way that no matter what particular words we draw we get an English sentence. For example:

Article	Human Noun	Verb That Takes Human Subject	Article	Animate Noun
The	chairman	saw	a	dog.
A	man	ate	the	beetle.
The	lawyer	hired	a	boy.
A	boy	loved	the	chairman.

These may not all make good sense, but they make good grammar.

WORD CLASSES OF ENGLISH

This is all by way of explaining what word classes are and how they operate. Word classes are groups of words which function in certain ways with other groups of words so as to make grammatical sentences. Different languages have different kinds of word classes.

English has four very large classes — *noun, verb, adjective, adverb.*
These can be subdivided in various ways — nouns, for example, as
human or nonhuman, animate or inanimate, countable or not
countable, and so on. In addition, English has a number of much
smaller word classes, called "structure groups" — *determiners,
auxiliaries, prepositions, conjunctions, subordinators, relatives, in-
tensifiers.* Some of these can be subdivided too. Finally, there are
a number of words whose behavior is so special that they can't be
put into word classes but must be dealt with separately. Examples
are *please, let's, not, to* (in *to go, to eat*), *oh,* etc.

In Chapter 1 we remarked that one thing a grammar might be
is a machine, an electronic English-speaking machine. Suppose we
wanted to build such a machine, one that could produce all the
grammatical sentences of English and could not produce ungrammatical sentences. In one way or another, we would have to give
the machine all the information about the classification and sub-
classification of English words. The machine would have to know
about nouns, what words occur in English as nouns and what at-
tributes each one has — whether it is human, animate, countable,
plural, abstract, etc. The machine would have to have an understanding of verbs and the subclasses of verbs and instructions about
which go with which subclasses of nouns and in what ways. Pro-
ceeding thus, we could eventually build into the machine all the
necessary grammatical information about English. Of course, it
would be an extremely complicated machine, requiring great numbers of high-speed drums.

Well, this is what you are. You are a machine like this. You have
all this built into you — the classes and subclasses with their lists
of words and the directions for putting them together. Your lists
may be long or short — that is, your vocabulary may be large or
small — but the classes and subclasses you have, and you have had
them since you were five or six years old. The proof is that you
regularly produce the grammatical sentences of English: "The man
shot a wolf," "The boy was a genius." Except for slips of the

tongue, you don't go even a little off. You don't say "The resentment hurried an house" or "An onion occurred the dog," let alone
"House of a go plenty" or "To sunny dream picnic around."

How you learned to do this is a mystery and a miracle. If we
knew all about it, we would know what man is. But it is a fact that
somehow or other, between the ages of one and six, every human
child builds the grammar of the language he hears spoken. From
the sentences uttered by his parents and brothers and sisters and
playmates, he figures out the sound system, the word classes, the
tense system, the number system, and all the rest of it. Then he
can use this machinery to produce infinitely many new sentences,
ones that he has never specifically learned, that no one has perhaps
ever pronounced before, and all will be recognizable as grammatical
English sentences.

In the chapters that follow, we will try to get a rough notion of
this machinery and how it operates. The notion will be necessarily
rough because the system is so very complex. We will notice the
main classes but by no means all the subclasses, the main sentence
patterns but not all the variations. When you get a grasp of the
chief outlines of the system, you will yourself be able to see how
the details fall into place.

EXERCISE 3

This is a kind of do-it-yourself exercise — how to be your
own grammarian. First write each of the following words on a separate
piece of paper: *face, my, never, his, dog, usually, car, struck, the, liked, a,
washed, window, sometimes, seldom, George, stroked, he, she, Annabelle, her,
goldfish, often, Sam, touched.* Now put the slips in a box or a pile and draw
them at random so as to make five-word sequences. Your chance of
getting a grammatical English sentence is mathematically very small.
Record your results in five columns, like this:

X	X	X	X	X
A. her	stroked	never	Sam	seldom

Now consider this sentence: "Edith frequently ignored our son." Arrange your slips in five piles according to whether the words will substitute grammatically for *Edith, frequently, ignored, our,* or *son.* You should have five slips in each pile. Each pile represents an English word — class or subclass. You could give them names if you wanted, or you could just refer to them as "words like *Edith,*" "words like *frequently,*" etc. Now draw words again, this time the first word from the *Edith* pile, the second from the *frequently* pile, and so on. Every sentence you draw this way should be a grammatical English sentence. Record your results in the same way as before, but this time label your columns with the words of the test sentence:

Edith   frequently   ignored   our   son.

A. _____   _____   _____   _____   _____

Now lengthen the lists. Find ten more words like *Edith,* two like *frequently,* five like *ignored,* five like *our,* ten like *son.* You must be careful to avoid ungrammaticality. For example, if you put *woman* in the *Edith* list, you will get "Woman frequently ignored our son," which is not English. If you put *married* in the *ignored* list, it will be all right in "Edith frequently married our son," but it would also give you "Edith frequently married my face," which is only partly grammatical, since verbs like *married* must have human nouns as objects.

EXERCISE 4

A. Here is another set of words: *father, very, ladder, looked, his, a, seemed, rather, your, short, strange, appeared, somewhat, this, pretty, building, the, old, ugly, quite, became, grew, umbrella, stride.* There is a common five-word sentence pattern which can be composed from these words. Figure out what the pattern is. Now list the words in each of the five word classes involved. There are five words in each list, with one word appearing in two lists. You can refer to the groups by number in the order of their appearance in the sentence pattern. List the words in this form on a separate sheet:

    1st Class
    2nd Class
    3rd Class
    4th Class
    5th Class

B. Make ten sentences by choosing at random from each class in order. If you have classified correctly, each sentence should be grammatical, if not sensible.

C. Lengthen the lists you made for Part A of this exercise by finding other words that will fit the sentence pattern.

SUMMARY OF TERMS • CHAPTERS 1–3

In these summaries, the major terms used in the book are defined with what are called "stipulative definitions." This means that the definitions simply specify or stipulate how the terms are used *in this book*. For some of them there may be other definitions just as reasonable, perhaps better for some purposes. But for the purposes of this book, the terms must be taken to mean just what they are said to mean and no more. Confusion often results when the student, perhaps unconsciously, is taking a term in a sense different from the one given.

The references in parentheses are to the pages on which the terms are first used.

Dialect (p. 7)   A variety of a language. The term is not used here in any bad sense. We can speak of the dialect of the Ozark mountains, the dialect of a street gang in New York, the dialect of the President of the United States, the dialect of the Queen of England.

Grammar (p. 1)   Something that produces the sentences of the language. The "something" may be thought of as a book, as an electronic machine, or as a human being who speaks the language natively. The grammar is correct if it never produces sentences which are not grammatical sentences of the language. It is complete if it can produce all the grammatical sentences. It is easy to construct a book or a machine which is correct. It is theoretically possible to construct a book or a machine which is also complete. But practically speaking, the only available grammar which is both correct and complete is a native speaker.

Grammatical (p. 1)   Conforming to the system of a particular language, or, more specifically, to a dialect of the language. Grammaticality has nothing to do with elegance or social acceptability. We may speak, for example, of grammatical substandard English, which would mean sentences that conform to the system of English dialects which are not socially acceptable. Grammaticality also has nothing to do with truth or reason, since one can lie or be mistaken or talk nonsense in grammatical sentences.

Native speaker (p. 1)   Someone who learned the language as his first language.

Word class (p. 13)   Groups of words that can occur, in certain specifiable positions, with other groups of words so as to make grammatical sentences. For English, such groups as nouns, verbs, adjectives, and adverbs are word classes. Some of these can be further subdivided into subclasses. For example, we have different kinds of nouns (common, proper, animate, inanimate, countable, not countable, etc.), different kinds of verbs, pronouns, etc. Ultimately, any word class or subclass can be fully defined only by listing the possible positions in which the class or subclass occurs, and listing the particular words that occur in those positions. In the summaries following, we shall identify word classes merely by listing typical words that occur in the positions for the class.

4 BASIC SENTENCE PATTERNS

We begin our description of the English grammatical system with what are called basic sentences. These are all statements (that is, not questions or requests or greetings or calls or exclamations), and they are all active, not passive (that is, like "Bill saw Jim," not like "Jim was seen by Bill.") Later on we will describe some of the ways in which these basic patterns can be built into more elaborate patterns.

These patterns are not basic in the sense that they occur more frequently than other kinds of sentences. For example, one basic pattern is represented by sentences like "Birds sing," "Snakes crawl," "Buildings crumble." But such sentences are actually rarely spoken. You might ask yourself how often you have had occasion to say, simply, "Birds sing," or how often you have heard it. You are much more likely to say something like "Can that bird sing?" or "The birds kept singing all the time." Yet we would probably all agree that "Birds sing" is somehow more fundamental, more basic, than these more common and more complicated sentences.

SUBJECT AND PREDICATE

All the basic sentences consist, first of all, of two parts. The first part is called the *subject* and the second part is called the *predicate*. Here are examples:

Subject	Predicate
Birds	sing.
Snakes	crawl.
The bird	sang.
The bird	was singing.
The building	might crumble.

Subject	Predicate
John	left.
He	left.
He	went away.
His mother	washed the car.
That bird	is stupid.
That bird	is an oriole.
He	preferred to go away.
She	enjoyed washing the car.

The simplest kind of a subject is a noun (sometimes preceded by a word like *the, that, his*) or a pronoun.

NOUNS

A noun is a word like *birds, snakes, building, John, mother,* as used in the sentences above. Other examples of words commonly used as nouns are *man, child, lawyer, chairman, beetle, grass, house, fire, time, danger, courage, resentment, Sally, Angela, Ambrose, Reginald, Harrison, Fielding.* Some of these words occur in other word classes too. Thus *man* is a noun in "The man went away" but a verb in "They manned the boat." On the other hand, *child* occurs only as a noun. Nobody ever says anything like "They childed" or "They will child it."

We saw in the last chapter that nouns can be divided into subclasses and that they have to be for a full description of English. Obviously *Sally* and *Ambrose* are a different kind of word from *grass* and *house* and all are different from *courage* and *resentment.* However, this book doesn't pretend to be a full description of English, and we will do as little subclassifying as possible.

DETERMINERS

Some of the nouns in the sentences above are preceded by the word *the, his,* or *that.* These words belong to the word class called *determiners.* Other common determiners are

a	their	no	all
an	this	both	most
my	these	some	more
our	those	many	either
your	every	much	neither
her	each	few	
its	any	several	

Determiners can be subdivided too and often are. Thus grammars speak of articles (*a, an, the*), possessives (*my, your, her, its, their, our, his*), demonstratives (*this, that, these, those*). These are all subclassifications of the determiner class.

Determiners commonly — and always in the basic patterns —

occur with nouns. But not all of them will occur with all nouns. For instance, *both, many, few, several* will occur only with plural nouns (*snakes, birds*), not with singulars. *Every, each, a, an* occur only with singulars. *A* and *an* do not ordinarily occur with nouns like *courage, resentment, gladness* or with nouns like *gravel, mush, oxygen.* Proper nouns like *Sally* and *Ambrose* — that is, personal names — are not usually modified by determiners of any kind.

PRONOUNS

The only examples of pronouns in the basic sentences given above are *he* and *she.* Many other words occur as pronouns; there are three chief subdivisions:*

Personal Pronouns:	I (me, mine), you (yours), he (him, his), she (her, hers), it (its), we (us, ours), they (them, theirs)
Demonstrative Pronouns:	this, that, these, those
Indefinite Pronouns:	either, neither, each, both, all, some, many, few, something, somebody, someone, anything, anybody, anyone, nothing, nobody, no one, one, none

However, the pronouns *me, him, her, us,* and *them* never occur as subjects in standard English — i.e., in what we called Grammar 1 in the second chapter.

You will perhaps have noticed that all of the demonstrative pronouns, many of the indefinite pronouns, and some of the personal pronouns appear also on the list of determiners. These words are determiners when they modify nouns; they are pronouns when they replace nouns in sentences. Compare these:

---

* What are usually called *relative pronouns* are here called simply *relatives* and are treated separately (Chapter 12). These do not occur in the basic sentences; nor do interrogatives.

Determiner: *That* building is crumbling.
Pronoun: *That* is crumbling. (The *that* must refer to something mentioned or otherwise indicated elsewhere.)
Determiner: *Each* missile had been tested.
Pronoun: *Each* had been tested.
Determiner: *His* birds sing.
Pronoun: *His* sing.

Not all words used as determiners occur also as pronouns: for example, *my, no, every* never do. And not all words used as pronouns occur also as determiners: for example, *he, mine, somebody* never do.

EXERCISE 5

This is another be-your-own-grammarian exercise. You are given a set of what are called "frames," that is, sentences with blanks in them. The words that grammatically can fill these blanks comprise subclasses of nouns. Copy each frame on your paper and write below it twelve words that can grammatically appear in the blank. Three examples are given to start you off. You are to find nine more. Traditional names for the categories are given in parentheses.

A. (Countable Nouns) How many _____ were there?
apples
houses
men

B. (Noncountable Nouns) How much _____ was there?
resentment
mush
gravel

C. (Animate Nouns) It terrified the _____
man
dog
lawyer

D. (Proper Nouns) His (her, its) name is _____.
Ambrose
Eleanor
Fido

E. (Datable Nouns) The _____ was on Saturday.
game
appointment
rehearsal

EXERCISE 6

The following are all basic sentences. Number your paper from 1 to 35, find the subject of the sentence, and write it beside the corresponding number. To the right of the subject, indicate whether it is a noun (**N**), a pronoun (**P**), or a determiner and a noun (**D - N**).

EXAMPLES: A. He went away.
He   **P**
B. Jack went away.
Jack   **N**
C. The man went away.
The man   **D - N**

1. Birds sing.
2. The bird sang.
3. The canary preferred to eat suet.
4. Neither understood it well.
5. Everybody liked her.
6. My uncle shook his head.
7. That's strange.
8. We enjoyed talking to her.
9. Every caller was buttered up.
10. Someone called you on the phone.
11. Hope springs eternal.
12. Much courage will be needed.
13. Neither caller wanted to leave his name.

14. Some like it hot.
15. Such dreams never come true.
16. Fortune smiled on her.
17. Angela had to weed the garden.
18. The child bit me.
19. Our mule went lame.
20. All men are mortal.
21. Exercise keeps people healthy.
22. No good can come of it.
23. Nothing succeeds like success.
24. Both beetles ignored the warning.
25. His date stood him up.
26. The umpire called it a ball.
27. Fate touched him on the shoulder.
28. Camels don't lay eggs.
29. Any assistance would be welcome.
30. Your father must have been surprised.
31. Either will do.
32. Edith wanted to learn to play the banjo.
33. He sells dictionaries to orphans.
34. Few answered the call.
35. Ebersole buttoned his vest.

5 THE PREDICATE

The subjects we have noticed in the basic sentence patterns are rather simple, consisting of either a noun, with or without a determiner, or a pronoun. We shall see that subjects can grow very much more complicated; nouns can be modified in intricate ways, and other structures can be made subjects in place of nouns or pronouns. However, in the basic patterns, subjects are simple.

Predicates, however, are complicated from the start. The predicate can be composed of several different structures, even in very simple sentences. It is this variety in the predicate that requires us to recognize not just one basic English sentence pattern but several. All predicates in the basic patterns contain either some form of a verb or some form of the word *be*. They may contain other items also, but they always contain at least one of these two: a verb or *be*.* English verbs are words like *go, try, die, hope, feel, become, see, resist, dilate, quicken, antagonize, emanicipate, bedevil, understand, vitiate, polish, quarrel.* Some of these words, though by no means all, occur also as members of other word classes. Thus *quarrel* is a verb in "They quarreled" but a noun in "They had a quarrel." *Feel* is a verb in "I couldn't feel it" but a noun in "I didn't like the feel of it."

VERBS

An English verb has five possible forms. These are traditionally named as follows:

Simple or Infinitive Form: drive, sing, go, put, walk, wait
Third Person Singular Form: drives, sings, goes, puts, walks, waits
Present Participle Form: driving, singing, going, putting, walking, waiting
Past Tense Form: drove, sang, went, put, walked, waited
Past Participle Form: driven, sung, gone, put, walked, waited

---

* It will surprise, and perhaps annoy, some readers that the word *be* is not called a verb, since it is traditional practice to speak of "the verb *be*." However, recent studies of English syntax have shown that a more efficient description of English results if *be* is treated quite separately. It differs markedly from verbs in its forms, in the sentence patterns built with it, and in its employment in the machinery for asking questions, stating negatives, and the like. We will not explore all of this complexity, and we could no doubt get on tolerably well calling *be* a verb and just making the necessary special statements about it. But even in this brief sketch it is simpler to keep it separate, and this procedure will keep the end open for the student who might some day proceed to a more advanced study of English syntax.

Because these terms are cumbersome and not very illuminating, it is common to call the third person singular form simply the "*–s* form," the present participle the "*–ing* form," the past tense the "*–ed* form," and the past participle the "*–en* form." This is what we shall do in this book. Here is how the forms line up:

Simple	-s	-ing	-ed	-en
drive	drives	driving	drove	driven
fall	falls	falling	fell	fallen
sing	sings	singing	sang	sung
put	puts	putting	put	put
go	goes	going	went	gone
have	has	having	had	had
walk	walks	walking	walked	walked
wait	waits	waiting	waited	waited
lean	leans	leaning	leaned	leaned

You will notice differences. The last three verbs — *walk, wait, lean* — are what are called *regular* verbs. That is, they are formed according to the general system of English verb formation. The others on the list are all *irregular*, formed in special ways. English has about two hundred irregular verbs. A person learning English learns the regular verb formation as a system, but must learn the irregular forms as individual items. A child learning English will often demonstrate that he has learned the system by applying it where it doesn't go. For example, he may say "We drived downtown" or "He singed me a song."

Notice that for most verbs the *–ed* and *–en* forms are identical. They are identical for all regular verbs and most irregular verbs. But we must make the distinction because some verbs, including some very common ones, have different forms. Not many verbs actually have *–en* in the past participle: *drive, fall, write, choose, blow, ride,* and a few others. We just use *–en* as a convenient way to refer to this form.

The word *be* differs from verbs, among other ways, in that it has

eight forms rather than five: *be, am, are, is, being, was, were, been.*
There are correspondences, of course, between these and the five
verb forms. The forms *be, am,* and *are* occur where verbs would
have the simple form; *is* corresponds to the *–s* form of verbs and
being to the *–ing* form. *Was* and *were* correspond to the *–ed* form and
been to the *–en* form.

PATTERN ONE

The very simplest kind of predicate is that which consists of just
a verb. In such a predicate, the verb has, in the present, either the
simple form or the *–s* form, depending on the subject. When the
predicate is of this sort, we shall call the sentence pattern PATTERN
ONE. Here are examples:

Subject	Predicate
Birds	sing.
The bird	sings.
He	sings.
They	sing.
Lions	growl.
Edith	growls.

The simple form occurs when the subject is plural: *birds, they, lions;*
the *–s* form occurs when the subject is singular: *bird, he, Edith.* If
the past tense is used, there is just one form, no matter what the
subject is:

Subject	Predicate
Birds	sang.
The bird	sang.
Lions	growled.
Edith	growled.

This pattern can be varied by the addition of an adverb, usually
after the verb. Adverbs are words like *sweetly, quickly, pleasantly,
hopefully, angrily, fast, hard.* These sentences, then, are also examples of PATTERN ONE:

Subject	Predicate
Birds	sing sweetly.
The bird	sang beautifully.
Edith	growled impatiently.

Some verbs of PATTERN ONE may have a different kind of adverb following them, a word like *away, up, on, out, by, over, in, under, to, down.*

Subject	Predicate
John	went away.
The child	looked up.
The lion	came to.
He	dropped in.
The parade	passed by.
We	looked on.

Predicates of this kind are sometimes called verb-adverb combinations. An adverb of this type often changes the meaning of the verb markedly, much more than an adverb of the *sweetly* type changes the meaning of the verbs it accompanies. "He dropped in" has an entirely different meaning from "He dropped." A person learning English must obviously learn just which of these adverbs go with which verbs and how the meaning is affected. It is a considerable problem for a foreign student learning English, but it is not much of a problem for the native speaker, who learns these combinations at an early age along with the rest of his vocabulary.

The verbs that occur in PATTERN ONE — *sing, growl, go, come, pass, look, occur, live, die, cry, arrive,* etc. — belong to the subclass called *intransitive verbs.*

EXERCISE 7

A. Write ten examples of PATTERN ONE, like "Birds sing" or "Birds sing sweetly," using verbs not used in the example sentences of this chapter.

B. List twelve additional intransitive verbs — i.e., verbs that can occur grammatically in PATTERN ONE. A simple way is to think of verbs that can replace those in the examples in this chapter or in your sentences above.

C. List fifteen verb-adverb combinations — like *drop in*, *pass by*. Do not repeat any examples used in the chapter.

D. Give the forms of the verbs listed. The *–en* form, past participle, is the one that occurs after *has, had,* or *have: has driven, had walked;* the *–ed* form is the simple past tense: *he drove, he walked.* The forms are given for the first two verbs to get you started. Follow this form throughout. Do not write in your book.

Simple	-s	-ing	-ed	-en
1. drive	drives	driving	drove	driven
2. walk	walks	walking	walked	walked
3. sing				
4. come				
5. think				
6. do				
7. fail				
8. bend				
9. hope				
10. ride				
11. blow				
12. throw				
13. try				
14. stay				
15. become				
16. drop				
17. forget				
18. stand				
19. sleep				
20. choose				
21. strike				
22. bring				
23. repeat				
24. drink				

6 ANOTHER SENTENCE PATTERN

We can represent PATTERN ONE in a formula in this way:

(D)   N   V   (Adv)

D stands for determiner, **N** for noun or pronoun, **V** for verb, and **Adv** for adverb. The parentheses mean that the item enclosed sometimes occurs and sometimes doesn't; thus we have a determiner or not depending on what kind of noun the subject is, and we have an adverb or not, depending partly on what verb precedes.

PATTERN TWO

PATTERN TWO has the following formula:

(D)   N   V   Adj

Adj stands for adjective. Adjectives* are words like *beautiful, sweet, tall, ugly, handsome, nice, sincere, honest, deceitful, troublesome, popular, physical, remote, indignant, youthful, happy.* Some of these words occur on other word lists also. For example, *sweet* is an adjective in "She's sweet," but it is a noun in "She ate a sweet." Notice that **Adj** is not in parentheses. That means that an adjective must occur; otherwise we do not have the pattern. Here are examples of PATTERN TWO:

Subject	Predicate
Birds	seem beautiful.
The bird	seems beautiful.

---

* We are using the term *adjective* in a narrow sense in this book. It does not mean here "anything that modifies a noun," but only "the class of words that can occur after *seem* in such sentences as 'The man seems angry.'" For further discussion of this point see page 66.

Subject	Predicate
Ambrose	looked sad.
The children	grew troublesome.
The story	rang true.
He	remained silent.
The lion	appeared sullen.
The pie	tastes good.
Her breath	smelled sweet.
The explanation	sounded false.

LINKING VERBS

Verbs which occur in PATTERN TWO are called *linking verbs*. The list of linking verbs is much shorter than the list of intransitive verbs of PATTERN ONE. There are thousands of intransitive verbs, but only a dozen or so linking verbs in general use, plus some others used in special contexts.

We have had examples earlier of what might be called the multiple employment of words — that is, the use of the same word in more than one word class. For example, *man* occurs as a noun ("The man went away") and also as a verb ("They will man the ship"). This double use of *man* doesn't cause any confusion, because there are plenty of signals to tell whether the word is being used as a noun or a verb. In "The man went away" the *the* before *man* and the *went* after it mark it plainly as a noun. In "They will man the ship" the *will* before and the *the* after mark *man* as a verb. We use thousands of words this way — sometimes as nouns, sometimes as verbs — and don't often get confused.

AMBIGUITY IN THE PATTERNS

It can happen, however, that the signals will fail and that we won't be able to tell whether a word belongs to one word class or another. Look at this sentence:

The detective looked hard.

This has two possible meanings. It could mean (1) that the detective was a tough-looking person or (2) that he made a careful search. When a sentence has more than one possible meaning, it is called *ambiguous*. Ambiguity occurs when the signals that are supposed to keep the patterns or the word classes of a language straightened out for some reason fail to do so. We are touching here on something **very** fundamental to language, and it will pay us to take enough time to understand it.

In Chapter 5 we gave as examples of adverbs such words as *sweetly, quickly, pleasantly, hopefully*. It will be obvious that these are all formed according to a simple pattern. They are composed of adjectives — *sweet, quick, pleasant, hopeful* — plus the ending *–ly*. If all adjectives and adverbs had this simple relationship, one could always easily tell which was which and such ambiguities as "The detective looked hard" could not occur.

However, English is by no means so simple. Adverbs are not the only words that end in *–ly*. Some adjectives do too: *elderly, manly, friendly, lordly*, most of these being composed of a noun plus the ending. Furthermore, not all adverbs end in *–ly*. We have noted the quite different group of adverbs — *up, by, down, in* — that occur in the verb-adverb combinations. Some adverbs consist of a noun plus the ending *–wise* or *–ways: lengthwise, sideways*. Finally, a few words have exactly the same form as adjective or as adverb: *hard, fast, straight*, and a few others. These words are adjectives when they occur in adjective patterns, adverbs when they occur in adverb patterns:

> John worked fast. (This is like "John worked quickly," PATTERN ONE; *fast* is an adverb.)
> John seemed fast. (This is like "John seemed happy," PATTERN TWO; *fast* is an adjective.)

A further complication is introduced by multiple employment of verbs. Not only do some words, like *man*, occur either as noun or verb, but some words occur in more than one subclass of verbs.

Grew, for example, can occur as an intransitive verb in PATTERN ONE or as a linking verb in PATTERN TWO:

The boy grew steadily. (PATTERN ONE)
The boy grew tall. (PATTERN TWO)

Now we should be able to see exactly why "The detective looked hard" is ambiguous. *Looked* is a word that occurs both as an intransitive verb (occurring alone or before an adverb) and as a linking verb (occurring before an adjective). *Hard* is a word that occurs both as an adverb (after intransitive verbs) and as an adjective (after linking verbs). If *looked* is intransitive, *hard* is an adverb; if *looked* is linking, *hard* is an adjective; if *hard* is an adverb, *looked* is intransitive; if *hard* is an adjective, *looked* is linking. But all signals fail, and the sentence is ambiguous.

Note that the following sentences are not ambiguous. There is in each one a signal sufficient to identify the pattern.

The detective looked careful. (*Careful* is a recognizable adjective — PATTERN TWO.)
The detective looked carefully. (*Carefully* is a recognizable adverb — PATTERN ONE.)
The detective seemed hard. (*Seemed* is a recognizable linking verb — PATTERN TWO.)
The detective worked hard. (*Worked* is a recognizable intransitive verb — PATTERN ONE.)

We go into this matter not to warn you against ambiguity but to demonstrate something basic to language. Ambiguity in writing is of course a fault, but this particular type doesn't represent much of a danger. The point to grasp is that the patterns and word classes of a language are not artificial things dreamed up by grammarians. They are realities. The user of the language, whether he has ever studied grammar or not, must and can distinguish adverbs from adjectives, verbs from nouns, adjectives from nouns, determiners from pronouns, PATTERN ONE from PATTERN TWO. He must do this to use the language understandably.

In a real language, as distinguished from an artificial or invented language, the signals that separate the categories — separate adjectives from adverbs, for example — are very complicated, much too complicated to be detailed in a book the size of this one. For native speakers of English, such specification is, in any case, unnecessary. If you speak English natively, you can distinguish the word categories and the sentence patterns all right. If you couldn't, you couldn't understand or be understood. All you need to do now is become aware of what you're doing.

EXERCISE 8

A. In the sentences "The boy worked hard," "Edith growled sullenly," *hard* and *sullenly* are adverbs. By substituting in these or other sentences of PATTERN ONE, find twenty more examples of adverbs. Do not duplicate the examples of Chapters 5 and 6.

B. In the sentences "The boy seemed happy," "Edith grew sullen," *happy* and *sullen* are adjectives. By substituting in these or other sentences of PATTERN TWO, find twenty more examples of adjectives. Do not duplicate the examples of Chapter 6.

C. The sentences below are all ambiguous. Most of them are the kind that might appear, if anywhere, in telegrams or newspaper headlines. For each sentence write two clear sentences, showing the meanings. Be prepared to discuss just what is unclear in the ambiguous sentences — i.e., what word or words might belong to two word classes.

EXAMPLE: A. The detective looked hard.
                    The detective looked tough.
                    The detective made a careful search.

1. Box leaves today.
2. John grew fast.
3. It's an orderly room.
4. College demands change.
5. Navy witnesses smoke.
6. The brave deserved the reward.

EXERCISE 9

The sentences following are all examples of PATTERN ONE or PATTERN TWO. Number your paper to 35 and identify each sentence as PATTERN ONE or PATTERN TWO. Indicate which by writing 1 or 2 in the margin. Some of the sentences contain forms not explicitly discussed in the preceding chapters. For these, you must simply decide whether the sentence seems more like "The lions growled," "The lions growled angrily," "The boy went away" (PATTERN ONE) or more like "The lions seemed sullen," "The boy grew tall" (PATTERN TWO).

1. The shipment arrived.
2. He felt sad.
3. The milk tasted sour.
4. Something must happen.
5. He replied courteously.
6. Ambrose ambled in.
7. He remained quiet.
8. Mr. Hoskins looked foolish.
9. Sally stayed out.
10. It smelled good.
11. It smelled very good.
12. Rover sniffed cautiously.
13. Roses smell sweet.
14. Bloodhounds smell well.
15. Alfred went home.
16. He went downtown.
17. The beetle died quietly.
18. The garage burned down.
19. That sounds interesting.
20. The milk turned sour.
21. John turned quickly.
22. The milk turned sour quickly.
23. The milk must have turned sour.
24. The minister seemed rather elderly.
25. The party grew boisterous.
26. The pace quickened.

27. The kings departed.
28. They went out.
29. They went to the store.
30. Alfred became somewhat insolent.
31. John turned around quickly.
32. The party ended in a fist fight.
33. David spoke up earnestly.
34. David occasionally spoke up rather earnestly.
35. Someone must have been moving around outside.

7 MORE SENTENCE PATTERNS

We now have two basic sentence patterns with the following formulas:

PATTERN ONE: **(D)   N   V   (Adv)**
PATTERN TWO: **(D)   N   V   Adj**

In PATTERN ONE, the verb is an intransitive verb; in PATTERN TWO the verb is a linking verb.

PATTERN THREE

PATTERN THREE has the formula

(D)   N   V - b   (D)   N

The symbol **V - b** stands for a very small class of verbs which have no agreed-on name in traditional grammar, though they are sometimes listed as a type of linking verb. For many speakers of English, the only words that occur in the **V - b** category are *become* and *remain*. We take the **b** of the symbol **V - b** from the more common word, *become*. Here are examples of PATTERN THREE:

Subject	Predicate
The boy	became a man.
Alfred	remained my friend.
The milk	became cheese.

The nouns occurring in the predicate in this pattern are sometimes called *predicate nouns.*

Some Americans also use the verb *seem* in this pattern:

The boy	seemed my friend.

Others, however, would say instead "The boy seemed to be my friend," which is a variation of a pattern we have not yet considered.

British English has a considerably longer list of words in the **V - b** category. The following sentences are more normal in British than in American English:

The boy	looked a fool.
He	grew a fine young man.

PATTERN FOUR

PATTERN FOUR has the following formula:

(D)   N   V - t   (D)   N

V - t stands for transitive verb. In contrast to the **V - b** category, which contains, in American English, just two or three words, the transitive verb category contains thousands of words. Here are some examples of PATTERN FOUR:

Subject	Predicate
The man	shot the wolf.
Alfred	found his mother.
The building	cost money.
The doctor	cured Edith.
Birds	eat worms.
The explanation	puzzled us.
John	antagonized his friends.

The noun or pronoun in the predicate in PATTERN FOUR is called an *object.*

Note the difference in meaning between PATTERN THREE and PATTERN FOUR:

> THREE: John became my friend.
> FOUR: John antagonized my friend.

In THREE, the subject and the object refer to the same person or thing; in FOUR, the subject and the object refer to different persons or things. This is the effect of the verbs of the **V - b** category — to make the following noun refer to the same person or thing as the subject.

PATTERN FIVE

A complete grammar of English would have to distinguish quite a few more basic patterns, according to the different subclasses of verbs that can occur. In order to keep our discussion within limits that can be readily managed, we shall take up just three more fairly common ones. PATTERN FIVE is the pattern that contains what is called an *indirect object.* We symbolize the subclass of verbs in this pattern as **V - g,** the **g** from the word *give,* which is one of the most common verbs in this subclass. The formula of PATTERN FIVE is:

(D)   N   V - g   (D)   N   (D)   N

Here are examples:

Subject	Predicate
The man	gave his son a car.
He	gave him a car.
Henry	brought his mother some flowers.
I	wrote my sister a letter.
We	sent them the money.
My uncle	found me a job.

The first noun or pronoun in the predicate in this pattern (*son, him, mother, sister, them, me*) is called an *indirect object*. The second noun (*car, flowers, letter, money, job*) is called a *direct object*.

PATTERN SIX

PATTERN SIX is similar to PATTERN FIVE in having two nouns in the predicate. It differs in the type of verb that occurs. PATTERN SIX verbs are verbs like *consider, think, believe, call, suppose*. We shall label these verbs **V - c,** after the first word on this list. This is the formula:

$$\textbf{(D)} \quad \textbf{N} \quad \textbf{V - c} \quad \textbf{(D)} \quad \textbf{N} \quad \textbf{(D)} \quad \textbf{N}$$

Here are examples:

Subject	Predicate
My uncle	considered me a fool.
He	thought her an angel.
I	believed it the truth.
The principal	called my brother a genius.
I	supposed him an honest man.

Notice a difference between PATTERN FIVE and PATTERN SIX: in FIVE, the two nouns or pronoun and noun in the predicate refer to different people or things; in SIX, they refer to the same people or things. This is the effect of the different subclasses of verbs. The first noun or pronoun in the predicate of PATTERN SIX is an object; the second noun is usually called an *object complement*. One variation of PATTERN SIX has an adjective in place of the second noun:

Subject	Predicate
My uncle	considered me foolish.
He	thought her angelic.
I	supposed the man honest.

PATTERN SEVEN

PATTERN SEVEN, the last that we shall distinguish except for the patterns with *be,* differs in that the verb is one of the type *elect,*

choose, vote, make. We shall refer to these as **V - e** words after *elect.*
This is the formula:

(D)   N   V - e   (D)   N   (D)   N

Here are examples:

Subject	Predicate
They	elected my brother their president.
The club	chose Sam secretary.
They	voted Edith the most popular girl.
They	made him the scapegoat.

PATTERN SEVEN is quite similar to PATTERN SIX, and some grammarians consider them variations of the same class. In both patterns the last noun is called an object complement, and in both the
two nouns or the noun and the pronoun in the predicate refer to the
same person or the same thing. A difference between the patterns,
in addition to the different verbs that occur, is that an adjective
cannot replace the second noun in PATTERN SEVEN.

We shall not specify any other basic patterns, but in case you are
curious about what sort of thing is left, the following represent additional patterns:

They put it away.
They passed by the house.
They persuaded him to go.
They found John studying in the library.

Remember that there is considerable overlapping in the verb subclasses. That is, the same word often belongs to two or more subclasses. For example, the word *call* is both a **V - g** (PATTERN FIVE)
and a **V - c** (PATTERN SIX). That is why the following sentence is
ambiguous:

He called me a slave.

This could have a PATTERN FIVE meaning: he summoned a slave to wait on me; or a PATTERN SIX meaning: he said that I was a slave. It is the basis for an old joke:

"Call me a taxi."

"Okay, you're a taxi."

EXERCISE 10

Write three examples of each of the seven basic sentence patterns. You may use verbs occurring in the chapter examples if you can't think of others, but make the rest of the sentences original.

PATTERN ONE:	**(D)**	**N**	**V**	**(Adv)**		
PATTERN TWO:	**(D)**	**N**	**V**	**Adj**		
PATTERN THREE:	**(D)**	**N**	**V - b**	**(D)**	**N**	
PATTERN FOUR:	**(D)**	**N**	**V - t**	**(D)**	**N**	
PATTERN FIVE:	**(D)**	**N**	**V - g**	**(D)**	**N**	**(D)**	**N**
PATTERN SIX:	**(D)**	**N**	**V - c**	**(D)**	**N**	**(D)**	**N**
PATTERN SEVEN:	**(D)**	**N**	**V - e**	**(D)**	**N**	**(D)**	**N**

EXERCISE 11

Number 1 to 35 on a sheet of paper. Indicate what basic pattern each sentence illustrates by writing 3, 4, 5, 6, or 7 beside the number of each sentence.

1. They shot a moose.
2. She became a movie star.
3. George gave me his pencil.
4. The mayor appointed Jorgensen coroner.
5. Nobody heard the shot.
6. We admired her poise.
7. He sent me his address.
8. She remained my closest friend.

9. Sally rubbed her nose.
10. We thought him a coward.
11. We thought him cowardly.
12. He was learning French.
13. Smathers suddenly got an idea.
14. The bride wore a veil.
15. His mother mailed him a package.
16. His mother mailed him a package on his birthday.
17. The Board named him president.
18. It seemed a shame.
19. He found a match.
20. He found a match in his coat pocket.
21. I asked you a question.
22. I occasionally asked a question.
23. I asked the teacher a question once in a while.
24. I never asked the teacher a question during class.
25. They found him reliable.
26. His lawyer requested another hearing.
27. He just shrugged his shoulders.
28. The news had not yet reached Finsterwald.
29. He must have become a thief.
30. He told us his troubles.
31. Colonel Stewart surrendered the garrison.
32. He had spent all his money.
33. Stanley considered it a pretty good idea.
34. Somebody should show him the way.
35. They should not have chosen Morrison their spokesman.

EXERCISE 12

Number to 35. Indicate which basic pattern each sentence illustrates by writing 1, 2, 3, 4, 5, 6, or 7 beside each sentence number.

1. He closed the door.
2. She yawned wearily.

3. The car looked new.
4. The enemy retreated.
5. He gave me a beetle.
6. We elected him president.
7. Ambrose became a vestryman.
8. Edith swallowed some ink.
9. The principal thought me a churl.
10. She sang well.
11. She sang me a song.
12. Somebody killed Sammy.
13. We thought him foolish.
14. The water felt very good.
15. Freddie remained the sergeant at arms.
16. They chose him their leader.
17. He seemed an interesting chap.
18. I found her dull.
19. He must have fallen in.
20. They kept quiet.
21. He wounded the stag.
22. He wounded him badly.
23. I'll mail her a check.
24. We believe him a saint.
25. The cry resounded loud and clear.
26. They withdrew in haste.
27. He acted insane.
28. The camel laid an egg.
29. He eventually became a grandfather.
30. We voted Sam the boy most likely to be average.
31. They ought to find the cobra a new home.
32. Nobody ever called Charlie a chump.
33. He bought his grandfather some dancing shoes.
34. We made Edith our leader.
35. No birds sang.

8 BASIC PATTERNS WITH *BE*

We said in Chapter 5 that every predicate in the basic sentence patterns contains either a verb or the word *be*. In Chapters 5, 6, and 7 we described patterns with verbs. We turn now to the three main basic patterns that have *be*.

PATTERN EIGHT

The first pattern with *be*, which we will call PATTERN EIGHT, has the following formula:

(D) N be Adv

You will notice that this is similar to PATTERN ONE. A difference, in addition to the presence of *be*, is that **Adv** is not in parentheses. This means that it must occur to produce this pattern. Furthermore, the adverb that occurs must be one of those with place or time meaning — *here, there, in, out, away, later*. Adverbs like *quickly, carefully* do not occur.

Recall that *be* has eight forms: *be, am, are, is, was, were, being, been*. In the simple pattern, *am* occurs when the subject is *I; are* occurs when the subject is *you* or any plural noun or pronoun; *is* occurs when the subject is any singular noun or any singular pronoun other than *I* or *you*. In the past tense, *were* occurs with *you* and any plural; *was* occurs with any singular subject, including *I*. Here are examples of PATTERN EIGHT:

Subject	Predicate
The boy	was here.
I	was there.
He	is outside.
You	are up.
It	was nearby.

Subject	Predicate
The eagles	were inside.
They	are off.
We	were out.

PATTERN NINE

PATTERN NINE has this formula:

(D) N be Adj

Notice that it is just the same as PATTERN TWO except that *be* occurs in place of a verb. It is, however, much more common than PATTERN TWO. Here are examples:

Subject	Predicate
The lions	were hungry.
Ambrose	was insolent.
I	am tired.
Edith	was ill.
She	is well now.
The boxes	are empty.
The syringe	is ready.
The chocolates	were poisonous.

PATTERN TEN

PATTERN TEN, the last of the basic patterns that we shall specify, has this formula:

(D) N be (D) N

It is thus very similar to PATTERN THREE, with *be* in place of *become* or *remain*. As in PATTERN THREE, the two nouns or pronouns in PATTERN TEN refer to the same person or the same thing. TEN is much more common than THREE. Here are examples:

Subject	Predicate
Ambrose	is my friend.
My uncle	is an Elk.

Subject	Predicate
I	am a senior.
You	are a liar.
These men	are ushers.
It	was a turkey.
They	were history teachers.

Just as we left some predicates with verbs unclassified, so we leave some predicates with *be*. The following sentences, for example, might be associated with some of the patterns described in this chapter or might better be treated separately:

> The party was over.
> We were through.

THE *THERE* TRANSFORMATION

Before we leave the patterns with *be*, we must notice one pattern that derives from one of them. This is not a basic pattern, since it derives from a basic pattern, but it is very common in modern English. You remember that PATTERN EIGHT has this form:

(D)   N   be   Adv

The symbol **Adv** here, and also in PATTERN ONE, can stand for an adverb — *here, there, outside* — or it can stand for a phrase — *in the house, on the lawn, by the mailbox.* "He worked eagerly" is an example of PATTERN ONE, and so is "He worked with a will." "He is here," "He is in the house," "He is in charge," "It was for us" are all examples of PATTERN EIGHT. Now some PATTERN EIGHT sentences, though not all, can be changed in the following way:

(D)   N   be   Adv

becomes

There   be   (D)   N   Adv

The chief restriction is that the determiner, if there is one, is usually a word of general meaning, like *a, some, many*, not a determiner with specific meaning, like *the, my, this.*

Here are examples:

A man is here.	**(D N be Adv)**
There is a man here.	**(There be D N Adv)**

Some men are outside.

There are some men outside.

A boy is in the room.

There is a boy in the room.

Many letters are in the mailbox.

There are many letters in the mailbox.

A glint was in his eye.

There was a glint in his eye.

The word *there* in this construction is not an adverb. In fact it doesn't belong to any of the common word classes. It is unique, in a class by itself. It is just the word that gets this peculiar English construction started.

One point to notice is the form of *be* that occurs. The relationship between *be* and the noun in the sentence is exactly the same in the *there* pattern as in PATTERN EIGHT. In standard English the form *is* or *was* occurs if the noun is singular; *are* or *were* occurs if the noun is plural.

The development of **There   be   (D)   N   Adv** out of **(D)   N   be   Adv** is what is called a *transformation*. All of the complicated English sentences are transformations of one kind or another of the basic sentence patterns. We shall have more examples of transformations later.

Note that the *there* transformation can be made from PATTERN EIGHT only. The other nine patterns in their basic forms never — or very rarely — produce the *there* construction. For example, from "The people wait" we cannot derive "There wait the people." However, we shall see in the next chapter that all the predicates can be expanded so as to include *be* as an auxiliary and some may then undergo the *there* transformation. "Some people are waiting" becomes "There are some people waiting."

EXERCISE 13

A. Write five sentences each to illustrate PATTERNS EIGHT, NINE, and TEN.

EIGHT: **(D)   N   be   Adv**   (Remember that the **Adv** can be an adverb of place or time — *here, inside, early* — or a phrase of similar meaning — *in the house, at five o'clock*.)

NINE: **(D)   N   be   Adj**

TEN: **(D)   N   be   (D)   N**

B. Write ten sentences illustrating the *there* transformation of PATTERN EIGHT. Remember that the number of the noun (singular or plural) controls the form of *be* that occurs.

There   be   (D)   N   Adv

EXERCISE 14

Number to 35.   Indicate which of the ten basic patterns each sentence illustrates by writing 1, 2, 3, 4, 5, 6, 7, 8, 9, or 10 at the right of the number.

1. Mabel is upstairs.
2. I supposed her the maid.
3. It was inside.
4. He is a minister.
5. The coyotes howled at the moon.
6. It seems rather sad.
7. He became a different person.
8. The men chose Kaufmann their spokesman.
9. I considered it an insult.
10. Bradbury lowered the boom.
11. Harold was in his room.
12. It was foolish.
13. The collection agency sent him a threatening letter.
14. Murphy remained silent.
15. The bride wore red.
16. That's nice.

17. The boiler exploded.
18. We mailed him the package.
19. The troops fought back.
20. Gorrell arrived in the nick of time.
21. Someone was in the office.
22. He's still here.
23. He's still.
24. He's here.
25. I found her a good conversationalist.
26. I found her a crowbar.
27. Ambrose had a date.
28. Zumas stroked his mustache.
29. It was an inspiring message.
30. Nothing remained behind.
31. I took him the rabbits.
32. Henry became a musician.
33. The roof blew off.
34. The lawn needed water.
35. We urged his election.

SUMMARY OF TERMS • CHAPTERS 4–8

Adjectives (p. 30)   Words like *good, true, lovely, sensitive, amiable, original*. Adjectives can be identified as the group of words that can occur in PATTERN TWO, after verbs like *seem, sound, taste*. Note that in this text *adjective* does *not* mean "that which modifies a noun."

Adverbs (p. 27)   Words like *sweetly, hopefully, fast;* or *up, in, away;* or *never, sometimes, recently*.

Basic sentence (p. 18)   A sentence that is not derived from some more fundamental sentence. In English, basic sentences are all statements in the active voice without much modification.

Demonstrative pronouns (p. 21)   *this, that, these, those.*

Determiners (p. 20)   Words like *the, his, that,* in structures like *the man, the old man, his indignation, that oatmeal*. Determiners usually occur with nouns. Some of them sometimes occur with other word classes, as in *the poor, the brave*.

- ed form (p. 26)   Same as the past tense.

- en form (p. 26)   Same as the past participle.

Indefinite pronouns (p. 21)   *either, neither, each, both, all, some, many, few, something, somebody, someone, anything, anybody, anyone, nothing, nobody, no one, none, one.*

Indirect object (p. 38)   The first noun or pronoun following the verb in PATTERN FIVE.

Infinitive (p. 25)   Such verb forms as *see, think, relieve, industrialize.*

- ing form (p. 26)   Same as the present participle.

Intransitive verbs (p. 28)   The subclass of verbs that occur in PATTERN ONE.

Linking verbs (p. 31)   The subclass of verbs occurring in PATTERN TWO.

Nouns (p. 20)   Words like *John, man, snake, laundry, business, oatmeal, indignation.* Some of these words occur in other word classes too. In English it is very common for words to occur in more than one class or subclass.

Object (p. 38)   The noun or pronoun following the verb in PATTERN FOUR.

Object complement (p. 39)   The second noun after the verb in PATTERN SIX.

Past participle (p. 25)   Such verb forms as *seen, thought, relieved, industrialized.* For most verbs, the past tense and past participle forms are identical.

Past tense (p. 25)   Such verb forms as *saw, thought, relieved, industrialized.*

Pattern One (p. 27)   A sentence pattern consisting of a subject and an intransitive verb — i.e., a verb like *sing, go, arrive, occur.* "The ship arrived," "John went away."

Pattern Two (p. 30)   A sentence pattern consisting of a subject, a verb, and an adjective: "The man seemed young," "The dinner smelled good."

Pattern Three (p. 36)   A sentence pattern consisting of a subject, the verb *become* or *remain*, and a noun or pronoun: "John became a teacher," "He remained our friend."

Pattern Four (p. 37)   A sentence pattern consisting of a subject, a transitive verb, and a noun or pronoun: "John ate lunch," "We enjoyed the movie."

Pattern Five (p. 38)   A sentence pattern consisting of a subject, a verb of the *give* class, and two nouns or pronouns: "He gave me the book," "John sent us a message."

Pattern Six (p. 39)   A sentence pattern consisting of a subject, a verb of the *consider* class, and two nouns or pronouns: "John considered me a bore," "We thought him our friend."

Pattern Seven (p. 39)   A sentence pattern consisting of a subject, a verb of the *elect* class, and two nouns or pronouns: "The class elected John secretary," "We chose her our spokesman."

Pattern Eight (p. 44)   A sentence pattern consisting of a subject, some form of the word *be*, and an adverb: "John is here."

Pattern Nine (p. 45)   A sentence pattern consisting of a subject, some form of the word *be*, and an adjective: "John is angry."

Pattern Ten (p. 45)   A sentence pattern consisting of a subject, some form of the word *be*, and a noun or pronoun: "John is a man."

Personal pronouns (p. 21)   *I, me, mine; you, yours; he, him, his; she, her, hers; it, its; we, us, ours; they, them, theirs.*

Predicate (p. 19)   The second of the two main parts of English sentences: *went away* in "John went away"; *intended to be here* in "John intended to be here."

Predicate noun (p. 37)   The noun or pronoun occurring after the verb in PATTERN THREE.

Present participle (p. 25)   Such verb forms as *seeing, thinking, relieving, industrializing.*

Pronouns (p. 21)   Words like *I, that, somebody, each.* Pronouns are sometimes considered a subclass of nouns, since they regularly occupy noun positions. Some words which occur as pronouns occur also as determiners.

- s form (p. 26)   Same as the third person singular.

Simple form (p. 25)   Same as the infinitive.

Standard English (p. 21)   The dialects of English normally used by educated native speakers.

Subject (p. 19)   The first of the two main parts of English sentences: *John* in "John went away"; *the old man* in "The old man went away."

There construction (p. 46)   A sentence derived or transformed from PATTERN EIGHT: "There are some men here" (from "Some men are here"); "There's a mouse in the closet" (from "A mouse is in the closet").

Third person singular (p. 25)   Such verb forms as *sees, thinks, relieves, industrializes.*

Transitive verb (p. 37)   The subclass of verbs occurring in PATTERN FOUR.

V - b (p. 36)   The subclass of verbs occurring in PATTERN THREE. For many speakers of American English, only two verbs occur in this subclass — *become* and *remain.* For British English, the **V - b** list is longer.

V - c (p. 39)   The subclass of verbs occurring in PATTERN SIX.

V - e (p. 40)   The subclass of verbs occurring in PATTERN SEVEN.

V - g (p. 38)   The subclass of verbs occurring in PATTERN FIVE.

Verb-adverb combination (p. 28)   A verb plus an adverb of the type *up, in, away: look up, drop in, go away.*

Verbs (p. 25)   Words like *see, think, wait, relieve, endure, anticipate, industrialize.* The word *be* (*am, is, are, was, were, been, being*) is not considered a verb in this text. Neither are such words as *can, may, will, must, could, should.*

 EXPANDING THE PREDICATE

We will now note several operations that can be performed on predicates to produce more complicated structures. All of these can be performed on all predicates of the basic patterns, and all are done in the same way.

ADDING A MODAL

First, all of the predicates can be preceded by what is called a *modal auxiliary* or simply a *modal.* The modals are *shall, will, can, may, must, should, would, could, might.* Any of these can occur before any of the predicates of the basic patterns. If a modal is used, the verb has the simple form. *Be* has the form *be.*

	Subject	Predicate
ONE:	John	went away.
	John	may go away.
TWO:	The boy	looks sick.
	The boy	will look sick.
THREE:	He	became my friend.
	He	could become my friend.
FOUR:	My father	shot a moose.
	My father	may shoot a moose.
FIVE:	I	gave the boy a dollar.
	I	shall give the boy a dollar.
SIX:	They	considered John a fool.
	They	would consider John a fool.
SEVEN:	They	elected Jim treasurer.
	They	should elect Jim treasurer.
EIGHT:	He	is here.
	He	may be here.
NINE:	Margery	is pretty.
	Margery	might be pretty.
TEN:	The boss	is a bore.
	The boss	can be a bore.

ADDING *BE* PLUS *–ING*

Another addition that can be made to all the basic patterns, and all in the same way, is *be* plus *–ing*. In this, an appropriate form of *be* — *am, are, is, was,* or *were* — precedes the verb and *–ing* is added to the simple form of the verb — i.e., the verb takes the present participle form. Examples:

	Subject	Predicate
ONE:	John	went away.
	John	was going away.

	Subject	Predicate
THREE:	He	became my friend.
	He	is becoming my friend.
SEVEN:	They	elected Jim treasurer.
	They	are electing Jim treasurer.
TEN:	The boss	is a bore.
	The boss	is being a bore.

Note that this works on *be* patterns as well as on verb patterns.

ADDING *HAVE* PLUS *–EN*

A third addition possible to all the predicates is *have** plus *–en*. In this an appropriate form of *have* occurs before the verb or *be* and the verb or *be* occurs in the *–en* (past participle) form. Examples:

	Subject	Predicate
ONE:	John	went away.
	John	has gone away.
THREE:	He	became my friend.
	He	had become my friend.
SEVEN:	They	elected Jim treasurer.
	They	have elected Jim treasurer.
TEN:	The boss	is a bore.
	The boss	has been a bore.

So, to any of the predicates we can add a modal, a *have* and an *–en*, or a *be* and an *–ing*. The modal is followed by the simple form, the *have* by an *–en* form, and the *be* by an *–ing* form. We can show this in a formula as follows:

$$\text{Subject} \quad \text{(M)} \quad \text{(have plus - en)} \quad \text{(be plus - ing)} \quad \left\{ \begin{array}{c} \text{be} \\ \text{V} \end{array} \right\} \quad \text{X}$$

This looks complicated, but if you work it out, you see an in-

---

* On page 25 (footnote) we remarked that *be* is not a verb but just a *be*. *Have*, however, is both a verb and a *have*. That is, in some sentences it behaves specially, and in others it behaves just like verbs.

teresting and graspable structure. The parentheses mean that the item can occur or not. To have a sentence, we must have a subject and either a *be* or a verb, since these items are not in parentheses. The brackets around *be* and **V** mean that one or the other of these must be chosen but that both cannot be. In addition, we may have a modal or not, *have* plus *–en* or not, *be* plus *–ing* or not. Or we may have any two of these or all three, provided we take them in the order shown. The *–en* and the *–ing* always go on what follows, whether it is a *be*, a *have*, or a verb. The **X** in the formula stands for whatever may follow the verb in any particular pattern — object, adjective, adverb, or nothing.

Suppose we start with **Subject** plus **V** — e.g., *John walks*. Add **M**, and we get:

> **Subject M V** John may walk.*

Now add *have* plus *–en*. This must follow the **M**, according to the formula. The *–en* will be added to what follows the *have*, in this case a **V**. That is, the verb will have the past participle, or *–en*, form — *walked, sung, driven*, etc. So:

> **Subject M have V - en** John may have walked.

Now add *be* plus *–ing*. This must follow the *have* plus *–en* and precede the **V**. So the *be* now takes the *–en* form and the verb the *–ing* form:

> **Subject M have be - en V - ing** John may have been walking.

Here are more examples:

Subject Predicate

John   goes away.   (**N   V   Adv**)
John   may go away.   (**N   M   V   Adv**)
John   has gone away.   (**N   have   V - en   Adv**)
John   may have gone away.   (**N   M   have   V - en   Adv**)

* You may wonder what happens to the *s* of *walks* when we derive " John may walk " from " John walks." If you are curious, you may want to look ahead to the more precise explanation of these structures given in Chapter 32.

Subject	Predicate
John	is going away.	**(N be V - ing Adv)**
John	may be going away.	**(N M be V - ing Adv)**
John	has been going away.	**(N have be - en V - ing Adv)**
John	may have been going away.	**(N M have be - en V - ing Adv)**

There are other things we can do to all the predicates. There is a class of verbs of the type *prefer, want, try, begin, seem.* Any of these verbs can occur at the beginning of any predicate. If one does, it is followed by the word *to* and then the simple form of the verb or the *be* of the predicate. Examples:

	Subject	Predicate
ONE:	He	went away.
	He	preferred to go away.
FIVE:	He	lent me the money.
	He	tried to lend me the money.
NINE:	She	was pretty.
	She	wanted to be pretty.

There is another class of verbs of the type *avoid, enjoy, endure, begin.** These also can occur at the beginning of any predicate. When one does, it is followed by the *–ing* form of the verb:

	Subject	Predicate
ONE:	He	went away.
	He	avoided going away.
FIVE:	He	lent me the money.
	He	enjoyed lending me the money.
NINE:	She	was pretty.
	She	endured being pretty.

* Note that some verbs, like *begin,* belong to both classes. That is, both *begin going* and *begin to go* are grammatical. Most of the verbs have also other uses in the grammar. Thus, *prefers* is simply a PATTERN FOUR verb — i.e., a transitive verb — in "John prefers milk." *Seems* is a PATTERN TWO verb in "John seems angry." We thus note again the multiple use of words in the grammar — the occurrence of words in several different word classes or subclasses.

These verb classes can occur before any verb (or any *have* or any *be*). The only requirement is that the *prefer* type must be followed by a *to* and then a simple form of the verb (or *have* or *be*) and the *avoid* type must be followed by the *–ing* form of a verb (or *have* or *be*). Furthermore, this operation may be performed any number of times in a sentence. There is no rule in English that says we can have only one *prefer* or *avoid* per sentence or only two or only ten or only a million. Thus the following sentence, though it is far from elegant and tends to become meaningless, is perfectly grammatical: "John may prefer to avoid wanting to try to enjoy going away."

EXERCISE 15

Write sentences from the following formulas. **M** stands for modal; *prefer* means any verb of the *prefer* type. *Avoid* means any verb of the *avoid* type. Use a little variety.

Indicate the number — 1 to 10 — of the basic sentence pattern.

1. **D   N   V   Adv**
2. **N   M   be   Adv**
3. **D   N   be   V - t - ing   D   N**
4. **D   N   have   V - g - en   N   D   N**
5. **N   M   have   be - en   D   N**
6. **N   M   have   be - en   V - g - ing   D   N   D   N**
7. **D   N   prefer   to   be   Adj**
8. **N   M   avoid   V - ing   Adv**
9. **N   have   be - en   V - c - ing   N   D   N**
10. **D   N   M   be   D   N**
11. **N   M   have   be - en   Adj**
12. **D   N   prefer   to   avoid   V - t - ing   D   N**
13. **D   N   M   have   V - b - en   D   N**
14. **D   N   M   have   V - e - en   N   D   N**
15. **D   N   M   have   be - en   prefer - ing   to   V   Adv**
16. **N   have   be - en   V - ing   Adj**
17. **D   N   be   V - g - ing   D   N   D   N**

10 TRANSFORMATION

Most of the sentences that we have studied so far have been basic sentences. The single exception was the *there* construction described in Chapter 8: "There is a man here." "A man is here" is a basic sentence. So is "A man must have been intending to be here." But "There is a man here" is not. It is what we will call a *transformed sentence* or a *transformation* — that is, a sentence that is made out of or that derives from a basic sentence.

In the rest of this book we shall be dealing mainly with transformations of one kind or another. But before going on, we should try to get as clear an idea as we can of the essential difference between basic sentences and transformed sentences. Why are "A man is here" and "John can go" basic sentences, whereas "There is a man here" and "John can't go" are transformed sentences?

THE SYSTEM OF A LANGUAGE

One of the most puzzling things about languages is that human beings are able to learn to speak them. Listen to any English conversation and note the tremendous diversity of the structures that occur. There seems to be no end to the variety. Scholars who have tried to put all of English into grammar books have sometimes found that four or seven or ten large volumes are not enough. When we look at this apparently immense complexity, we wonder how anyone can be bright enough or have a powerful enough memory to learn a language and use it.

Yet we all do this. Even those of us who are not very bright and those who have poor memories manage somehow or other to learn at least one language. We master virtually all of its grammar (though of course not all of its vocabulary), and we achieve this without conscious study and at a very early age. Some children do more than this. If their homes are bilingual, they learn two languages. In some parts of the world — the Middle East, for instance — it is not uncommon to find children of six or seven speaking four languages — perhaps Greek, Arabic, Turkish, and French. Nor are such children necessarily of high intelligence. Some of them are quite dull, incapable of learning arithmetic or history, perhaps even incapable of learning to read. Yet they have somehow fathomed the apparently complicated structures of four vastly different languages.

If there is any explanation at all, it must be that language structure is not really as complicated as it looks at first. There must be some kind of system to it simple enough to be grasped and held by any human mind, however ordinary. The grammarian's task is therefore to seek out this system, to be always trying to describe languages in the shortest and simplest way possible. If we have two grammars of a language, both of which describe the language fully but one of which is half as long as the other, the assumption is that the shorter one is twice as good. For, being shorter and simpler, it must come closer to what is contained in the mind of a speaker of the language. The child learning the language presumably does not take a long route when a shorter one is available to him.

BASIC AND TRANSFORMED SENTENCES

When we try to describe English, we find that we get the shortest and neatest description if we suppose that it consists of two fundamentally different kinds of sentences. There is first of all a kernel or base — a rather small set of sentence types which we have here called basic sentences. The bulk of these we have here described in a few short chapters. All the rest of English is transformation. That is, all the more complicated sentences of English can be explained as deriving from the basic sentences. Given the kernel, the set of basic sentences, we can describe the great variety of English by explaining the rules by which complicated sentences are made out of basic sentences. For example, from any sentence of the type "A man is here," we can derive a *there* construction. The rule is to add the word *there* and to reverse the positions of the subject and the *be:*

A man is here. → There is a man here.

The child somehow learns the basic structure and the transformation rule. This is simpler than learning the two structures separately, as if they were unrelated. It also makes him capable of producing new sentences, correct sentences, which he has never specifically learned.

Or take the passive construction. Given any PATTERN FOUR basic sentence, like "John loves Mary," we can derive a related construction called the passive. The rule is to make the second noun the subject, to add *be*, to put the verb in the *–en* form, and to express the original subject in a *by* phrase:

John loves Mary. → Mary is loved by John.

This is true for any PATTERN FOUR, and thus the passive is not learned separately but as a possible product of PATTERN FOUR. Given knowledge of the system, the child can produce sentences he has never learned. If he knows "The policeman arrested John," and knows the rule, he can produce "John was arrested by the policeman" without ever having heard it before.

"The man seemed kind" is a basic sentence, but "The kind man left" is a transformation. Given any sentence like "The man seemed kind" we can derive a related structure: "the kind man."

The man left.
The man seemed kind. } → The kind man left.

But the reverse is not true. It is not a fact that any word occurring as a modifier of a noun will also occur in PATTERN TWO after *seemed.*

From "the main reason" we cannot derive "The reason seemed main."

Let us return once again to the metaphor of the electronic English-producing machine, a machine capable of producing all the grammatical sentences of English and incapable of producing ungrammatical ones. If we actually tried to produce such a monster, we would find that we needed two distinct kinds of mechanism. The machine that produced the basic sentences would be a fairly simple one, performing just one operation at a time. For example, it could produce easy variations of "They drive":

They drive. plus modal   ⟶ They can drive.
They drive. plus *be* and *–ing*   ⟶ They are driving.
They drive. plus *have* and *–en* ⟶ They have driven.

Or it could add these in various combinations: "They may be driving," "They have been driving," "They might have driven," "They might have been driving." It is a matter of simple additions.

However, the machine that produces transformations would have to be more powerful. It would have not only to add things, but also to subtract and often to switch things around. It would have to be able to look forward and backward so as to make subjects and verbs agree, to produce the proper forms of personal pronouns, etc. Also, it would have to have a memory and an ability to recognize structures. Given the sentence "The man became the boss," it would have to perceive not only that *man* and *boss* are nouns and *became* a verb, but also that the sentence is an example of PATTERN THREE, not PATTERN FOUR. Otherwise it could apply the passive transformation, producing the ungrammatical sentence "The boss was become by the man."

We assume that the human mind contains machinery of both types. We know how to produce the kernel, the basic sentences, and then we are able to recognize what we have produced and to know what transformations we can make and where. Whether we have studied grammar or not, we recognize that "The man loved the girl" is different from "The man became the boss" and that we can make the first sentence passive but not the second.

In describing a language, we naturally describe the basic sentences first and then the transformations. No one would think of beginning a grammar with "The girl was loved by the man" and going on to "The man loved the girl." But of course we don't mean to suggest that this is the order in which the child learns. He does not learn to make basic sentences first and then to transform them. He may very likely hear the transformation "Did you see the horse?" before he hears the basic sentence "You see the horse." The language comes to him jumbled up in all kinds of ways. But however it comes, he eventually sorts it out into a kernel and rules for making other sentences out of the kernel.

In succeeding chapters, we shall have many explanations of different kinds of transformations. We will finish this one by showing how the structures of a complicated sentence can be viewed as being composed through transformation of basic sentences. Consider this sentence:

> The young working people upstairs who gave my mother the information knew they had nothing to gain from refusing to name the person who told them.

This has as its base the PATTERN FOUR sentence "The people knew it." All else is a series of transformations, as follows:

> The people knew it.
> The people seemed young. ⟶ The young people knew it.
> The people work. ⟶ The young working people knew it.
> The people are upstairs. ⟶ The young working people upstairs knew it.
> The people gave the mother → The young working people the information.   upstairs who gave the mother the information knew it.

I have a mother. ⟶ The young working people upstairs who gave my mother the information knew it.

They had it. ⟶ The young working people upstairs who gave my mother the information knew they had it.

They gained nothing. ⟶ The young working people upstairs who gave my mother the information knew they had nothing to gain.

They refused to name the ⟶ The young working people person. upstairs who gave my mother the information knew they had nothing to gain from refusing to name the person.

The person told them. ⟶ The young working people upstairs who gave my mother the information knew they had nothing to gain from refusing to name the person who told them.

EXERCISE 16

A. Apply the *there* transformation to each of the following PATTERN EIGHT sentences.

EXAMPLE: A. A man is outside. (kernel sentence)
There is a man outside. (*there* transformation)

1. Some men are here.
2. Some dogs are on the lawn.
3. A letter is in the box.
4. A meeting is at eleven o'clock.

5. A few cookies are in the jar.
6. No one is home.

B. Apply the passive transformation to each of the following PATTERN FOUR sentences.

EXAMPLE: A. John beat Sam. (kernel sentence)
                    Sam was beaten by John. (passive transformation)

1. The policeman stopped the car.
2. The Harrisons hired Albert.
3. The Queen opened Parliament.
4. Wolves nursed the infants.
5. Bradley won the second game.
6. The last survivor had left an account of the ordeal.

C. Each of the following sentences consists of transformations of three basic sentences. See if you can figure out what they are.

EXAMPLE: A. The young man who was here went away.
                    The man went away.
                    The man seemed young.
                    The man was here.

1. The people who remained had a nice talk.
2. The family upstairs complained when the party grew noisy.
3. Weeping widows need quiet consolation.

11 NOUN CLUSTERS

We have shown that the basic English sentence consists of two parts, a subject and a predicate, and we have described the principal variations in the predicate that distinguish the basic sentence patterns of English. We want now to examine the processes by which the material of these basic patterns is used to create the great complexity of English sentences.

We will begin by describing some of the ways in which nouns can be expanded into what we call *noun clusters*. We have noted how nouns (with or without determiners) or pronouns occur in the basic patterns. They occur as subjects in all the patterns. In addition, we have the objects of PATTERNS FOUR, FIVE, SIX, and SEVEN; the predicate nouns of PATTERNS THREE and TEN; the indirect object of PATTERN FIVE; the object complements of PATTERNS SIX and SEVEN. We shall see that nouns in any of these positions can be expanded into complicated noun clusters, and that the machinery of expansion is the same, no matter what the function of the noun in the basic pattern.

HEADWORDS AND MODIFIERS

A noun cluster consists of a noun *headword* plus one or more *modifiers*. *Headword* simply means "that which is modified." We have already had examples of one kind of noun modifier — determiners. Expressions like *the birds, my car, several snakes* are small noun clusters in which the nouns *birds, car,* and *snakes* are headwords and the determiners *the, my, several* are modifiers.

Adjectives also occur as modifiers of noun headwords. We have had examples of adjectives — words like *old, honest, elderly, beautiful* — in our illustrations of PATTERNS TWO and NINE. Adjectives in noun clusters can be thought of as deriving from either PATTERN TWO or NINE. We will take as our test frame PATTERN TWO sentences with the verb *seem*, a verb which happens not to occur in any of the other basic patterns. (Its only other use is as a member of the *prefer* class: "He seems to be in charge here.") Wherever we have an instance of PATTERN TWO, we have the possibility of a corresponding noun cluster containing an adjective, in this fashion:

The birds seem beautiful.	the beautiful birds
The boy seems honest.	an honest boy
The snake seems dangerous.	every dangerous snake
The man seemed elderly.	an elderly man

Notice that we restrict the term adjective to these words — the words that occur as the last part of PATTERN TWO.* This means that we don't call *main* in *the main reason* an adjective. *Main* is a different kind of word from *beautiful, honest,* etc., as is seen in the fact that we don't say "The reason seems main." *Main* belongs to a different class of words (to which we will give no name in this book) including such items as *principal, chief,* and perhaps others. If we told a foreign student of English that these words were in the same class as *beautiful* and *honest,* he would have to suppose that they behaved in the same way, and he would be betrayed into such ungrammatical sentences as "The reason seems main," "The idea is chief."

NOUNS AS MODIFIERS

In English, nouns may also occur as modifiers of nouns and often do. That is, we have constructions in which a noun is a headword and another noun is the modifier. The nouns that modify other nouns derive mostly from PATTERNS ONE, FOUR, EIGHT, and TEN, in a wide variety of ways. Here are examples:

ONE:	The worker works in the field.	field worker
ONE:	The child goes to school.	school child
FOUR:	The dog hunts birds.	bird dog
FOUR:	The inspector inspects buildings.	building inspector
FOUR:	The salesman sells soap.	soap salesman
EIGHT:	The eraser is for the blackboard.	blackboard eraser
EIGHT:	The food is for dogs.	dog food
EIGHT:	The lamp is on the ceiling.	ceiling lamp

---

* Many books use *adjective* in a much wider sense: any modifier of a noun. It is not impossible to describe English with this terminology, but it is much easier if we restrict the term as we have above. When we need a term embracing all the words that modify nouns, we say *noun modifier*.

TEN:	The girl is a servant.	servant girl
TEN:	The convertible is a Plymouth.	Plymouth convertible

Sometimes we can derive the same noun modifier from two different basic patterns — for example, from TWO (an adjective pattern) and from FOUR (a noun pattern). When that happens the noun cluster may have two meanings:

TWO:	The salesman seems sweet.	sweet salesman
FOUR:	The salesman sells sweets.	sweet salesman

The expression *sweet salesman* is ambiguous — i.e., has two possible meanings. The reason it has two possible meanings is that we can't tell whether *sweet* is a noun or an adjective. The reason we can't tell whether it is a noun or an adjective is that we can't tell which of the basic patterns it derives from.

VERBS AS MODIFIERS

Verbs may also occur as modifiers of noun headwords. Such verbs have either the *–ing* (present participle) form, the *–en* (past participle) form, or sometimes the simple form.

The *–ing* verbs used as modifiers derive most simply from PATTERN ONE:

The woman weeps.	weeping woman
The boy grows.	growing boy
The rain falls.	falling rain

From PATTERN FOUR we get *–ing* verbs modifying nouns in a more complicated construction. In these, the verb has the object it has in PATTERN FOUR. In the modification structure, the object precedes its verb, usually, in the writing system, being joined to it by a hyphen:

FOUR:	The rancher raises cattle.	a cattle-raising rancher

FOUR: The seamen sing
          psalms.   some psalm-singing seamen
FOUR: The woman packs a
          pistol.   a pistol-packing woman

We often have *–ing* verbs of a different sort modifying nouns. For example, *reading room, moving van, resting place.* We would probably all agree that *weeping woman* is somehow different from *reading room.* If we ask why or in what way it is different, the answer is that the two derive from different sources:

ONE: The woman weeps.   weeping woman
EIGHT: The room is for reading.   reading room*

The expression *moving van* is actually ambiguous, because it can come from either source:

ONE: The van moves.   moving van
EIGHT: The van is for moving.   moving van

Noun clusters with *–en* verbs as modifiers come mostly from PATTERN FOUR through the passive transformation. Whenever we have an instance of FOUR we can transform it in the following fashion:

1st N   V   2nd N

      becomes

2nd N   be   V - en   (by   1st N)

That is, the object of PATTERN FOUR becomes the subject of the passive transformation of FOUR, *be* is added, the verb takes the past participle form, and the original subject may or may not be expressed in a phrase with *by:*

---

* To be precise, we must say that *reading room* is a double transformation:

    They read in the room.   (PATTERN ONE)
      becomes
    The room is for reading. (a variation of EIGHT)
      becomes
    the reading room

FOUR   PASSIVE OF FOUR
John hates Jim.   Jim is hated by John.
The wind drives the snow.   The snow is driven by the wind.
She sang a song.   The song was sung.

PATTERNS FIVE, SIX, and SEVEN can become passives in slightly
more complicated transformations:

FIVE: He gave Mary the money.   Mary was given the
                                                            money.
SIX: We thought Al a fool.   Al was thought a fool.
SEVEN: We elected Al chairman.   Al was elected chair-
                                                            man.

The passives of FOUR supply –*en* form verbs as noun modifiers:

The snow was driven.   driven snow
The guests were invited.   invited guests
The cat was stunned.   stunned cat

These come ultimately from such basic sentences as "The wind
drives the snow," "They invited the guests," "It stunned the cat."

Sometimes simple forms of verbs appear as noun modifiers. These
derive mainly from PATTERN ONE:

ONE: The horse works.   a work horse
ONE: The boy flies.   a fly boy

In our writing system, most clusters derived from this source are
spelled as one word: *scrubwoman, gocart, watchdog.*

There is much more variety than we have shown here in the
words that can modify following noun headwords. But they all
come from the same general source; in one way or another, they all
derive from one or another of the basic sentence patterns. A person learning English — infant or foreigner — learns the patterns
and also, somehow or other, learns the machinery by which the
stuff of the patterns can be built into noun clusters.

If several modifiers modify the same noun headword, fairly rigid
rules of order must be followed. For example, if a determiner, an

adjective, and a noun modify another noun, they must occur in that order:

> a beautiful servant girl
> an old blackboard eraser
> some tasty dog food

Remember that any noun cluster can occur anywhere the noun headword can occur. For example:

PATTERN ONE:	The girl was dancing.
	The beautiful servant girl was dancing.
PATTERN THREE:	The girl became a bride.
	The beautiful servant girl became a bride.
PATTERN FIVE:	I gave the girl a kiss.
	I gave the beautiful servant girl a kiss.
PATTERN TEN:	She is a girl.
	She is a beautiful servant girl.

EXERCISE 17

The items given below all consist of a determiner, a modifier of some sort, and a noun headword. Copy each item and write after it a basic pattern from which it might derive. Identify the basic pattern by number, 1 to 10.

EXAMPLES: A. an old man
              The man seems old. — 2
              B. a shoe salesman
              He sells shoes. — 4

1. a weeping child
2. an attractive girl
3. a house builder
4. a punctured tire
5. a sewing room
6. a nasty bruise

7. a smiling villain
8. a playroom
9. a lordly manner
10. a table lamp
11. an awkward situation
12. a singing bird

13. some drifting snow
14. a writing desk
15. a loosened necktie
16. a beetle-hater
17. his glasses case
18. the growling lion
19. a splendid sunset
20. a quickening breeze
21. a mean dog
22. a dogcatcher
23. a stiff breeze
24. her gym clothes

25. a crybaby
26. a driving lesson
27. a driving iron
28. some drying clothes
29. an overlooked bet
30. a bookmark
31. her generous uncle
32. a startled fawn
33. a charming girl
34. a frowning girl
35. an Indiana girl

EXERCISE 18

Take the following noun cluster: *the young service station man.*
This is built from such patterns as these:

The man is young.   (NINE)
The man works in the station.   (ONE)
The station gives service.   (FOUR)

This noun cluster, like any noun cluster, can be used in most of the noun
positions in the basic sentence patterns. Write sentences using it as directed.

EXAMPLE: A. Subject in ONE
            The young service station man works hard.

1. Subject in TWO
2. Subject in THREE
3. Predicate noun in THREE
4. Subject in FOUR
5. Object in FOUR
6. Subject in FIVE
7. Indirect object in FIVE
8. Subject in SIX

9. Object in SIX
10. Object complement in SIX
11. Subject in SEVEN
12. Object in SEVEN
13. Subject in EIGHT
14. Subject in NINE
15. Subject in TEN

12 NOUN CLUSTERS — MODIFIERS AFTER THE HEADWORD

In our discussion of noun clusters in the preceding chapter, all the noun modifiers were types that generally occur before the noun headword. Various other kinds of modifiers occur generally or always after the headword.

For example, certain kinds of adverbs modify nouns. Those that do derive chiefly from PATTERN EIGHT and occur after the noun they modify:

EIGHT:	The boy is here.	the boy here
EIGHT:	The dog is outside.	the dog outside
EIGHT:	A barn was nearby.	a barn nearby
EIGHT:	The dinner was later.	the dinner later

Some of these adverbs can also occur before the noun: *a nearby barn, a later engagement,* and *an outside chance.* But mostly they come after.

TRANSFORMATIONS THAT PRODUCE MODIFIERS

The transformations that produce modifiers are more complicated than such transformations as the passive, and it may be worthwhile to pause to examine their nature carefully. In a modification transformation, two sentence patterns are always involved: the pattern from which the modifier is derived and the pattern in which the modification structure is used. We call the first the *source* sentence and the second the *consumer* sentence. Thus *the boy here* is not a sentence pattern itself. It derives from PATTERN EIGHT (the source) and will be used in some other sentence pattern (the consumer):

EIGHT: The boy is here.

TEN: The boy is my brother.

The boy here is my brother. (TEN expanded with material from EIGHT.)

EIGHT: The dog was outside.

FIVE: I gave the dog some food.

I gave the dog outside some food. (FIVE expanded with material from EIGHT.)

PATTERN EIGHT is also the principal source of the prepositional phrases that modify nouns. The resulting noun cluster can be used in any of the noun positions of the various sentence patterns:

Source: The bird is in the tree. (EIGHT)

Consumer: The bird sang beautifully. (ONE)

Result: The bird in the tree sang beautifully. (ONE expanded from EIGHT.)

Similarly:

EIGHT: The man is from Toledo. His guest is a man from Toledo.

EIGHT: The door was to his right. He took the door to his right.

PREPOSITIONAL PHRASES

Prepositional phrases deriving from various sources other than PATTERN EIGHT may also modify nouns. We give some examples without trying to specify the sources:

the city *of Toledo*

the first *of the month*

some *of the boys*

You will note that a prepositional phrase consists of a preposition (*on, from, to, with, of*, etc.) plus a noun or pronoun. The noun in the prepositional phrase, like all the nouns in the basic patterns, can also be modified, can itself become the headword of a noun cluster with modifiers deriving from the basic patterns in the ways we have discussed:

> the boy with the girl
> the boy with the servant girl
> the boy with the beautiful servant girl

A noun in a prepositional phrase can itself be a headword modified by a prepositional phrase:

The boy is on the horse.	the boy on the horse
The horse is by the barn.	the boy on the horse by the barn
The barn is in the meadow.	the boy on the horse by the barn in the meadow

This process can go on indefinitely, the number of prepositional phrases being limited only by considerations of style or comprehension. Any noun in the string of phrases can be modified with any of the modification machinery used on other nouns.

RELATIVE CLAUSES

Another important kind of noun modifier is what is called a *relative clause*. If you have understood the basic sentence patterns that we have described, you will find nothing difficult in relative clauses. A relative clause is just one of the basic sentence patterns with the word *who, that, which,* or *whom* occurring in place of one of the nouns or with the word *whose* occurring in place of a determiner. *Who, that, which, whom,* and *whose* make up the group of structure words called relatives.

The machinery that produces relative clauses is similar to that producing other modifiers. Again two sentences are involved. The relative clause is derived from a source sentence and used in a consumer sentence:

Source: He went away. (ONE)
Consumer: He came back. (ONE)
Result: The man who went away came back.

Source: It looked odd. (TWO)
Consumer: I bought a picture. (FOUR)
Result: I bought a picture that looked odd.

The two examples above illustrate the simplest kind of relative clause, that in which the relative replaces the subject of the source sentence. In such a clause, the relative is *who, that,* or *which. Who* replaces a human noun or pronoun of the source sentence; *which* replaces a nonhuman noun; *that* replaces any noun. Here are more examples. We give just the source sentence and a resulting noun cluster. The cluster could be used in any noun position in which its headword could be used:

THREE:	He became my friend.	the boy *who became my friend*
FOUR:	He was eating an apple.	the chap *that was eating an apple*
FIVE:	He gave Sam the money.	the man *who gave Sam the money*
SIX:	He called Sam a fool.	the man *who called Sam a fool*
SEVEN:	They elected Sam chairman.	the committee *that elected Sam chairman*
EIGHT:	He was here.	someone *who was here*
NINE:	It was offensive.	a remark *which was offensive*
TEN:	It was a surprise.	a remark *which was a surprise*

Relatives can also replace the objects of PATTERNS FOUR, FIVE, SIX, and SEVEN. The relatives so used are *which, that,* and *whom,* and they come before the verb, not after it. In these constructions, the noun modified is one that could be the object in the basic pattern.

> **Source:** He ate an apple. (FOUR)
> **Consumer:** The apple was rotten. (NINE)
> **Result:** The apple which he ate was rotten.

Similarly:

FIVE:	He gave her a flower.	the flower *that he gave her*
SIX:	He called the man a fool.	the man *whom he called a fool*
SEVEN:	They elected him chairman.	the man *that they elected chairman*

Relative clauses of this type, in which the relative replaces an object, have an alternate form in which the relative is simply omitted, the position of the clause showing that it is a modifier:

> an apple he ate
> the man he called a fool

The relative *whose* can replace any determiner in a basic pattern and so convert the pattern into a relative clause. If the determiner replaced modifies an object, the relative and the object occur before the verb, as in the third example below:

ONE:	The dog barked.	the boy *whose dog barked*
FOUR:	The boy ate the apple.	the mother *whose boy ate the apple*
FOUR:	The boy ate the apple.	the child *whose apple the boy ate*

Relatives can also replace noun, pronouns, and determiners occurring in prepositional phrases. The relatives used are *whom*, *which*, and *whose*.

FOUR: He did it for her.   the girl *for whom he did it*

FOUR: He did it for her sake.   the girl *for whose sake he did it*

FOUR: He sent it to this address. the address *to which he sent it*

A relative clause and a prepositional phrase may both be used to modify the same noun. When this situation occurs, the prepositional phrase comes first and the relative clause second:

Headword		Prepositional Phrase	Relative Clause
the	girl	in the car	who was waving to us
the	boys	in back	who had been talking
the	goats	on the lawn	that were bleating

However, there is a danger of ambiguity in this construction. The relative will have two nouns ahead of it: the main headword and the noun in the prepositional phrase. There must therefore be some signal to tell which noun the relative clause refers to. In the following examples there is no such signal, and the constructions are ambiguous:

> the girl in the car that needed water
> the goats on the lawn that had recently been clipped
> the bird in the cage that belongs to me

We shall discuss this difficulty in greater detail in Chapter 21.

Be sure to distinguish between noun clusters and sentences. Noun clusters, no matter how complicated their modification, are not sentences. If you punctuate them with a capital letter at the beginning and a period at the end, you produce the writing error called a fragment. These constructions become parts of sentences only when they take **N** positions in consumer sentences.

TEN: *The girl in the car who was waving to us* is Sam's aunt.

FOUR: The teacher reprimanded *the boys in the back who had been talking.*

FIVE: He gave *the goats on the lawn that were grazing* a good scare.

EXERCISE 19

You are given below an assortment of basic sentences, each with an **N** position italicized. First identify the pattern by number. Then, by substituting a relative for the italicized word or words, make the sentence into a relative clause and rewrite it as part of a noun cluster. Do not punctuate the clusters as sentences.

EXAMPLES: A. *He* gave me the money.

5 — *the bank clerk who gave me the money*

B. He became *a* helper.

2 — *the electrician whose helper he became*

1. *He* just went away.
2. *They* were outside.
3. *It* ruined the table.
4. It ruined *the table.*
5. It ruined *the* table.
6. *He* remained an Elk.
7. He considered *the man* a wastrel.
8. They wanted *a cup of coffee.*
9. They were *cold.*
10. *She* seemed thoughtful.
11. The mailman gave me *some* letters.
12. The mailman gave me *some letters.*
13. I fixed it for *him.*
14. Belinda sang to *the baby.*
15. *The* parakeet looked unwell.
16. *The hen* must have laid an egg.

17. *They* had wanted to go away.
18. The mailman enjoyed bringing me *letters*.
19. *His* brother enjoyed pretending to think school a bore.
20. They must have been trying to repair *the* car.

EXERCISE 20

Number from 1 to 30. The following sentence patterns contain noun clusters as well as simple nouns and pronouns in **N** positions. Interspersed, and incorrectly punctuated as sentences, are some noun clusters. If the item is a sentence, write **S** beside the corresponding numbers. If it is a noun cluster, write **NC**. Identify the sentence patterns by number.

EXAMPLES: A. Her brother gave her a small bracelet which she liked very much.

        S — 5

       B. A small bracelet which her brother gave her.

        NC

1. The spokesman for the reporters requested an interview.
2. The people who have been visiting us seem very pleasant.
3. The man who ordinarily brings the laundry.
4. The ushers ejected the boys who had been throwing grapefruit.
5. The cars in the back which have already been sold.
6. He gave his fiancée a handsome diamond ring which had been in his family for centuries.
7. A box of oysters that his mother had given him for Christmas.
8. The people that live upstairs have been complaining.
9. The new treasurer of the club should be someone who already has a lot of money.
10. I thought her father a pompous old windbag.
11. The young acolytes who murdered the archbishop.
12. He had just purchased a rubber potato masher which had taken his fancy.
13. The old set of andirons which Father brought back from Spain.
14. This is the face that launched a thousand ships.

15. A book about bees that my mother had never allowed me to read.
16. The design of angleworms which dominated the bedroom wallpaper was quite unpleasant.
17. A haggard look which gave his friends great concern.
18. The porter that had gone off with his baggage never returned.
19. An interesting old man who in his younger days had been a well-known rabbit groomer.
20. The Argonaut Café became his favorite restaurant in Portland.
21. A trouble shooter is not exactly a man who shoots trouble.
22. The rather grimy individual in the last seat who claimed to be a Macedonian.
23. The gift he most appreciated was the cigarette lighter which his aunt had given him.
24. Dining-room tables of dark mahogany which were being sold at fantastic prices.
25. The foghorn in the outer harbor was going constantly.
26. He impassively read the note which had been handed to him.
27. They voted my brother the most popular man in the senior class.
28. A medical bill that he couldn't possibly pay.
29. The vice-principal to whom such unpleasant chores were simply part of the day's routine.
30. The fellow I spoke to you about may try to come later.

13 VERB CLUSTERS

In earlier chapters we studied the variations that occur in predicates and that distinguish the basic patterns of English. In Chapter 9 we saw how all of these predicates can be expanded through the addition of certain other forms according to fairly simple rules:

John   went away.
John   may go away.   **(M** added)

John	has gone away.	(**have** plus - **en** added)
John	is going away.	(**be** plus - **ing** added)
John	may have gone away.	
John	has been going away.	
John	may be going away.	
John	may have been going away.	
John	preferred to go away.	
John	enjoyed going away.	
John	preferred to enjoy going away.	
John	enjoyed preferring to go away.	
John	may have been enjoying preferring to go away.	
John	may prefer to have been enjoying to go away.	

And so on. This mechanism, which we can describe in a few lines, can be applied to any of the predicate patterns to produce infinitely many English sentences.

THE MAKE–UP OF A VERB CLUSTER

A predicate is one function of what we call a *verb cluster*. A verb cluster consists of a verb plus any of the stuff that may go with verbs in the various patterns: objects of any kind, predicate nouns, adjectives, adverbs, prepositional phrases; also the auxiliaries: modals, *have, be;* also verbs of the types *prefer* and *enjoy* as used above. All of these features that modify or otherwise consort with verbs make up the verb cluster.

We say that a verb cluster is used as a predicate when it has a subject — i.e., when, along with its subject, it makes a sentence pattern. All of the examples above are of verb clusters used as predicates. We shall see in later chapters that verb clusters have many other uses; with certain changes made, they can occur as modifiers of nouns, as subjects and objects, and so on. But before we go on to consider these other functions of verb clusters, we need to note certain other expansions possible in the verb cluster. We shall continue to illustrate with verb clusters used as predicates.

ADVERBS IN VERB CLUSTERS

Adverbs, which we have already encountered, are a common feature in verb clusters. There are several types. Adverbs like *up, away, down, in, out, home*, which are often called adverbs of place or direction, occur most prominently in PATTERNS ONE and EIGHT.

> ONE: John walked away (in, out, down, up, home).
> EIGHT: John is here (there, away, out, upstairs, home).

They occur also in some of the patterns that we haven't numbered:

> He put it away.
> He left it there.

Another subclass of adverbs are adverbs of time: *often, usually, sometimes, never, occasionally, frequently*. These can occur with all of the basic patterns. The most common position for them is before the verb, either directly before or somewhere amid the auxiliaries:

> ONE: John   usually walked away.
> FOUR: John   might never have seen the fellow.
> SIX: John   often thought his brother an imbecile.

In the *be* patterns, the most common position is right after the *be*:

> NINE: John   was never happy.

All of the time adverbs except *never* can occur also at the very end of the verb cluster:

> ONE: John   walked away sometimes.
> NINE: John   was happy occasionally.

The largest subclass of adverbs are the adverbs of manner: *courageously, hopefully, quickly, sweetly, fast*. Most of these are composed of an adjective form plus *–ly*. These occur with any of the first seven basic patterns; they are not so common with the *be* patterns. They can occur at many positions within the cluster, though they occur more commonly after the verb than before it:

ONE:	John	walked away angrily.
ONE:	John	angrily walked away.
ONE:	John	walked angrily away.
THREE:	John	courageously became my friend.
FIVE:	John	lent me the money reluctantly.

In place of an adverb we can usually have a prepositional phrase: *to the store, in the morning, with a will.* Prepositional phrases in a verb cluster regularly come after the verb rather than before it:

John	walked home.
John	walked to his house.
John	walked occasionally.
John	walked in the mornings.
John	worked steadily.
John	worked with a will.

Of course we can have more than one adverb in a verb cluster, though usually not more than one of any subclass. If more than one adverb occurs, certain rules of order prevail.

| John | walked home happily sometimes. |
| John | went to the store on his bicycle in the afternoon. |

Often we have a noun with a determiner performing the function of an adverb of time; such nouns occur after the verb in the cluster:

John	left early.
John	left this morning.
John	often worked.
John	worked this afternoon.

SUBORDINATE CLAUSES IN VERB CLUSTERS

Another structure that can occur in a verb cluster is what is called a *subordinate clause.* These are very simple to describe. They are simply sentence patterns of any kind preceded by a subordinator — that is, a word like *because, if, when, where, while, unless, until, after, before, whereas, since.* When one of these words is used before a sentence pattern, the sentence pattern is no longer a sentence but a part of a sentence. Any sentence pattern at all can become a subordinate clause in this way:

ONE: John went away.
        because John went away

FIVE: He gives me the money.
        if he gives me the money

SEVEN: We elected Sam president.
        when we elected Sam president

NINE: Birds are beautiful.
        although birds are beautiful

TEN: He is your friend.
        unless he is your friend

Subordinate clauses have several different functions. One is that of modifier in verb clusters. Any of the basic patterns can add a subordinate clause to the verb cluster:

ONE: John   went away.
        John   went away because he was angry.

FOUR: He   will see you later.
        He   will see you later if he has time.

EIGHT: Mary   was here.
        Mary   was here when I came.

NINE: He   'll be happy.
        He   'll be happy after he sees the letter.

EXERCISE 21

Certain problems of punctuation and of other aspects of writing can be solved if one is able to recognize fundamental structures through all the elaboration of which they are capable. Below you are given verb clusters — predicates — of increasing complexity. See if you can identify the basic patterns — ONE to TEN — that they represent. Remember that the pattern is determined by what follows the verb or *be*. If there is more than one verb or *be* (*preferred to go, is being, seemed to enjoy being*), it is what follows the last one. Thus "John goes," "John is going," "John prefers to go," "John seems to be going" are all instances of PATTERN ONE. "John is happy," "John enjoys being happy," "John seems to be happy" are all instances of PATTERN NINE. The pattern of a subordinate clause does not affect the pattern of the main part of the sentence. Write the number of the pattern of the sentence on a separate sheet of paper.

1. John   left.
2. John   was here.
3. John   gave me the money.
4. John   became a clerk.
5. John   went away.
6. John   felt sad.
7. John   faced the music.
8. John   was a flyer.
9. John   often rode his cycle.
10. John   thought me a coward.
11. John   sometimes behaved badly.
12. John   usually drove his car to the office.
13. John   was here this morning.
14. John   preferred to sleep.
15. John   seemed to be ill.
16. John   enjoyed telling old jokes.
17. John   forgot to send her his address.
18. John   did the dishes when he got home.
19. John   climbed the tree in ten seconds.
20. John   climbed the old elm tree in the back yard.
21. John   remained quiet all evening.
22. John   wanted to elect Sam chairman.
23. John   used to be a good friend of mine.
24. John   liked to recollect the adventures of his early youth.
25. John   will give you a hand if you can wait a few minutes.
26. John   refused indignantly to reply to the question.

27. John   hoped to raise cabbages in the back yard later on.
28. John   was feeling happy because there was only one more week of school.
29. John   very gracefully introduced us to his aged parents.
30. John   reluctantly showed us the letter that he had received from the principal.
31. John   was on his way to the hardware store when he heard the siren.
32. John   probably was the last fullblooded Paiute in the county.
33. John   bore a sharp resemblance to a fellow I had known in Henderson before the war.
34. John   decided to risk asking Mabel a rather personal question.
35. John   was hoping to see Paris once more before he died.

EXERCISE 22

One of the writing errors considered most serious by teachers of English, including those who read college entrance examinations, is the fragment — i.e., a structure which is not a sentence but which is punctuated as if it were. Obviously, learning to avoid fragments is a matter of learning to distinguish sentences from such nonsentences as verb clusters, noun clusters, relative clauses, subordinate clauses, and prepositional phrases. All of these structures, along with some sentences, are included in the items below. On a separate sheet of paper, identify each structure with the appropriate symbol: sentence **(S)**, noun cluster **(NC)**, verb cluster **(VC)**, relative clause **(RC)**, subordinate clause **(SC)**, prepositional phrase **(Prep)**.

1. he won second prize
2. the fellow that I was telling you about
3. that I was telling you about
4. because his uncle was a judge
5. won second prize because his uncle was a judge
6. the fellow that I was telling you about won second prize because his uncle was a judge
7. some codfish that had seen better days
8. before we realized what she was doing

9. in the lake that bordered the campus
10. the lake that bordered the campus
11. the lake that bordered the campus bred mosquitoes
12. was desperately trying to pick up the pieces
13. it was a hand-painted picture of his mother
14. a young fellow from Lapland who had never seen a toothbrush
15. desperate young inmates with murder in their eyes watched us from an upstairs window
16. the bride was obviously radiant with happiness
17. because Harold could hang by his heels
18. desperate young inmates with murder in their eyes who watched us from an upstairs window
19. wanted to meet the man who had been responsible for it all
20. within ten seconds of the pressing of the button
21. they seemed to be watching us constantly
22. since he had no idea that there was anyone else in the room
23. several aluminum-ware salesmen who were loudly demanding service
24. occasionally liked to order a large tenderloin steak with French fried potatoes
25. the first of the four bulls had already been killed in the arena
26. had tried patiently to peel the apple with a dull spoon
27. by a feeling of revulsion which he could not conceal from us
28. a large mackerel had somehow appeared in the goldfish bowl
29. a broad-shouldered youngster in uniform who had been standing nearby handed me a box which had been loosely wrapped in newspaper
30. a weary smile on his handsome young face

EXERCISE 23

By using the modification devices explained in the last few chapters, expand each of the sentence patterns given below to sentences of fifteen words or more. If you use just the kinds of modification we have so far examined, you will have no commas in your sentences. Identify each pattern by number.

EXAMPLE: A. Birds eat worms.
             The little canary birds that we have at our house sometimes
             refuse to eat the worms that we give them for supper. — 4

1. The man went away.
2. The police arrested the criminal.
3. The girl wrote her mother a letter.
4. The club chose my brother their president.
5. The child was in the yard.
6. The judge looked angry.
7. The man was the judge.
8. The teachers considered my sister a good student.
9. The village became a city.
10. The custodians were sad.

14
SUBSTITUTES FOR NOUNS

In the basic sentence patterns that we have examined, various positions have been occupied by nouns or pronouns. Each of the patterns has a noun or pronoun as subject; some patterns have them as objects, predicate nouns, or object complements. We have also seen that any noun can develop into a complex noun cluster through the mechanism of noun modification.

In addition, each of the noun positions can be taken by other structures: verb clusters, relative clauses, subordinate clauses.

VERB CLUSTERS IN NOUN POSITIONS

Verb clusters taking noun positions are of two types. We will refer to them as the *–ing* type and the *to* type. Any predicate can be transformed into a subject or predicate noun by the addition of an *–ing* to the simple form of a verb or *be:*

John milked the cows.
Milking the cows took a lot of time.
His chief chore was milking the cows.

Note that the last sentence, in which a verb cluster appears in the place of a predicate noun (PATTERN TEN), is different from "His oldest boy was milking the cows" (PATTERN FOUR).

He was punctual.
Being punctual was his principal virtue.
Being punctual bored him.

In a variation of this construction, the verb or *be* is preceded by a possessive noun (*John's*, *the boy's*, *the dog's*) or by a possessive determiner (*his*, *my*, *our*, etc.):

John was punctual.
John's being punctual saved us.
The thing that saved us was John's being punctual.

An *–ing* cluster can also be used as the object of a preposition:

John saved the day by being punctual.

In the *to* type, the simple form of the verb is preceded by the word *to*. Any of the ten patterns can occur after *to* in noun positions.

He called John a fool.
To call John a fool is absurd.

He knows John.
He likes him.
To know John is *to like him.*

He answered insolently.
To answer insolently was foolish.

The last example, in which the *to* cluster is subject of a predicate of PATTERN NINE (**Subject** plus **be** plus **Adj**) can be changed once more into the construction **it   be   Adj   to   cluster:**

To answer insolently was foolish.
It was foolish *to answer insolently*.

He was there on time.
To be there on time was unnecessary.
It was unnecessary *to be there on time*.

RELATIVE CLAUSES IN NOUN POSITIONS

Relative clauses can also occur in noun positions. The relative clauses that do are similar to those that occur in noun clusters but not identical. You remember that the relatives introducing clauses that modify nouns are *who, whose, whom, which, that*. The relative clauses that take noun positions in the basic patterns are introduced by *who, whose, whom,* and *which*, but not by *that*. They may also be introduced by *what, whatever, whoever, whichever*. Here are examples of relative clauses replacing nouns or pronouns:

He did that.   (Source — FOUR)
He is my hero.   (Consumer — TEN)
Whoever did that is my hero.

He found it.   (Source — FOUR)
He gave him a dime.   (Consumer — FIVE)
He gave *whoever found it* a dime.

He did that.   (Source — FOUR)
I know it.   (Consumer — FOUR)
I know *who did that*.
I know *what he did*.

He asked the question.   (Source — FOUR)
I have forgotten it.   (Consumer — FOUR)
I have forgotten *who asked the question*.
I have forgotten *what he asked*.

SUBORDINATE CLAUSES IN NOUN POSITIONS

Subordinate clauses may also occur in noun positions. Recall the difference between subordinate clauses and relative clauses. A rela-

tive clause is introduced by a relative like *who, which, whose, what.*
The relative takes the place of a noun or a determiner of the basic
sentence pattern. A subordinate clause is introduced by a subordinator like *because, if, unless, that.* The subordinator does not replace anything in the sentence pattern but precedes the whole
pattern.

Subordinate clauses taking noun positions are most commonly
introduced by the subordinator *that* (different from the relative
that which occurs in noun clusters) though other subordinators are
sometimes used.

> John stole the horse. (Source — FOUR)
> I know it. (Consumer — FOUR)
> I know *that John stole the horse.*
>
> They had plenty of money. (Source — FOUR)
> It was true. (Consumer — NINE)
> *That they had plenty of money* was true.

Like the sentences with *to* clusters, sentences like the last, in
which a subordinate clause occurs as subject of a PATTERN NINE
construction, are likely to go through a second change: **clause be
Adj** becomes **it be Adj clause:**

> That they had plenty of money was true.
> It was true *that they had plenty of money.*
>
> He was able to come. (Source — NINE)
> Something was nice. (Consumer — NINE)
> *That he was able to come* was nice.
> It was nice *that he was able to come.*

These, then, are some of the constructions that can occur in place
of the nouns of the basic patterns: verb clusters with *–ing;* verb
clusters with *to;* relative clauses; subordinate clauses. Notice that
everything derives from the basic sentence patterns. Given just the
stuff of the basic patterns plus the rules for transforming them, we
can make all sorts of complicated sentences. Looked at one way,

English sentences are very complex. But looked at another, the most complex of them is very simple, since it will inevitably boil down to the basic patterns.

We have not exhausted the possibilities of substitutions for nouns. For example, adjectives, derived from PATTERN TWO, can be preceded by *the* and used in any noun position:

> They seemed brave.
> They seemed fair.
> The boys deserved the girls.
> *The brave* deserved *the fair.*

Other structures occur in noun positions now and then, but the ones we have illustrated are the important ones.

EXERCISE 24

You are given below a number of sentence patterns. Copy these sentences and identify each pattern by number. Then write four different sentences using each pattern in a noun position as (1) an *–ing* verb cluster, (2) a *to* verb cluster, (3) a relative clause, (4) a subordinate clause.

EXAMPLE: A. John stole the horse.

> *John stole the horse.* — 4
> *He was arrested for stealing the horse.*
> *To steal the horse took a lot of nerve.*
> *I know who stole the horse.* (Or *I know what he stole.*)
> *It is true that he stole the horse.*

1. He found the money.
2. He sent her a letter.
3. He became a citizen.
4. He was argumentative.
5. He believed her innocent.
6. He was in the house all day.
7. They captured the monkey.
8. He talked back rudely.
9. She threw George a kiss.
10. He mowed the lawn on Sunday.

15 SUBJECT-PREDICATE AGREEMENT

We have seen that one use of a noun or pronoun is to occur as a subject, and that one use of a verb or verb cluster is to occur as a predicate. In the basic patterns, verb clusters occur only as predicates.

RELATION OF SUBJECT AND PREDICATE

In English, the subject-predicate relationship differs from other sentence relationships in that the form of the subject controls the form of the predicate. More exactly, the form of the subject controls the present-tense form of the first verb or *be* or *have* in the predicate:

> The bird sings.
> The birds sing.
>
> The bird is singing.
> The birds are singing.
>
> It has been singing.
> They have been singing.

After *bird* and *it*, the forms *sings, is, has* occur; after *birds* and *they*, the forms *sing, are, have* occur. We say that *bird* and *it* are *singular* forms, having the meaning "one." *Birds* and *they* are *plural* forms, having the meaning "more than one." Singular subjects are followed by the *–s* form of verbs and by the *am* (after *I*) and *is* forms of *be*. Plural subjects are followed by the simple form of verbs and the *are* form of *be*.

If the first word in the predicate is the past tense of a verb or any modal auxiliary, then the number of the subject has no effect:

The bird sang.
The birds sang.

The bird can sing.
The birds can sing.

But if the first word is a past tense of *be*, *was* occurs after singular subjects and *were* after plural subjects:

The bird was cute.
The birds were cute.

The bird was singing.
The birds were singing.

To say this much to the native speaker of English is to explain what is obvious. Speakers of English learn very early to make subjects and predicates agree in this way. After the age of four or five we automatically, as we speak, select the predicate form that suits the subject. It is virtually impossible for native speakers to say, for example, "The birds sings" or "The bird cans sing."

SPECIAL PROBLEMS IN AGREEMENT

However, in the frequently more elaborate structures of writing and with the time lag between the thinking of the sentence and the getting it down on paper, errors in agreement of subject and predicate are common enough. For example, though we might never go wrong with a basic sentence, we might get confused if the subject is developed into a complicated noun cluster. Remember that it is the *headword* of the noun cluster, not any other noun that the cluster may contain, which determines the form of the predicate. In the following examples, the headwords are italicized:

The young *choirboy* who is standing somewhat apart from the other lads *sings* beautifully. (*Lads* does not affect the form of the verb.)

The young *choirboys* who are shown here being decorated by the rector *sing* beautifully. (*Rector* does not affect the form of the verb.)

Notice in these examples that the *be* in the relative clause is also controlled by the headword in the cluster: *choirboy who is, choirboys who are.*

A complication occurs when the subject is *compound* — that is, when it is composed of two nouns or pronouns connected by *and* or by *or*. *And* and *or* belong to the structure group called *conjunctions*, of which we shall have more to say in Chapter 17. Here we shall notice merely their effect on subject-predicate agreement.

The effect of *and* is to make the subject plural:

The *boy* and the *girl* sing beautifully.

The little *choirboy* about whom we were speaking and the *girl* who appears with him in this picture sing beautifully.

Or (which occurs most commonly along with the word *either*) does not normally affect the number of the subject. If it connects two singular nouns, the subject is singular; if it connects two plural nouns, the subject is plural:

Either the *boy* or the *girl* is a good singer.

Either the *boys* or the *girls* are good singers.

The combination *neither . . . nor* works the same way:

Neither the *boy* nor the *girl* is a good singer.

Neither the *boys* nor the *girls* are good singers.

If a singular and a plural subject is compounded with *either . . . or* or *neither . . . nor*, the handbook recommendation is to make the verb agree with the part of the subject closest to it: "Neither the boys nor the girl is a good singer." However, most experienced writers would simply avoid the construction altogether.

Some difficulties in subject-predicate agreement result from differences between speech and writing. For example, the pronouns *either*, *neither*, and *each* are often treated as plurals in speech but regularly as singulars in formal writing. That is, many of us frequently *say*, "Neither of them are going." But in anything except a personal letter or dialogue, we would write, "Neither of them is going." And similarly:

Either of the alternatives is acceptable.
Each of the alternatives is acceptable.

The word *none*, however, which used to be in this category, is now treated in both ways. Both of the following might be found in serious writing:

None of the alternatives is acceptable.
None of the alternatives are acceptable.

The first might strike some readers as the more elegant.

The number of the word *half* depends on what follows in the prepositional phrase:

Half of the pie has been eaten.
Half of the boys have been beaten.

The expression *a number* is plural, but *the number* is singular:

The number of people who attended the service was very large.
A number of the people who attended the service were very large.

Another possible conflict between speech and writing involves the *there* transformation. This, you will remember, is a construction of the type "There is a man here," which derives from PATTERN EIGHT, "A man is here." In speech, the *there* is frequently treated as if it were a singular subject and is followed by *is* or *was*, whatever the number of the noun in the pattern. That is, many people say, "There's some men here" or "There was some mice in this room." If you do, you need to remember that the usage of serious writing is different. The noun is treated as the subject, determining the form of the predicate:

There *is* a *man* here.
There *are* some *men* here.
There *was* a *mouse* in the room.
There *were* some *mice* in the room.
There *is* only one acceptable *alternative*.
There *are* several possible *alternatives*.
There *is* *something* about her I like very much.
There *are* many *things* about her I would like to change.

EXERCISE 25

Write sentences from the following formulas, using the structure words given and being careful to choose the proper form of *be*. **Prep** stands for prepositional phrase, **R** for relative.

1. **There   be   D   N   Adv**
2. **There   be   D   N   Prep**
3. **There   be   N   Prep**
4. **Neither   of   D   N   be   D   N**
5. **D   N   and   D   N   be   V - ing   Prep**
6. **Both   of   D   N   be   N**
7. **Neither   D   N   nor   D   N   be   Adj**
8. **Either   D   N   or   D   N   be   Adj**
9. **Both   D   N   and   D   N   be   Adj**
10. **One   of   D   N   R   V   D   N   be   D   N**
11. **Some   of   D   N   R   V   D   N   be   Adj**
12. **A   number   of   D   N   R   V   D   N   be   Adj**
13. **The   number   of   N   R   V   D   N   be   Adj**
14. **None   of   D   N   R   V   D   N   be   Adj**
15. **D   N   R   V   D   N   and   D   N   R   V   D   N
    be   V - ing   Prep**
16. **Either   D   N   R   V   D   N   or   D   N   R   V
    D   N   be   V - ing   Prep**
17. **Neither   D   N   R   V   D   N   nor   D   N   R   V
    D   N   be   V - ing   Prep**
18. **D   N   Prep   and   D   N   R   V   D   N   be   N**

SUMMARY OF TERMS • CHAPTERS 9–15

Adverbs of manner (p. 82)   Words like *happily, courageously, indispensably.*

Adverbs of place (p. 82)   Words like *here, there, outside, away.*

Adverbs of time (p. 82)   Words like *now, later, usually, never.*

Compound subject (p. 95)   Two subjects joined by a conjunction so as to function with a single predicate: "The boy and the girl swim." The effect of the conjunction *and* is to make the subject plural. Other conjunctions do not ordinarily affect the number of the subject.

Consumer sentence (p. 73)   The basic pattern in which a transformation is used. "The man went away" is a consumer sentence in which the transformation *the man outside* might be used: "The man outside went away."

Headword (p. 65)   The key or central part of a modification structure; the part which has a function in relation to another part of the sentence outside the modification structure; that which is modified. Nouns, verbs, adjectives, adverbs, and certain structure words may be headwords of modification structures.

- ing form (p. 88)   The simple form of a verb plus the ending *–ing: going, driving, resigning.*

Modal auxiliary (p. 52)   One of the words *can, may, shall, will, must, could, might, would, should.*

Noun cluster (p. 65)   A construction consisting of a noun plus modifiers of the noun.

Noun modifier (p. 65)   Anything that modifies a noun. Determiners, adjectives, verbs, adverbs, other nouns, phrases, and clauses may occur as noun modifiers.

Number (p. 93)   A grammatical feature which applies, in English, primarily to nouns and pronouns and secondarily to verbs. English nouns and pronouns have number in the sense that they express the difference between one (*apple, boy, he*) and more than one (*apples, boys, they*). The forms that mean "one" are called *singular* forms; the forms that mean "more than one" are called *plural* forms. Verbs have number only in the sense that their forms change according to the number of the subject: "The boy swims," "The boys swim." Verbs have these changing forms only in the present tense. *Be* has them also in the past tense.

Passive (p. 60)   A particular transformation of sentence PATTERNS FOUR, FIVE, SIX, or SEVEN: "The man was arrested" (from FOUR), "John was given the money" (from FIVE), "John was considered a hero" (from SIX), "John was elected president" (from SEVEN). All passives contain in the predicate a form of *be* plus an *–en* (past participle) form of a verb.

Possessive noun (p. 89)   A noun plus an ending which indicates possession or some related meaning. In regular spelling, the possessive ending is spelled " 's " or, for regular plural nouns, just " ' ". *John's, boy's, man's, boys', men's* are examples of possessive nouns.

Prepositional phrase (p. 73)   A construction consisting of a preposition (*at, with, to,* etc.) plus a noun or a noun equivalent. The constructions *at the door, with the boy, to whoever wanted it* are prepositional phrases.

Relative clause (p. 74)   A transformation in which one of the relatives *who, whose, whom, which, that* replaces a noun or a determiner of a basic sentence pattern. Relative clauses either modify nouns or occur in noun positions in sentences. The constructions *who was here, whom we saw, that asked the question* are relative clauses.

Source sentence (p. 72)   The basic pattern from which a transformation is derived. "The man is outside" is the source of the modification structure *the man outside.*

Subordinate clause (p. 83)   A sentence pattern preceded by a subordinator — i.e., a word like *because, if, while, where, unless, although.* Subordinate clauses usually function as modifiers of verbs or of whole sentence patterns. Sometimes they occur in noun positions in sentence patterns.

To form (p. 88)   The simple form of a verb preceded by the word *to: to go, to drive, to resign.*

Transformation (p. 58)   A construction deriving from a basic sentence or a part of a basic sentence. Any construction that is not part of the basic sentences of English is a transformation.

Transformed sentence (p. 58)   A sentence that is made out of or derives from a basic sentence or a part of a basic sentence.

Verb cluster (p. 81)   A modification structure in which the headword is a verb.

16 FRAGMENTS

We have already, in the course of the last few chapters, had a good deal to say (though somewhat indirectly) about fragments. A fragment is a piece of a sentence punctuated as a complete sentence — that is, with a capital letter at the beginning and a period at the end. The fragment is considered — not only by teachers and readers of college entrance examinations, but also by editors and others who control writing standards — a grievous error.

USAGE DIFFERENCES IN SPEECH AND WRITING

Possibly one reason students tend to write fragments is that they are misled by the practices of speech. In speech we frequently — indeed, very frequently — utter sentences which lack the full structure of the patterns we have studied here. For example, if someone asks us, "Who is that fellow?" we are not at all likely to reply, "That fellow is my brother" or even, "He is my brother." Instead, we would probably say, simply and properly, "My brother." The conversation might go like this:

"Who is that fellow?"
"My brother."
"He go to this school?"
"No, he's in college."
"Which one?"
"Michigan State."

Of the six utterances, only two, the first and fourth, have the full forms that we have spoken of as sentences. But it must be emphasized that there is nothing at all wrong with such a conversation. The structures derive from the basic sentence patterns by regular rules, just as we have seen other structures derive. No one speaking in this way could possibly be therefore supposed to be uneducated or uncultured. The only point is that the usage of speech is not the same as the usage of writing. We would not *write* such structures as these, unless we were writing dialogue.

CONVENTIONAL PUNCTUATION OF SENTENCES

Yet it must be stated that even in serious writing many structures which do not have the patterns we have described are punctuated as sentences. Nor are such structures to be found only in the writing of such artists as Ernest Hemingway and James Joyce. Study of ordinary expository writing, such as articles in magazines like *Harper's* or the *Reader's Digest*, will reveal many subject-less or predicate-less structures punctuated as sentences. The student may therefore inquire why he is penalized for doing what the professional writer does with impunity.

What is true is that the wayward student and the professional writer are not doing precisely the same thing. The student is uncertain about the structure of English, has an insecure grasp of the conventions of punctuation, and therefore punctuates haphazardly and at random. The professional understands the structure of English perfectly well, and he is working with it on a more subtle and complicated level than the student is yet capable of. He is for the most part following conventional practices, but he now and then diverges from the norm, intentionally, in particular situations, in order to achieve calculated effects.

It would be perfectly possible to describe the professional writer's punctuation habits, including all his departures from the norm, but it would require much more space than is available in such a book as this one. All we can do here is describe average practices. This we have done by listing a number of basic patterns, showing typical ways in which they can be expanded, and defining sentence as one of these patterns, simple or expanded. The student is urged, for the present, to punctuate as sentences only these. If he continues to write and if he closely observes the practices of other writers, he will eventually learn how and when to depart from these norms.

Most of the fragments written by students consist of one of the following structures punctuated as sentences: noun cluster, verb cluster, prepositional phrase, relative clause, subordinate clause. What happens is that the student separates such a structure from the sentence of which it forms a part. Usually the fragment belongs with the preceding sentence, perhaps separated from it by a comma.

Here are examples of noun clusters written as fragments:

> All his life Jimson was the sole support of his seventeen brothers and sisters. *A fact which we should certainly not overlook.*
>
> I always enjoyed talking to Harry. *A man after my own heart.*

The second parts of these items are fragments. They should be written as follows:

> All his life Jimson was the sole support of his seventeen brothers and sisters, *a fact which we should certainly not overlook.*
>
> I always enjoyed talking to Harry, *a man after my own heart.*

Verb clusters which give this kind of trouble are usually those in which the verb or *be* has the *–ing*, or participial, form:

> Gordon seldom held a job longer than three months. *Being a lazy, irresponsible chap.*
>
> *Not having ever seen the man before in our lives.* We were surprised when he sat down at our table.

These also should be written with a comma in place of the period:

> Gordon seldom held a job longer than three months, *being a lazy, irresponsible chap.*
>
> *Not having ever seen the man before in our lives*, we were surprised when he sat down at our table.

Prepositional phrases are sometimes written as fragments, particularly when the object of the preposition is a long or complicated structure:

He was arrested in Los Angeles. *For being disorderly and noisy in the railroad station.*

He entered the restaurant in his usual fashion. *With a swaggering gait and a nasty little smile on his lips.*

Commas should replace the periods:

He was arrested in Los Angeles, *for being disorderly and noisy in the railroad station.*

He entered the restaurant in his usual fashion, *with a swaggering gait and a nasty little smile on his lips.*

Relative clauses should not be separated from their sentences:

We decided to ask Jones. *Who was supposed to be an authority on the subject.* (Corrected: We decided to ask Jones, *who was supposed to be an authority on the subject.*)

The bill for the operation came to ninety-three thousand dollars. *Which he thought a little high.* (Corrected: The bill for the operation came to ninety-three thousand dollars, *which he thought a little high.*)

And finally, subordinate clauses should not be punctuated as sentences:

He was a pretty good worker. *When he felt like it.* (Corrected: He was a pretty good worker *when he felt like it.*)

Because Leroy had never stayed away so long before. His parents were nearly frantic with worry. (Corrected: *Because Leroy had never stayed away so long before,* his parents were nearly frantic with worry.)

In some of these sentences, a dash might be used in place of a comma. The effect of the dash is to put more emphasis on what follows:

All his life Jimson was the sole support of his seventeen brothers and sisters — *a fact which we should certainly not overlook.* He entered the restaurant in his usual fashion — *with a swaggering gait and a nasty little smile on his lips.*

But a semicolon (;) should *not* be used. A semicolon in these positions is as bad an error as a period.

Remember that it is the nature of the structure, not its length, that counts. Don't just chuck in a period or a semicolon because you feel that the sentence is getting rather long. Put in the period only when you come to the end of the sentence.

EXERCISE 26

The following passage is incorrectly punctuated, many *parts* of sentences being punctuated as if they were full sentences. Number from 1 to 40 on a separate sheet and indicate which items are sentences and which are fragments. Use the symbol **S** for sentences and **F** for fragments.

1. Not very much is known in the United States about the Macedonians. 2. A colorful people whose ancestors once conquered most of the world. 3. They are a friendly, peace-loving people. 4. Living quietly in their native villages. 5. Amid the rugged mountains that they know and love so well.

6. The principal occupation of the Macedonians is the gathering and processing of lint. 7. An operation rather like woolgathering, only more difficult. 8. The lint-gathering is done almost exclusively by the women. 9. While the men stay in the village and do the processing. 10. The method employed in lint-gathering is very interesting. 11. As soon as she has finished breakfast, the lint-gatherer bathes her feet and ankles in mox. 12. A substance which has many of the properties of glue. 13. But which remains sticky for hours and does not harden. 14. With her feet completely covered with mox, the gatherer then goes into the field. 15. Around which she stamps all day, letting the lint attach to the mox on her feet. 16. By evening each foot will be covered with a ball of lint twelve or fourteen inches in diameter.

17. As one might guess, women with large feet are highly prized in Macedonia. 18. Since the amount of lint that can be gathered is directly proportional to the size of the feet. 19. For this reason, no Macedonian peasant is likely to marry a small-footed woman. 20. Who would be more a liability than a help to him in his work. 21. Female babies with small feet are often exposed on the mountainside. 22. Or sold to the slave traders who pass through the area periodically.

23. During the lint-gathering season, the men for the most part remain idle. 24. Sleeping in the warm sun near the town pump or singing ballads to the accompaniment of the groke, an instrument which resembles the banjo. 25. But when harvest time is over and all the lint is stored. 26. It is the man's turn to go to work. 27. It is he who does the processing. 28. Which consists principally of removing the mox from the lint. 29. All winter long the Macedonian peasant can be seen sitting at the doorstep of his hut, surrounded by great balls of lint. 30. From which he is patiently removing the mox. 31. Usually he will be also surrounded by his sons. 32. Who watch him keenly, learning the difficult art of mox removal. 33. They are diligent students, for they know that if they do not master the art they will have no means of livelihood when they grow up and will starve. 34. Or else have to go into the slave trade.

35. In the spring, when all the mox has been removed, the lint is packed in bales and transported by mules to the nearest port or railway station. 36. From which it is shipped to the great lint markets of the world. 37. Places like Istanbul, Cairo, Karachi, Amsterdam, and Trieste. 38. After the lint has been shipped, the Macedonians spend a month of joyous celebration. 39. During which they drink large quantities of strega, a powerful drink produced by the fermentation of melon juice. 40. Then once again the women bathe their feet in mox and go into the fields, and the whole glorious cycle of Macedonian life begins anew.

EXERCISE 27

The following items include sentences (**S**), noun clusters (**NC**), verb clusters (**VC**), relative clauses (**RC**), subordinate clauses (**SC**), and prepositional phrases (**Prep**). Using the abbreviations given, identify the structures on a separate sheet of paper. The last five items have nonsense words in place of real nouns, verbs, adjectives, and adverbs. This device is sometimes useful in enabling us to see structure apart from meaning. You should have no more trouble in identifying these than you have with the others.

1. whom we had not seen for several months
2. to the people hanging around the front entrance
3. one of the young men shouted something in Greek
4. thinking that no one was watching
5. although he had had some trouble with the lighting system before
6. the old gentleman that was always rocking on the front porch
7. the Ganderburys didn't seem at all pleased when we drove up
8. the committee appointed by the PTA in the fall of the preceding year
9. if you wouldn't mind just taking a look at these drawings
10. Jennings merely yawned rudely when I asked to be allowed to explain
11. feeling rather uneasy about what had taken place
12. from miles and miles up the broad, empty highway
13. excused from playing basketball because of her broken leg
14. who were probably expecting us to stop and help them
15. the missionaries in the village were beginning to feel they had waited too long to send for help
16. that his parents had been born in a small town in central Sicily
17. a good joke on all of us who accepted the invitation
18. having all the objectivity of a female lynx whose cubs are threatened
19. to know her even slightly was a most rewarding experience
20. that there might be some merit in the opposing view simply never occurred to him
21. a jorgle that was flimming the brax
22. flimming a flubsome brax while the nandle dreed
23. the jorgle in the rabbish might have preferred to sporkle a spale
24. because brappons very seldom sporkled spales in those drinips
25. by sporkling a spale that had been spathered in the rabbish

17 CONJUNCTIONS AND SENTENCE CONNECTORS

We come now to two more devices for expanding and complicating the basic sentence patterns. These are the structure groups called *conjunctions* and *sentence connectors*. Both have a bearing on conventions of punctuation.

CONJUNCTIONS

Conjunctions we have already noticed, briefly, in Chapter 15. There we saw that *and, or,* and *nor* are conjunctions and that they serve to join nouns or noun clusters, producing compound subjects. To be more precise, the process is this: if two subjects can occur in separate sentences as subject of the same verb, they can be joined by a conjunction and occur in the same sentence as a compound subject of the verb:

> The boy enjoyed the movie.
> His father enjoyed the movie.
> The boy and his father enjoyed the movie.

Furthermore, this process is not limited to subjects or to nouns. Any like parts of basic patterns or any like expansions of basic patterns can be similarly compounded.

> The boy felt hungry.
> The boy felt tired.
> The boy felt hungry and tired.

> The boy who was here disappeared.
> The boy who left the note disappeared.
> The boy who was here and who left the note disappeared.

But if two structures have different derivations, we ordinarily can't compound them. For example, it would be ungrammatical to say *a sagging and reading room,* because *sagging room* derives from *the room sags* (not from *the room is for sagging*), but *reading room* derives from *the room is for reading* (not from *the room reads*). We could of course say *a sagging reading room,* but we cannot compound the modifiers. We shall discuss this point in more detail in Chapter 29.

When a conjunction occurs between *parts* of sentence patterns in this way — that is, between two subjects, two predicates, two relative clauses, two subordinate clauses, two prepositional phrases, etc. — it is not customary to use a comma before the conjunction. Don't do it.

However, conjunctions are also used to join whole sentence patterns, either basic or expanded, and when they do, it is conventional to have a comma before (not after) the conjunction. Compare these:

> The men and boys whistled and danced.
> The men whistled, and the boys danced.

The first sentence is a compounding of two subjects and two predicates; there is no punctuation. But the second sentence is a simple joining by *and* of two sentence patterns: *the men whistled; the boys danced.* There is a comma before the *and.*

Seven words — *and, or, but, for, so, yet, nor* — occur as conjunctions between sentence patterns:

> The men whistled, and the boys danced.
> You can keep it, or you can throw it away.
> His mother was a peasant woman, but his father was a
>   renowned archaeologist.
> He decided to leave at dawn, for he had many miles to ride.
> We had heard that the railroad bridge had been washed out,
>   so we decided to go by car.

> Stanley was charming and courteous, yet there was something strangely repulsive about him.
>
> The children were tired and cross, nor were their parents in a much better humor.

Notice the structure of the second pattern in the last example. After *nor*, a modal or a *have* or a *be* reverses with the subject: "the parents were" becomes "were the parents." If there is no modal or *have* or *be*, we put in a *do, does,* or *did:*

> ... nor did their parents feel any better.

This is part of the same mechanism that is used in asking questions, in stating negatives, and in many other parts of English grammar.

In place of the comma, one may sometimes use a semicolon or a period before the conjunction. The following are all correct:

> The men whistled, and the boys danced.
> The men whistled; and the boys danced.
> The men whistled. And the boys danced.

The semicolon would be unlikely with patterns as short as these, but there is no general rule against it. Nor is there any rule against using a period before *and*. This is a commonly used device to throw a greater emphasis on the second sentence pattern.

SENTENCE CONNECTORS

Sentence connectors are words like *therefore, nevertheless, however, otherwise, moreover, indeed, in fact, consequently, accordingly, hence, thus.* Like conjunctions, these words are used to connect two sentence patterns. Before a conjunction joining two sentence patterns, you put usually a comma, possibly a semicolon or a period, never nothing. Before a sentence connector, you put a semicolon or a period — never a comma and never nothing:

> The men whistled; therefore the boys danced.
> The men whistled. Therefore the boys danced.

> We didn't like them very much; however, we had to invite them.
>
> We didn't like them very much; nevertheless we decided to invite them.
>
> We didn't like them very much. In fact, we couldn't stand having them in the house.

There is a structural difference between conjunctions and sentence connectors. The conjunction joining two sentence patterns *must* occur between the two patterns. In general, the sentence connector *may* occur between the patterns or it may come within or at the end of the second pattern:

> We didn't like them very much; however, we had to invite them.
>
> We didn't like them very much; we had, however, to invite them.
>
> We didn't like them very much; we had to invite them, however.

In the first sentence, *however* could be replaced by one of the conjunctions — *and, or, but, for, so, yet, nor*. But in the second and third sentences, *however* could not be replaced by a conjunction. We do not say, "We had, or, to invite them" or "We had, and, to invite them" or "We had to invite them, for." This structural difference has caused writers to feel the two groups of words as different and to punctuate them differently in the position that they share — between two sentence patterns.

A question that always arises at this point is whether one puts a comma *after* the sentence connector. There is no simple answer. It depends on the particular sentence connector and on the particular writer. Some writers like commas more than others do. *However* and *indeed* are more likely to be followed by commas than *therefore* and *nevertheless*. Notice in your reading what other writers do, and use your own judgment.

When the sentence connector comes at the end of the sentence pattern, it usually has a comma before it:

> ; we decided to invite them, therefore.
> ; we decided to invite them, nevertheless.

When the sentence connector comes within the sentence pattern, commas are sometimes required and sometimes not. Read the following patterns aloud:

> ; we nevertheless decided to invite them.
> ; we decided, nevertheless, to invite them.

In the first sentence, the voice passes from subject to verb through the *nevertheless* without a break. In the second sentence, where the *nevertheless* occurs after the verb, there is necessarily a sharp break before the *nevertheless* and after it. These breaks must be represented by commas.

EXERCISE 28

Number from 1 to 30. Each of the following sentences contains one sentence connector or one conjunction. Punctuation has been omitted. Write the sentence connector or conjunction on your paper beside the appropriate number. If it is a sentence connector, put a semicolon in front of it. If it is a conjunction connecting whole sentence patterns, put a comma in front of it. If it is a conjunction connecting parts of sentence patterns, do not put any punctuation in front of it.

EXAMPLES: A. He knew what he wanted but he didn't know how to get it.
   , but
   B. He knew what he wanted however he didn't know how to get it.
   ; however
   C. He was a man who knew what he wanted and who intended to get it.
   and

1. They were very tired and they still had miles to ride.
2. The plan had certain weaknesses nevertheless we decided to adopt it.
3. The water and the food supplies were running low.
4. She was very pretty but rather hard to get along with.
5. The spaghetti itself was good but the sauce was rancid.
6. There seemed no chance of coming to an agreement therefore it was decided to break off negotiations.
7. Angela had lived all her life in Lyonesse however she didn't really know the city.
8. We simply told him that he had to shape up or ship out.
9. Sue's father had always been active in politics indeed he had once run for governor.
10. He was a man of great energy yet he remained a simple curriculum vice-principal all his life.
11. The table had not been cleared moreover the sink was full of dirty dishes.
12. We decided to fish Herbert out of the river for we loved him very much despite his faults.
13. He was a most entertaining conversationalist but not a very good writer.
14. The village was beautiful when winter came and the snow began to fall.
15. Each attack left him weaker than the one before thus he crept softly into the arms of death.
16. The new city administration has been six months in office yet not one of the promised reforms has been put into effect.
17. His mother was the daughter of a New England minister and his father had been a missionary in China.
18. The floods had damaged many of the railroad bridges consequently all trains were running late.
19. She had never been out of Ireland in fact she had never been more than twenty miles from Dublin.
20. We couldn't find any firewood so we simply chopped up some of the furniture.
21. You will have to report this immediately or you will be in serious trouble with the police.

22. The coach was not on speaking terms with any of the players hence team morale was rather low.
23. They knew perfectly well that dropping smoke bombs in the cafeteria was against the rules and that they could be suspended for it.
24. Clarence's new automobile had no motor but it was in very fine condition in other respects.
25. The rebels didn't have enough men to make a stand anywhere furthermore they were running short of ammunition.
26. None of the teachers knew what had happened nor could the students offer any explanation.
27. Uncle Horace was by then fully recovered from the ague accordingly the family set forth once more for Winnipeg.
28. Stanley didn't know the first thing about putting a high-pressure boiler on the line nevertheless he decided to try it.
29. Motorists who fail to renew their licenses or who drive when their licenses have been suspended will be subject to severe penalties.
30. Spring had come once again to Klamath Falls and the chipmunks were gamboling in the town square.

EXERCISE 29

Using the connecting words given, write sentences composed of two sentence patterns each. Punctuate according to the recommendations of Chapter 17.

1. and
2. therefore
3. but
4. moreover
5. or
6. indeed
7. furthermore
8. yet
9. however
10. for
11. in fact
12. consequently
13. thus
14. so
15. hence
16. nevertheless
17. nor
18. otherwise

18 RUN–ON SENTENCES

A run-on sentence is a construction in which two sentence patterns are written together without proper punctuation between them. In the crudest form of the run-on sentence, the two patterns are put together with nothing at all between them:

> The vice-principal was a fine speaker he was chosen to deliver the Commencement Address.

The construction is still a run-on sentence, though not so crude, if a comma appears between the patterns:

> The vice-principal was a fine speaker, he was chosen to deliver the Commencement Address.

This is what is sometimes called a *comma fault*.

The construction is still a run-on sentence if a sentence connector appears with a comma between the patterns:

> The vice-principal was a fine speaker, therefore he was chosen to deliver the Commencement Address.

This is a more subtle (and therefore a more common) variety of the error than the first two. But it is still an error in the sense that most American editors would object to it and correct it.

WAYS OF CORRECTING RUN–ON SENTENCES

Errors of this type can be corrected in several ways. (The following are all correctly punctuated, though some are stylistically much poorer than others.) A semicolon or a period may be inserted between the sentence patterns:

> The vice-principal was a fine speaker; he was chosen to deliver the Commencement Address.

The vice-principal was a fine speaker. He was chosen to deliver the Commencement Address.

A conjunction — preceded by a comma, semicolon, or period —
may be inserted between the sentence patterns:

The vice-principal was a fine speaker, and he was chosen to
deliver the Commencement Address.
The vice-principal was a fine speaker. And he was chosen to
deliver the Commencement Address.

A sentence connector — preceded by a semicolon or period — may
be inserted between the sentence patterns:

The vice-principal was a fine speaker; therefore he was chosen
to deliver the Commencement Address.
The vice-principal was a fine speaker. Therefore he was
chosen to deliver the Commencement Address.

Or one idea may be expressed in a subordinate construction:

Since he was a fine speaker, the vice-principal was chosen to
deliver the Commencement Address.
The vice-principal, a fine speaker, was chosen to deliver the
Commencement Address.

This last is the most sophisticated kind of revision of such an error
and often the best. We shall discuss subordination in Chapter 31.

HOW RUN–ON SENTENCES HAPPEN

It will be seen that a great many, though by no means all, errors
in fragments and run-on sentences result from a confusion of three
structure classes: conjunctions, sentence connectors, and subordinators. One might keep these separate by memorizing the three
lists. However, since some of the lists are rather long and since there
is some shifting about of individual items, it is well to understand
the structural differences. Anyway, it is always better to understand than to learn by rote.

The reason that the three classes are confusable is that they have a shared position: they all occur between two sentence patterns:

Conjunction:	The girls wept, and the boys went away.
Subordinator:	The girls wept when the boys went away.
Sentence Connector:	The girls wept; however the boys went away.

If this were all there was to it — if this were the only position for these words — they would all belong to the same class and presumably be punctuated alike. They are different because sentence connectors and subordinators occupy positions not shared by conjunctions or by each other.

We saw in the last chapter that sentence connectors can move around in the second pattern:

The girls wept; the boys, however, went away.
The girls wept; the boys went away, however.

These are not positions for conjunctions or subordinators. We do not say "The boys, for, went away" or "The boys went away, because."

The subordinator always occurs at the beginning of its pattern, but the pattern itself can occur at the beginning of the sentence:

When the boys went away, the girls wept.

This is not a position for the other classes. We do not say "However, the boys went away, the girls wept" or "And the boys went away, the girls wept."

We can sum up the positional possibilities as follows, using **C** for conjunction, **S** for subordinator, and **SC** for sentence connector:

Conjunction:	Sentence pattern **C** sentence pattern
Subordinator:	Sentence pattern **S** sentence pattern
	S sentence pattern sentence pattern

Sentence Connector: Sentence pattern **SC** sentence pattern
                               Sentence pattern sentence **SC** pattern
                               Sentence pattern sentence pattern **SC**

As for punctuation in the shared position, all of the following are conventional, the difference being one of emphasis:

Sentence pattern **,** **C** sentence pattern **.**
Sentence pattern **;** **C** sentence pattern **.**
Sentence pattern **.** **C** sentence pattern **.**

Sentence pattern **;** **SC** sentence pattern **.**
Sentence pattern **.** **SC** sentence pattern **.**

When a subordinator occurs in the shared position, it may be preceded by a comma or by nothing, but the difference is not just one of emphasis. Other differences will be described in Chapter 27. It is important not to use a semicolon or a period in this position, however. If one does, the result is a fragment.

EXERCISE 30

Some of the following items are correctly punctuated. Others (or parts of others) are run-on sentences or fragments. On a separate sheet of paper, write **S** for the correct ones, **R** for the run-ons, and **F** for the items that are fragments or contain fragments.

1. The men were very tired they had ridden hard all day.
2. When Sherman marched from Atlanta to the sea.
3. Rick wanted to own his own garbage truck, however he didn't have enough capital.
4. She seemed a shy little thing; yet she was capable of great violence when aroused.
5. The Turkish bath is a dying institution, it is slowly disappearing from American cities.
6. He was gazing absently at some papers on his desk. When suddenly the building started to shake.

7. David's beard was beautiful to behold; however, it was unfortunately not very comfortable.

8. He paused for a few moments in the middle of the Calvert Street Bridge, then he proceeded slowly down Connecticut Avenue.

9. We were all surprised by the wedding announcement. For we had heard George say he would always be a bachelor.

10. Gilbaugh turned and walked away. Because there was just nothing more to say.

11. The bus driver would do nothing to help them, so the passengers summoned a policeman.

12. As if that were all there was to it.

13. Frangiopane was very skillful at cleaning and repairing clocks; but he didn't know the first thing about watches.

14. They were not able to get into their hotel room until just before dinner, hence the first day was a total loss.

15. We were astounded to learn that Corelli had been given the tenor role in *Trovatore*. However, we decided to see the opera anyway.

16. You might separate the herring from the anchovies. If you really want to be helpful.

17. We had no idea who the redhaired man was, none of us had ever seen him before.

18. *Antony and Cleopatra* is the greatest of Shakespeare's plays. With the possible exception of *Hamlet*.

19. Nothing had been done about hiring an orchestra, though the Prom was only three weeks away.

20. Since the villagers speak very little English and the visitors seldom know any Macedonian.

21. He knew that entering the cave meant probable death. Yet he did not hesitate.

22. Barlow felt that he had no right to propose marriage to the princess, for he was only a commoner.

23. Williams rode up on his new toy, a motor scooter that he had bought in Toronto.

24. The lad could not produce a ticket, consequently he was asked to leave.

25. Mabel was a good housekeeper and an excellent cook, furthermore she had the prettiest blue eyes in East St. Louis.

EXERCISE 31

In the following account, some items are sentence patterns correctly punctuated; others are run-on sentences or fragments. Number your paper from 1 to 35 and mark the sentence patterns **S**, the run-ons **R**, and the fragments **F**. Then rewrite the passage, eliminating the fragments and run-ons. In some places this will best be done by simply changing the punctuation; in others revision of the structure will be preferable.

1. Outdoor living and increased travel are two important features of modern American life. 2. Sherman Livingston, a young businessman from Sioux Falls, South Dakota, became aware of these tendencies, furthermore he found a way to combine them through an ingenious new rental service called Rent-A-Pat. 3. Livingston had statistics to show that most Americans, when at home, spend their leisure time barbecuing meat in their patios. 4. Would it not be a good idea, he asked, to provide them a means of barbecuing meat when away from home? 5. The answer was Rent-A-Pat. 6. An organization designed to put a patio at the disposal of the tired traveler in most of the important cities of America.

7. It works like this. 8. A traveling family, desirous of barbecuing meat, simply goes to the nearest office of Rent-A-Pat. 9. Where numerous photos of available patios are on display. 10. The customers choose the patio best suited to their needs, then they drive out to it and barbecue their meat. 11. Rent-A-Pat provides the meat free. 12. Provided that the customer is satisfied with hamburger. 13. Steaks and chops are available at an additional charge, however Livingston finds that most customers are content with hamburger. 14. It is the *barbecuing* of the meat, not the eating of it, that counts. 15. Since the customer could get meat much cheaper in a restaurant. 16. If all he wanted was to eat it.

17. Recently Rent-A-Pat has set up offices in many of the major air terminals. 18. Having discovered that traveling businessmen are among its best customers. 19. The tired traveler gets off the plane in Dallas or Chicago and goes to rent a car, at the next desk he notices the pretty face of the smiling Rent-A-Pat girl. 20. Suddenly he thinks how nice it would be to barbecue his dinner in a patio. 21. Instead of going to a dull restaurant, as he had intended. 22. Almost before he knows what he is doing.

23. He moves to the counter, rents a patio, and goes off happily with his hamburger. 24. For the commercial traveler, Rent-A-Pat provides many little extras. 25. Like comic aprons and chef's hats and the lyrics of songs to be sung while barbecuing the meat.

26. Leading sociologists all over the country have heartily endorsed the efforts of Sherman Livingston. 27. For, as they point out, the backyard patio and barbecue pit are a means of keeping the family together. 28. While travel tends to pull the family apart. 29. Rent-A-Pat counteracts the latter tendency and strengthens the former. 30. The father traveling alone feels close to his family. 31. As he turns his hamburger over the glowing briquets. 32. His little ones at home, he muses, are turning their hamburgers over their briquets at the very same time, thus it is almost as if they were all together.

33. As soon as radio-television is sufficiently developed. 34. Rent-A-Pat hopes to make it possible for members of a family to see and talk to one another as they barbecue. 35. However, this service will probably not be available for some time.

19 IMMEDIATE CONSTITUENTS

Part of understanding an English sentence is understanding what goes with what. Part of composing an English sentence is making clear what goes with what. This seems perfectly simple and obvious, but actually the mechanism by which English keeps its lines clear is rather interesting and delicate. By studying this mechanism, one can perhaps avoid certain mistakes and clumsy constructions in writing.

An English sentence is not just a collection of words. Rather it is a series of groupings of words, a series of constructions that cluster and nest inside other constructions. The nature of the clustering is connected with the fundamental distinction between basic sentences and transformed sentences. All basic sentences have what is called a *binary construction*. This means that each basic sentence is composed of two parts. Each of these two parts (if more than one word) is composed of two parts; each of these is composed of two parts, and so on, until we get down to single words. Many transformed sentences have this kind of construction too, but not all do.

WHAT ARE IMMEDIATE CONSTITUENTS?

Let's take basic sentences first. You remember that we said that a basic sentence pattern consists first of all of a subject and a predicate. These are what are called the *immediate constituents* of the sentence. They are *constituents* in the sense that they constitute, or make up, the sentence. They are *immediate* in the sense that they act immediately on one another: the whole meaning of the one applies to the whole meaning of the other.

Since the subject of a basic sentence is a noun cluster and the predicate is a verb cluster, we can say that the immediate constituents (IC's, for short) of a sentence are a noun cluster and a verb cluster. These are the two parts of a sentence that apply their meaning directly to each other. Each of the IC's of the sentence can in turn be divided to get IC's at the next lower level. For example, the noun cluster of a sentence may consist of a determiner plus a noun (*the man* . . .). In this case, the construction may be cut between the determiner and the noun:

the   /   man

The IC's of this noun cluster are *the* and *man*. The verb cluster of the sentence may be a verb plus a noun cluster (*liked the movie*). This cluster can be cut into IC's as follows:

liked   /   the movie

The IC's of the construction are the verb and the noun cluster that function as its object. The diagram that follows displays the successive breaking down of each unit into two immediate constituents:

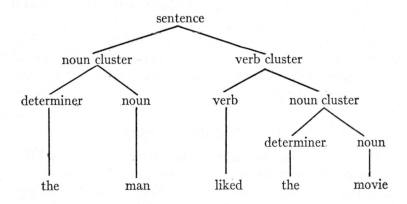

The IC's of the whole sentence are *the man* as one and *liked the movie* as the other. The IC's of *the man* are *the* and *man.* The IC's of *liked the movie* are *liked* and *the movie.* The IC's of *the movie* are *the* and *movie.* A group of words are a constituent of something if they go back to some division point. If they do not, they aren't. Thus *the man, liked the movie,* and *the movie* are all constituents of something. But *man liked, man liked the, the man liked* are not. They do not go back to any single point of division in the development of the sentence.

We have seen how nouns can be expanded into long noun clusters and verbs into long verb clusters. If the subject and predicate of a basic pattern are so expanded, we might get something like this:

> The old man who rented the room upstairs apparently likes
> the movie at the Grand Theater very much.

The IC's are still the subject and the predicate. The subject is not just *man* but the whole noun cluster of which *man* is the headword. It is the subject not just of *likes* or of *likes the movie* but of the whole verb cluster. The meaning of the whole noun cluster applies as a unit to the meaning of the whole verb cluster.

SENTENCE MODIFIERS

However, it is not always true that the IC's of an expanded sentence are the subject and the predicate. Consider this sentence:

Apparently the man liked the movie.

If we were to divide this sentence between the subject and the predicate, we would get as one constituent the string of words *apparently the man*. But as a unit this is meaningless. There is no construction, no single division point it can derive from. *Apparently* does not apply its meaning to *the man*. It is not the man that is apparent. What has happened is that from a source sentence, like "It was apparent," *apparent* has been converted into an adverb, and applied to the consumer sentence "The man liked the movie."

Source: It was apparent.
Consumer: The man liked the movie.
Result: Apparently the man liked the movie.

What is apparent is the whole idea — that the man liked the movie. *Apparently* is therefore, in this sentence, a *sentence modifier*. Its meaning applies to the whole sentence pattern that follows.

Sentence modifiers come mostly — and are most easily recognized — at the beginning of sentences. They can come inside and at the end of sentences too, but only when certain signals occur. Since these signals are somewhat subtle and complicated, we shall postpone discussion of them until later and here exemplify sentence modifiers in the initial position only. The slant line indicates the division between the immediate constituents:

Unfortunately **/** he had no money.
When she got there, **/** the cupboard was bare.
Racing into the room, **/** Stanley collided with Mrs. Kreeton.
The gate being locked, **/** we called the porter.

It will be seen that various constructions occur as sentence modifiers: adverbs, prepositional phrases, subordinate clauses, verb clusters. All of these structures derive from various features found in the basic sentence patterns. Some sentence modifiers occurring before the sentence pattern they modify are regularly set off with commas; others are not always set off. We shall discuss the punctuation practices in detail in Chapter 23.

The third example above is somewhat different from the others in that there is a close connection between the sentence modifier — *racing into the room* — and the subject of the main pattern, *Stanley*. Stanley is the one who races. This is not a modification relationship, however. Compare "Smiling, the man nodded" and "The smiling man nodded." *Smiling* is a sentence modifier in the first but a noun modifier in the second. We shall consider this matter in more detail in Chapter 24.*

Other constructions besides sentences can be cut into their immediate constituents. The division in many constructions is quite obvious. For example, a subordinate clause consists, plainly enough, of the subordinator as one part and the sentence pattern it subordinates as the other. For example, the subordinate clause *because the boy went away* would be cut thus:

because   **/**   the boy went away

The subordinator *because* contributes its meaning to the whole sentence pattern that follows, making it no longer an independent sentence but a part of some other sentence.

With the subordinator cut off, we could then go on to the next level and cut the sentence pattern remaining into *its* IC's:

the boy   **/**   went away

---

* The relationship can perhaps be more clearly seen, if the nature of the transformation is considered. There are two ideas involved, one coming from a source sentence and one from a consumer:

Source: Stanley raced into the room.
Consumer: Stanley collided with Mrs. Kreeton.
Result: Racing into the room, Stanley collided with Mrs. Kreeton.

In the result, the one subject serves to name the performer of both actions.

Relative clauses are somewhat more complicated, because their derivation from basic patterns is more complicated. If the relative replaces the subject of a basic pattern, the construction is cut just like a sentence:

The boy   **/**   went away.
who   **/**   went away

But how should we cut *whom he saw* which derives from a sentence like "He saw Jim"? If we must divide it, we would probably choose to do so thus: whom   **/**   he saw. But it is probably more realistic not to extend the principle of division into immediate constituents to derivations of this sort or to such others as "There was a man in the room" or "Didn't he see you?" The patterns from which these derive can of course be cut: "A man   **/**   was in the room," "He   **/**   saw you."

IC'S OF PREPOSITIONAL PHRASES

A prepositional phrase always has as its two IC's the preposition as one and the object of the preposition as the other. The division is perfectly obvious in simple phrases:

by   **/**   the tree
in   **/**   the house

But the rule holds also when the object of the preposition is more complicated:

by   **/**   the tree which my father had planted behind the barn

Here the object of the preposition is not just a simple noun with its determiner, but a complicated noun cluster. Nevertheless, the IC's are still the preposition as one and everything else as the other.

Notice also that English is capable of something like this:

by   **/**   the tree near the barn across the stream in the meadow

This illustrates how constructions may nest inside one another in English sentences. The preposition *by* has as its object the noun cluster that follows, with *tree* as its headword; *the tree* is modified by the prepositional phrase beginning with *near*, and so on in this fashion:

> by **/** the tree near the barn across the stream in the
> meadow
> the tree **/** near the barn across the stream in the meadow
> near **/** the barn across the stream in the meadow
> the barn **/** across the stream in the meadow
> across **/** the stream in the meadow
> the stream **/** in the meadow
> in **/** the meadow

Such a piling up quickly becomes clumsy and obscure, but there is no rule of English grammar which says that one can do it only a particular number of times.

EXERCISE 32

Cut each of the following constructions into its two immediate constituents and write the word *preceding* the cut on a separate sheet of paper. The constructions are all either sentence patterns (with or without sentence modifiers), prepositional phrases, or subordinate clauses.

EXAMPLES: A. some of the boys went home early
                           boys
                      B. in the meantime we started the fire
                           meantime

1. his father owns a Jaguar
2. since he had plenty of time
3. unfortunately no one was at home
4. he had a hard time starting the car
5. with the flower which she held in her teeth
6. in the early spring the valley is very beautiful
7. at his best Gilbaugh is unbeatable

8. the delegates from New York left in a huff
9. the Huff is a small car made in Norway
10. after everyone had sampled the ice cream
11. when the guests had all arrived Gordon began to barbecue the meat
12. the plan of attack that General Grapefield had worked out left much to be desired
13. looking at his watch David began making noises about going home
14. in the twinkling of his left eye
15. he polished up the handle so carefully that now he is the ruler of the Queen's Navy
16. a delegate from Toledo whom no one had previously noticed stood up and requested to be heard
17. beyond the sunset and the western stars
18. what you do with it is your own business
19. he made a fortune in lint
20. in spite of all his efforts Murchison was unable to get out of the third grade
21. when the paper underneath began to burn
22. nearly all the African tribesmen who were playing bridge inside the tent were friends of my brother Ralph's
23. Corelli had hired his own claque for the performance
24. people who know the opera well usually refer to it simply as *Trovatore*
25. that she didn't know how to shift gears soon became painfully apparent
26. a claque is a group of people who have been paid to applaud
27. stealing candy from children is not as easy as it sounds
28. from the man to whom it had originally been sold
29. bounding up the stairs Randolph collided with his elderly aunt
30. since tempers were beginning to flare it was decided to adjourn the meeting
31. by measuring the distance very carefully before he bought the materials
32. in the opinion of some of the reporters who attended the briefing
33. those of us who knew Simpson when he played the organ at St. James Cathedral in Vancouver were simply shocked to learn of his illness

34. smiling a contemptuous little smile Sir Tolbert arose and opened the case for the defense
35. livid with rage at being called a bounder William hit his tormentor in the nose

20   IMMEDIATE CONSTITUENTS OF NOUN AND VERB CLUSTERS

The meaning conveyed by a noun cluster will depend not only on what is in the noun cluster but on how it is put together. In other words, it depends on what the IC's are. Suppose, for example, we examine the following cluster:

the man from the garage who called about your car

The cluster contains ten words, but obviously they are not in free relationship with one another. The cluster contains several internal relationships building together in complicated ways to the total meaning. Thus the first word, *the*, is more closely related to *man* than it is to *from* or *called* or *car; from* is more closely related to *garage* than it is to *man; who* is more closely related to *called* than to *garage.*

CUTTING NOUN CLUSTERS

We can show these relationships by breaking the cluster into its immediate constituents, layer by layer. On the top layer, the IC's are these:

the man from the garage   **/**   who called about your car

This is to say that the relative clause *who called about your car* modifies all the rest of the noun cluster. It doesn't modify just *man* but the whole thing, *the man from the garage.* The whole meaning of the clause applies to the whole meaning of the rest of the cluster.

The two parts of the original cluster can then be broken into *their* parts:

> the man   **/**   from the garage
> who   **/**   called about your car

The remnant of the cluster consists of a prepositional phrase modifying *the man*. The relative clause consists of the relative *who* plus the predicate.

Cutting further, we find these structures:

> the   **/**   man
> from   **/**   the garage
> called   **/**   about your car

And then, on the next level:

> the   **/**   garage
> about   **/**   your car

And on the last level:

> your   **/**   car *

Most of this is pretty obvious. Anyone can see that a phrase like *from the garage* breaks naturally into the preposition as one

---

* Students are often bothered by the term *level* and by the order of cutting. For any construction, we have one *first* level cut. Having cut the construction into its two parts, we can turn our attention next to either one of these or to both of them. If both are made of more than one word, we have then two *second* level cuts. If both of these are made of more than one word, we have four *third* level cuts, then eight *fourth* level cuts, and so on. In actuality, we are always running out of material here and there along the line. One just keeps going through the sentence, each time on another level. For example:

Level 1   The man from the garage who called about your car│ was rather angry.

Level 2   The man from the garage│who called about your car│was│rather angry.

Level 3   The man│from the garage│who│called about your car│was│rather│angry.

Level 4   The│man│from│the garage│who│called│about your car│was│rather│angry.

Level 5   The│man│from│the│garage│who│called│about│your car│was│rather│angry.

Level 6   The│man│from│the│garage│who│called│about│your│car│was│rather│angry.

part and the noun and its determiner as the other. No one would suggest that *garage* is the object of *from the*. But obvious or not, analysis shows a great deal of complexity built into the simple-looking noun cluster.

Sometimes the analysis is not quite so obvious. Compare these noun clusters:

> the little boy with the red hair who was being beaten
> the little boy with the red hair which was being cut

These look similar but are actually quite different. In the first, two modifiers relating to *boy* follow the headword: the prepositional phrase and the relative clause. But in the second, there is only one modifier of *boy* after *boy*. *Which was being cut* is a modifier, but it doesn't modify *the little boy with the red hair*. It modifies *the red hair*. The two structures are cut like this:

> the little boy with the red hair **/** who was being beaten
> the little boy **/** with the red hair which was being cut

In the second one, the prepositional phrase *with the red hair which was being cut* functions as a unit, modifying *the little boy*. Its IC's are the preposition and its object:

> with **/** the red hair which was being cut

The object of the preposition is another noun cluster, imbedded in the original one. We are now down to the level on which the relative clause is a constituent:

> the red hair **/** which was being cut

Thus even in this simple example we can see very clearly the nesting characteristic of English structure: a noun cluster consists of a noun modified by a prepositional phrase, which consists of a preposition and its object, which is another noun cluster and consists of the headword and a relative clause.

We could easily think of much more complicated examples:

> the little boy with the red hair which was being cut by a

barber who always got faintly ill whenever a little boy with red hair wandered into his shop

Here are the chief elements:

the little boy / with the red hair which was being cut by a barber who always got faintly ill whenever a little boy with red hair wandered into his shop (The prepositional phrase modifies the rest of the noun cluster.)

with / the red hair which was being cut by a barber who always got faintly ill whenever a little boy with red hair wandered into his shop (The preposition has another noun cluster as its object.)

the red hair / which was being cut by a barber who always got faintly ill whenever a little boy with red hair wandered into his shop (A relative clause modifies the rest of the second cluster.)

which / was being cut by a barber who always got faintly ill whenever a little boy with red hair wandered into his shop (The clause consists of a relative and a predicate.)

cut / by a barber who always got faintly ill whenever a little boy with red hair wandered into his shop (The verb of the predicate is modified by a prepositional phrase.)

by / a barber who always got faintly ill whenever a little boy with red hair wandered into his shop (The preposition has another noun cluster as its object.)

a barber / who always got faintly ill whenever a little boy with red hair wandered into his shop (Another relative clause modifies the headword.)

who / always got faintly ill whenever a little boy with red hair wandered into his shop (The clause consists of a relative and a predicate.)

got faintly ill **/** whenever a little boy with red hair wandered into his shop (A subordinate clause modifies the rest of the predicate.)

whenever **/** a little boy with red hair wandered into his shop (The clause consists of a subordinator and a sentence pattern.)

a little boy with red hair **/** wandered into his shop (The sentence pattern consists of a subject and a predicate, each of which contains another prepositional phrase, each of which, in turn, contains a little noun cluster.)

CUTTING VERB CLUSTERS

The cutting of verb clusters is somewhat complicated because of the occurrence of auxiliaries. Auxiliaries include not only modals and *have* and *be* but also the forms added to the verb whenever *have* and *be* are used — i.e., *–en* and *–ing*. In a careful description, all auxiliaries, including *–en* and *–ing*, must be taken as a unit wherever they occur, and therefore we will have some constituents in which some elements are separated from others and in which some make up only parts of words. In order to keep the description from being sloppy on the one hand or too complicated on the other, we shall simply not consider in this book the constituents of verb clusters containing auxiliaries.

Apart from auxiliaries, a verb cluster consists of a verb headword, plus one or more modifiers, objects, or complements. A modifier occurring before the verb is cut off first:

often **/** visit us when they're in town

Then the last unit after the verb is cut:

visit us **/** when they're in town

The only difficulty lies in recognizing the number of units occurring. Note the difference between these structures:

took a ship **/** because he liked the sea
took **/** a ship that was going to Bombay

went to the store   **/**   in the morning
went   **/**   to the store in the shopping plaza

went to the store in the shopping plaza   **/**   in his car
went   **/**   to the store in the shopping plaza in his home town

As we cut a complicated construction into its constituents, we see something important in the nature of language, something which helps explain how it can work as well as it does. At each level we keep cutting out one or another of a few familiar structure types, for the most part these: sentence patterns, noun clusters, verb clusters, relative clauses, subordinate clauses, prepositional phrases. Any of these can contain within it any of the others or all of them or all of them several times. Even a very long and complex sentence will not present new constructions but rather a half dozen familiar ones capable of infinite variation. Each of these constructions will turn out to be made of the material found in the basic sentence patterns. Each will be formed according to its own simple rules. And they will nest in one another according to the rules of nesting — the rules, in other words, that govern immediate constituents.

EXERCISE 33

Number from 1 to 35. Each of the following constructions can be divided into two immediate constituents. Find the place where the cut should be made and write the word preceding the cut on your paper.

EXAMPLES: A. he knew what he was doing
            he
            B. with a smile on his face
            with
            C. behaved rather well when the time came
            well

1. the older people went home early
2. youngsters who helped with the haying
3. when his friends came to see him
4. at the sound of the chimes
5. men with guns who were looking for trouble
6. men with guns which were loaded
7. men with guns in shoulder holsters
8. coming in to dinner without washing his hands
9. coming in to a dinner which his sister had cooked
10. with the crowd that he has been going around with
11. fortunately there was a bag of oranges in the cupboard
12. prosperity often comes to those who deserve it least
13. animals in the foreground that reminded us of gazelles
14. perfectly good scientific explanations
15. the views of the delegates from Lyonesse apparently were not widely supported
16. wanted a doll that could speak French
17. by measuring the distance between those two points
18. that he came originally from Barcelona
19. bricks made of glass that were used in the superstructure
20. they might have stopped by to see how we were getting on
21. when the guests finally went home we started doing the dishes
22. from the rear of the crowd in front of the courthouse
23. where he buried the money is a secret that died with him
24. complaining about the children because their games interfered with his afternoon nap
25. for selling bales of lint without a license
26. all night long the garbage trucks rumbled down the street outside our window
27. realizing with mild surprise that he was growing old
28. in the first place cows do not have prehensile tails
29. dishes on the top shelf that were there when we bought the house
30. rather giddy airplane hostesses
31. though he had lived in Lyonesse all his life he had very few friends there

32. on the very day on which they were to be married
33. places he had never visited on the occasion of his first journey
34. letters from the bank written in green ink
35. gossiping idly with the mailman when the paper boy rode by

EXERCISE 34

Divide your paper into two columns and number from 1 to 35 down the left-hand margin. In the first column, identify each construction: sentence pattern (**S**), noun cluster (**NC**), verb cluster (**VC**), subordinate clause (**SC**), relative clause (**RC**), prepositional phrase (**Prep**). Decide how each construction can be cut into its two immediate constituents and write the word preceding the cut in the second column.

EXAMPLE: A. near the man who was waving his hat
          Prep   *near*

1. anxiety about what was going to happen next
2. got a job because he was going broke
3. most of the girls declined the invitation
4. in the best interests of all who have invested their money
5. wishing earnestly that he had kept his mouth shut
6. if you have finished we might join the ladies
7. since no one really knew much about it
8. preparations for the dance which would take place in the evening
9. preparations for the dance which were occupying everyone's time
10. went to the store on his bicycle
11. went to the store on the corner
12. went to the store on the corner on his bicycle in the afternoon
13. that he had acted foolishly was apparent to everyone
14. very beautiful harvest moon
15. if you like spaghetti with clam sauce
16. the building on the left houses the poultry
17. taught French to the children of the very rich
18. Alaskans who had made all their money in lumber
19. in the early mornings the valley was often blanketed in white fog

20. during the speeches that followed the dinner
21. because not one stone was left standing upon another
22. realized that an uproar would ensue when he communicated the news
23. the baby sitter simply popped Jack into the tub and sloshed him about a bit
24. since he didn't have the slightest idea what to do next General Grapefield maintained a mysterious silence
25. that eventually we had to face the problem squarely
26. finding himself outnumbered twenty-five to one Gilbaugh resorted to a stratagem
27. with the exception of Bernini Borromini was the greatest Italian architect of the seventeenth century
28. returned to the house in the early evening
29. for having turned in a false alarm
30. in the pages of a book that he had been reading the day before
31. if it was a dream she did not wish to waken
32. prisoners in a wagon that were being transported to a camp in the rear
33. in the middle of the meadow which extended northward from our camp
34. who had never been noted for tact
35. skimming lightly over the water for the last half hour

21 AMBIGUITY — IMMEDIATE CONSTITUENTS

A sentence, or a part of a sentence, is ambiguous when it carries more than one meaning. Occasionally, writers use ambiguity intentionally. Puns are examples of intentional ambiguity; poets sometime deliberately use expressions carrying multiple meanings. For the most part, however, ambiguity is unintentional, resulting from a careless use of the sentence structure, a failure to include the signals that would make the meaning clear. This kind of ambiguity is a feature of bad writing and is of course to be avoided if possible. Often a sentence is only, as one might say, mildly ambiguous. That is, the writer's intent can be discerned but only at some effort on the part of the reader, who must go back and consider the larger context in order to know what is meant. Such a weakness distracts the reader's attention from what is being said and directs it to the sloppiness of the expression.

DIFFERENT KINDS OF AMBIGUITY

There are several kinds of ambiguity. We discussed one kind in talking about word classes, where we saw that a sentence becomes ambiguous if the reader or hearer cannot tell what class the words belong to. "Box leaves immediately," "He looked hard," "an orderly room" are examples of this kind of confusion. Such ambiguities are not much of a danger to the writer, except perhaps to the writers of telegrams and headlines, because in ordinary, fully expressed prose, a superabundance of signals keeps the word classes sorted out.

Ambiguity can also occur, however, when the constituents of a sentence are not clearly shown, and the writer can fall into this trouble quite easily. He can avoid it only by learning to be alive to the possibilities and to make sure that his meanings are clearly signaled. We shall describe in this chapter some typical ambiguities involving immediate constituents and indicate the kind of signal that might make the meaning clear.

Consider this sentence:

The people who saw the play frequently praised it.

This sentence cannot be cut into its IC's, because we cannot tell whether to cut before or after *frequently*. Either of the following might be intended:

The people who saw the play **/** frequently praised it.
The people who saw the play frequently **/** praised it.

The difficulty is that the adverb *frequently* comes between two verb clusters — *saw the play* and *praised it* — and it could go logically and grammatically with either. The following are not ambiguous:

> The people who frequently saw the play praised it. (*Frequently* in this position must apply to *saw*.)
>
> The people who saw the play praised it frequently. (In this position, *frequently* must apply to *praised*.)
>
> The people who saw the play never praised it. (It happens that *never* occurs only at the beginning of verb clusters, not at the end; hence it must here modify *praised it*.)
>
> The people who saw the play many times praised it. (The expression *many times* rarely occurs before the verb; it would here normally be taken as modifying *saw the play*.)

In speech, intonation can serve as a signal, indicating in this example whether *frequently* goes with *saw* or *praised*. Punctuation often symbolizes the intonation of speech, but not in this structure. There is no conventional way of solving this problem by punctuation.

AMBIGUITY IN NOUN CLUSTERS

Noun clusters offer various possibilities of ambiguity. Consider this:

> the girl in the car that had moved

Was it the girl that had moved or the car? We can't tell, because we can't tell what the IC's are. They could be either of these:

> the girl / in the car that had moved
>
> the girl in the car / that had moved

This difficulty arises because of a particular requirement of noun clusters: if a prepositional phrase and a relative clause are used to modify a noun headword, the prepositional phrase must come first and the clause second. This means that the clause will have two nouns in front of it — the first noun and the noun that is object of the preposition — and there must be a signal to tell which noun it goes with. Note that the following are unambiguous and could be cut into their IC's:

> the girl in the car who had moved (*Who* links the clause to the person, not the thing.)
> the girl in the car which had moved (*Which* links the clause to the thing, not the person.)
> the girls in the car that were moving (*Were* links the clause to the plural, not the singular.)
> the girls in the car that was moving (*Was* links the clause to the singular, not the plural.)

Often the meaning of individual words will be signal enough:

> the girl in the car that was waving

Since we think of girls, but not cars, as wavers, we would presumably take this structure only one way. Reliance on such a signal is risky, though. Sometimes the writer's intention is clear enough, but a ridiculous alternative teases the reader. The following are all at least doubtful:

> the girl in the car that needed water
> the girl in the car that reminded me of Aunt Sally
> the girl in the car that had broken down
> the girl in the car that had no bonnet (This one would be ambiguous in England, where *bonnet* can mean "hood.")

Notice that it is not simply a matter of putting the modifier next to what it is supposed to modify. Suppose that the writer *means* that the car, not the girl, reminded him of Aunt Sally — perhaps because it was long and sleek and gaudy. Still "the girl in the car that reminded me of Aunt Sally" is ambiguous, even though the clause is right next to its intended headword.

AMBIGUITY IN VERB CLUSTERS

Ambiguity can easily occur in verb clusters:

> defended the man she loved with all her heart

Did she defend him or love him with all her heart?

Sometimes a very slight change is the difference between an ambiguous construction and an unambiguous one. The first member of the following pairs is ambiguous; the second is not.

> washed the boat on the shore
> washed the boat onto the shore

> the chair in the room in which she usually sat
> the chair on the porch in which she usually sat

Frequently ambiguity can be avoided only by a radical change in the structure. Sometimes such a change will correct other faults besides ambiguity. The following construction is not only ambiguous but wordy:

> the book in the car that is red

Either meaning can be expressed unambiguously in a simpler construction:

> the red book in the car
> the book in the red car

EXERCISE 35

Some of the following are ambiguous and some are unambiguous. On a separate paper, mark the ambiguous ones **A** and the others **U**. Be prepared to explain the two meanings of those that are ambiguous.

1. The people we met now and then were very kind to us.
2. Now and then the people we met were very kind to us.
3. The people we met were very kind to us now and then.
4. He drove up in a car with a souped-up motor that he had recently bought.
5. He buried the knife he found in the cellar.
6. I looked at the letter Maxwell was reading with unfeigned astonishment.
7. He put away the golf tees in his pocket.

8. He put the golf tees in his pocket away.
9. We watched them march away proudly.
10. We proudly watched them march away.
11. The women with the children who were complaining were told to move along.
12. The men with the dogs that were barking were told to move along.
13. The party later was a great success.
14. The man with the truck which was waiting at the curb lit a cigar.
15. He was fond of playing a radio that he had made himself during the winter.
16. Nobody discovered the books that he had stolen that morning.
17. Tipton presented the girl that he was escorting to the dance with a bauble that he had bought in New York.
18. She decided to send the sheets to the cleaners that were dirty.
19. The police have found the child that was kidnaped in Sioux Falls, South Dakota.
20. He lived on a street near the post office which was always full of people.
21. He arrived accompanied by a Russian wolfhound with a big smile on his face.
22. Cows that eat cornflakes frequently have stomach trouble.
23. Cows that eat cornflakes frequently rarely have stomach trouble.
24. Cows that eat cornflakes never have stomach trouble.
25. We were grateful for the blinds that covered the windows on sunny days.
26. The party for the winning candidate was attended by a large throng.
27. He couldn't find the key to the jewel case which he had left on the table.
28. A man in a brown hat pulled up alongside the policeman on a motorcycle.
29. We found the man who had lost his way in the mountains with the help of two Boy Scouts.
30. The lengthening shadows on the wall of the church near the corner warned us that it was nearly dinnertime.
31. Nobody likes girls that pout a great deal.
32. We suddenly noticed a man in a space suit which should have been sent to the cleaners.

33. The police have trouble with the people who occupy these cottages all the time.
34. Children who stay out all night sometimes should be punished.
35. Children who stay out all night should seldom be punished.
36. She spoke to the boy with a warm smile.
37. She spoke to the boy with the warm smile.
38. She spoke to the boy with the warm smile that she reserved for children.
39. He had a date with a girl from the country that he had never seen.
40. He had a date with a girl from a country that he had never seen.

EXERCISE 36

Each of the following sentences is ambiguous. Rewrite each one twice, so as to show both meanings. Make whatever structural changes you like, but try to write smooth and pleasing sentences.

EXAMPLE: A. We saw a boy with a book that had no jacket.
          We saw a boy with a book who had no jacket.
          We saw a boy with a jacketless book.

1. People who visit Rome frequently like it very much.
2. Teachers of elementary school children that do well naturally expect to be rewarded.
3. He often strolled through the woods that he liked so much in rainy weather.
4. He introduced us to a girl with a shy smile that we found rather lovable.
5. The social get-together afterward got rather lively.
6. I was next introduced to an Italian with a mustache that completely captivated me.
7. He carefully washed the stones he had found in the river.
8. We were urged seriously to fight back.
9. We encountered a child with a bag of candy that was turning green.
10. A man who had just entered the room briskly delivered a little pep talk on sales quotas.

SUMMARY OF TERMS • CHAPTERS 16–21

Ambiguous (p. 136)   Having more than one meaning. There are several different kinds of ambiguity. The sentence "The train was long" is ambiguous because of the possibilities of the noun *train:* e.g., that which runs on the railroad, or that which is attached to a bridal gown. This kind of ambiguity is lexical, not grammatical. That is, the grammatical structure is perfectly clear, but the meaning of one of the words is not. The sentence "The boy looked fast," however, is an example of grammatical ambiguity. We don't know whether *fast* is an adjective (*speedy*) or an adverb (*speedily*). The cluster "the men with the boys who were laughing" is a grammatical ambiguity of a different sort; we can identify the word classes, but we do not know what goes with what — i.e., what the immediate constituents are. A very common kind of ambiguity is that in which the reference of a pronoun is not clear: "John told his father he had acted foolishly." We do not know whether *he* refers to *John* or *father*.

Auxiliary (p. 132)   All of the material — words or endings — used to alter the meaning or relationship of a verb or *be*. The modals (*can, may, will*, etc.) are part of the auxiliary. So are *have* and *be*, though these words may also be the headword of the predicate. Verbs which modify other verbs (*prefer* in *prefer to go*) are part of the auxiliary. The endings, *–s, –ed, –ing, –en* are part of the auxiliary. In *might have been preferring to go*, everything but *go* is auxiliary.

Conjunctions (p. 107)   The words *and, or, but, nor, for, yet, so* used to join sentence patterns or parts of sentence patterns. All seven are used to join sentence patterns, but only *and, or, but* are used alone to join parts of patterns. (*Nor* will join sentence parts in combination with *neither.*) The words *and, or, nor* occur only as conjunctions; the others occur also in other word classes. The combinations *both . . . and, not . . . but, either . . . or, neither . . . nor* are called *correlative conjunctions.*

Constituent (p. 121)   That which makes up or constitutes something. In grammar, the term refers to functioning parts of sentences or of words. Such items as subjects, objects, prepositional phrases, nouns, prefixes may all be constituents on some level of a sentence.

Fragment (p. 100)   A part of a sentence punctuated as if it were a complete sentence. The parts of sentences so punctuated are likely to be noun clusters, verb clusters, prepositional phrases, relative clauses, and subordinate clauses. Though writers use some types of fragments intentionally and effectively, their haphazard occurrence is generally thought to constitute a serious writing error.

Immediate constituents (p. 121)   The largest functioning units in a construction. The sentence "The boys seem friendly" has nine constituents, but it has only two *immediate* constituents: *the boys* and *seem friendly*. These are the parts of the whole sentence that apply their meaning immediately to each other. The immediate constituents of *the boys* are *the* and *boys;* of *boys, boy* and *–s;* of *seem friendly, seem* and *friendly;* of *friendly, friend* and *–ly*. The abbreviation of immediate constituent is IC. Thus we speak of the IC's of a construction or of IC analysis.

Run-on sentence (p. 114)   Two sentence patterns written with neither a conjunction to join them nor a semicolon or period to separate them. Other terms for run-on sentence are *run-together sentence, fused sentence, comma fault, comma splice*. Like the fragment — of which it is, in a sense, the opposite — the run-on sentence is considered a serious writing error.

Sentence connectors (p. 109)   Such words as *therefore, nevertheless, however, moreover*. In some books these words are called *conjunctive adverbs, adverbial conjunctions*, or *introductory adverbs*. All these terms refer to essentially the same group of words. Sentence connectors are like conjunctions in that they join sentence patterns. However, the connection is looser, as is shown by the fact that sentence connectors may occur not only between the patterns but also inside or at the end of the second pattern. Conjunctions cannot. Two sentence patterns joined by a sentence connector are separated by a semicolon or a period.

Sentence modifier (p. 123)   A construction which applies its meaning to the whole of a sentence pattern. In "Fortunately they came early," *fortunately* modifies the whole pattern *they came early*, not just part of it. The immediate constituents of the complete sentence are *fortunately* and *they came early*. Structures of many different kinds may occur as sentence modifiers — for example, adverbs, prepositional phrases, subordinate clauses, verb clusters.

22 AMBIGUITY — PRONOUNS

Another kind of ambiguity that the writer must guard against involves the use of certain pronouns — the personal pronouns (*he, she, it, they*, etc.) and the demonstratives (*this, that, these, those*).

ANTECEDENTS

Personal and demonstrative pronouns pattern very much like proper nouns (*John, Sally, Germany*) except in one respect: the pronouns have *antecedents*.* That is, a word like *he* will not occur unless some such word as *Sam* or *the boy* or *my brother* has previously occurred. To put it another way, you can start a discussion with *Sam* or *the boy* or *my brother*, but you cannot start a discussion with the word *he*.

In conversation, the antecedent may lie unexpressed in the physical context. For example, if two people observe a man walking in the street, one may remark, "He looks like Simpson, doesn't he?" But there is no such exception in writing. *He* occurs in writing only if an antecedent for *he* occurs.

Difficulties arise when the pronoun has more than one possible antecedent, as in the following sentence:

> Sam told his brother that he wasn't going to get a typewriter for Christmas.

It is possible that a larger context might make this sentence clear, but as it stands it is ambiguous. *He* is preceded by two nouns, either of which might be the antecedent, and we do not know whether it is Sam or the brother that will miss out on the typewriter.

* First and second person pronouns — *I, me, you, we* — do not have antecedents, for they refer unmistakably to the speaker or the person spoken to.

There are several ways of eliminating this ambiguity. The crudest way is this one:

> Sam told his brother that he (Sam) wasn't going to get a typewriter for Christmas.

One would usually seek a more felicitous solution:

> When Sam heard that he wasn't going to get a typewriter for Christmas, he told his brother.
>
> Sam broke the news that his brother would not get a typewriter for Christmas.

The situation might permit a subtler solution:

> Sam complained to his brother about not getting a typewriter for Christmas. (Sam expected the typewriter.)
>
> Sam sympathized with his brother about not getting a typewriter for Christmas. (Clarence expected it.)

The English system works naturally in many ways to prevent this type of ambiguity. For instance, if words for a boy and a girl or a person and a thing or animal lie ahead of the pronoun, there need be no trouble:

> Sam told his sister that she wasn't going to get a typewriter for Christmas.
>
> Sam told the dog that it wasn't going to get any supper.

It is only when words for two males or two females or two things or two groups precede the pronoun that one must take care to avoid ambiguity.

OTHER PRONOUN PROBLEMS

Certain other problems with personal pronouns involve not so much clarity as conventions of writing. For example, writers often avoid letting a possessive noun stand as antecedent to a pronoun. Instead of this:

> When I tried to remove the dog's dish, it bit me.

one would do better to choose another construction:

The dog bit me when I tried to remove its dish.

Editors usually object to such uses of *they* as the following:

In Italy they are all individualists.

It is perfectly clear what is meant, but it would be better to say it this way:

All Italians are individualists.

However, it would be misleading to set down a simple rule on this point. When tone and context permit, writers do use *they* with this *vague reference*, as it is called. The following might well come intentionally from the pen of a good writer:

They are saying in Plainfield today that Gubser has no chance of re-election.

We must be similarly tentative in describing the use of the demonstratives. We do not usually have a clear-cut difference between clarity and ambiguity but instead a gradual shading off into fuzziness and confusion. The following sentence, for example, is rather soggy:

He greeted me by my first name and handed me a letter, but this didn't surprise me.

What didn't surprise me? What does *this* refer to? Does it mean his greeting me by my first name or his handing me the letter or both, or does it refer to the letter itself? It would be better, in such a circumstance, to avoid *this* and state the idea more explicitly:

I was not surprised by his using my first name or by his handing me the letter.

He greeted me by my first name and handed me the letter, but his familiarity didn't surprise me.

He greeted me by my first name and handed me a letter, the contents of which did not surprise me.

The demonstratives *this* and *that,* unlike the personal pronouns, often refer, quite properly, not to nouns but to whole sentences or to ideas expressed in verb clusters:

> He had a most unhappy home life. This may account for his personality problems.

It is perfectly clear that what may account for his personality problems is his having had an unhappy home life. Such usage is frequently to be observed in professional writing, and it is to be preferred to the clumsiness which might result from trying to avoid it. Nothing much is gained, for example, either in clarity or in style, by making the pronoun into a determiner followed by a vague noun, like *fact* or *condition:* "This fact may account for his personality problems."

Here, as in other areas, what is wanted is both clarity and grace, not just one or the other, or one at the expense of the other. The inexperienced writer will do well to be conscious of his use of *this* and *that, these* and *those,* and be sure that, whatever they refer to, the reference is clear. Sometimes one can get rid of the demonstrative and express the idea more clearly and neatly another way. Sometimes the demonstrative, even though it has no noun as its antecedent, is the best way of expressing the meaning.

EXERCISE 37

Number from 1 to 30. Some of the following items contain examples of faulty reference of pronouns. Some do not. Write **F** for the faulty ones and **G** for the good ones.

1. Mabel asked her sister if she had been invited to the dance.
2. Mabel asked her sister if she wanted to go to the dance.
3. Mabel asked her sister not to bother her.
4. When the dog came upon the cat, it got frightened.
5. When I tried to stroke the cat's fur, it scampered away.
6. Murchison indicated to the teacher that he didn't know what conditions were like in the third grade.

7. Murchison informed the principal that he intended to do something about the conditions in the third grade.

8. Smiling quietly, Sir Tolbert told the judge that he didn't understand the case at all.

9. Civilians are not permitted to talk to the prisoners until they have been thoroughly indoctrinated.

10. She showed me a picture of her mother, but that wasn't what surprised me.

11. When Jim's son was a year old, he decided to get married again.

12. He had eaten a dozen oysters an hour before, but this could hardly have caused his illness.

13. When we saw Fred leading Danny by the hand, we knew that he had been up to something.

14. The General informed his aide that he was leaving on the next plane for Karachi.

15. The sauce with which the meat had been covered had lost its savor.

16. He had visited some countries so backward that they actually sold bread without wrapping it in wax paper.

17. In the morning, Darlingbrooks was able to drink a little tea, but it didn't really agree with him.

18. A policeman walked over and handed us a paper on which a message had been written in Arabic, but this didn't frighten us.

19. Burton did his best to persuade Mr. Krabble to let him marry Febbria.

20. The housemother warned Eliza that her thoughtlessness could get her into trouble.

21. Maria led the pony up the stairs and tied her to the front door.

22. When I tried to put the baby's teddy bear away, it bit me.

23. Peters removed the fork from the saucer and held it against the light.

24. He read the blurb on the dust jacket of the book and decided that it wasn't very good.

25. His father wouldn't give him a dime, though he had plenty of money.

26. His father wouldn't give him a dime because he had plenty of money.

27. The lad was playing "Dixie" on a harmonica, and this made Carruthers weep.

28. He bought a new car with a radio, but it wasn't in good condition.

29. In the school I was in before, they were always threatening us.

30. Before he could remove the thorn from the lion's paw, it ate him up.

EXERCISE 38

Each of the following items contains an ambiguity. Rewrite each sentence twice, expressing each possible meaning clearly.

EXAMPLE: A. Elsa told her mother that she was losing her mind.

Fearing that she was losing her mind, Elsa confided in her mother.

Elsa thought her mother was losing her mind and told her so.

1. Frances remarked to Sally that she would look good with gray hair.
2. Before the tourists mingle with the natives, they should be inoculated.
3. He removed the stone from the cloth and washed it carefully.
4. Elaine had to stay home with her little sister because she had been naughty.
5. The judge didn't want to give Smathers a heavy sentence because he was very kind.
6. It was decided to turn on the water in the fountain in the town square because it attracted many visitors.
7. The teacher wrote his name on the blackboard, and this amused the students very much.
8. When Mr. Parker caught his six-year-old son smoking a cigar, he tried to be nonchalant.
9. When the eggs were served to the customers, they often looked green.
10. Sally told Eleanor that she would have to run the rest of the way.

23 PUNCTUATION OF SENTENCE MODIFIERS

The concept of the sentence modifier was explained in Chapter 19. We saw there that if the sentence "Apparently the man liked the movie" is cut into its two parts, the cut must necessarily come between *apparently* and *the:*

Apparently   /   the man liked the movie.

No other cut would make any sense. If we cut between subject and predicate, we would get the string of words *apparently the man*, which is clearly not a unit, not a meaningful part of anything. The meaning of *apparently* does not apply just to *the man* or just to *liked the movie* but to the whole sentence pattern: *the man liked the movie.* All of that is what is *apparent.*

Sentence modifiers can occur, as we shall see, at the end of the sentence they modify or in the middle of it. But they occur most frequently and most obviously before the sentence pattern, and in this chapter we shall consider them only in this initial position. A number of different kinds of constructions can occur here as sentence modifiers: adverbs, prepositional phrases, subordinate clauses, verb clusters, noun clusters, adjective clusters. The punctuation of sentence modifiers depends on the type of modifier. Some constructions are regularly separated by a comma from the sentence patterns they modify. Other types sometimes are and sometimes are not.

SUBORDINATE CLAUSES

A subordinate clause occurring as a sentence modifier is regularly followed by a comma:

> When he finally arrived at school, classes had already started.
> Though we didn't have much time, we decided to call on Smathers.
> Since it was obvious that no progress was being made, the meeting was adjourned indefinitely.

You will find this rule transgressed in professional writing sometimes, but not often.

VERB CLUSTERS

Verb clusters also occur as sentence modifiers and are also regularly punctuated. The verb headword in such a cluster, like the headword in verb clusters in other nonpredicate uses, has the *–ing* (present participle) form, the *–en* (past participle) form, or the simple (infinitive) form with *to*. In the function of sentence modifier, the *–ing* form is probably most common:

> Shinning up the tree, Bertram rescued the cat.
> Being a shy little thing, she twisted her handkerchief and said nothing.
> Strolling down Piccadilly one day, Darlingbrooks saw a walking stick that took his fancy.

Verb clusters of the *–ing* type, like subordinate clauses, can derive from any of the basic patterns:

> ONE: John sat down.
> Sitting down . . .
> When John sat down . . .
>
> FIVE: John gave Mary the flowers.
> Giving Mary the flowers . . .
> Because John gave Mary the flowers . . .

Verb clusters of the *–en* type, however, derive only from PATTERNS FOUR, FIVE, SIX, or SEVEN, and in a more complicated way. First of all, any of these patterns can be transformed into the *passive* construction described in Chapter 10.

> FOUR: John saw Mary.
> Mary was seen by John.
>
> The children ate the peanuts.
> The peanuts were eaten by the children.
>
> FIVE: John gave Mary some flowers.
> Mary was given some flowers (by John).
>
> SIX: John called Mary a fool.
> Mary was called a fool (by John).
>
> SEVEN: The members elected Sam president.
> Sam was elected president (by the members).

Any such passive can now provide a verb cluster for use as a sentence modifier. The verb cluster will consist of the verb in the *–en* form plus whatever follows it:

Seen by John, Mary removed her disguise.
Elected president by the members, Sam promised reforms.

As sentence modifiers, such clusters are also set off from the sentence they modify.

Verb clusters with the *to* form, deriving from any of the basic patterns, can occur as sentence modifiers. They are regularly punctuated:

To understand Asia, one must begin by understanding India.
To put an end to the argument, Davis struck his opponent on the head.

ADJECTIVES

Adjectives can also occur as sentence modifiers and are also punctuated. Such adjectives are usually themselves modified by something — that is, they constitute the headword of what we can call an adjective cluster:

Angry at the delay, Hopkins refused to participate.
Eager to please her new friends, she planned the party very carefully.

Like all adjectives, these derive ultimately from PATTERN TWO: "Hopkins seemed angry," "She seemed eager."

Students of grammar have often been puzzled by words like *alarmed, terrified, chagrined* in sentences like "Alarmed at having heard nothing, he sent a wire." Is *alarmed* an adjective like *angry*, or an *–en* verb like *seen* or *elected?* It is somewhat different from both, but more like *angry* than like *elected*. There is a group of transitive verbs which can have *it* as subject and a human noun as object: "It alarmed John," "It terrified John," "It interested John." All of these verbs in the *–ing* form or the *–en* form can go into PATTERN TWO:

It seemed alarming.
He seemed alarmed.
He seemed terrified.

From there on they can function like any adjective. The difference between *angry* and *alarmed*, to use a metaphor, is that *angry* is born in PATTERN TWO, whereas *alarmed* is in PATTERN FOUR and comes to TWO in a second step. But words like *seen, elected, sung* are not PATTERN TWO words by either birth or adoption, and therefore are not adjectives.

NOUN CLUSTERS

Noun clusters are somewhat rare as sentence modifiers. They suggest a formal and elaborate style. When they do occur, they are punctuated:

A man who was willing to risk all to get what he wanted, Renfrews did not hesitate a moment.

In a special kind of noun cluster, the noun is modified by a verb cluster with an *–ing* headword. This is traditionally called a *nominative absolute*. It is regularly punctuated:

The minister being ill with a touch of flu, the sermon was delivered by his assistant.

ADVERBS AND PREPOSITIONAL PHRASES

One cannot be so definite about the punctuation of adverbs and prepositional phrases used as sentence modifiers. They are often but not always set off in this position. Punctuation depends somewhat on the individual items. *Fortunately*, for example, is more likely to be set off than *then:*

Fortunately, we had had a good breakfast.
Then we all went to breakfast.

Punctuation may depend also on the individual writer or on the medium for which he is writing.

There is a tendency to punctuate long prepositional phrases occurring as sentence modifiers but not to punctuate short ones:

> At the time such matters were of little interest.
> At the time of which we are speaking, such matters were of little interest.

If the object of the preposition is a verb cluster, the prepositional phrase is regularly punctuated:

> By working nights, Harley managed to stay in school.
> In looking for a cure for the common cold, Wilson discovered a new method of tranquilizing rabbits.

Sometimes the omission of a comma after an adverb or a prepositional phrase will permit misreading:

> Inside the cathedral was beautiful.
> Before eating Sam took a pill.
> In writing subordinate clauses are very common.

To keep the reader from momentarily taking the constructions as *inside the cathedral, before eating Sam,* and *in writing subordinate clauses,* one would use commas:

> Inside, the cathedral was beautiful.
> Before eating, Sam took a pill.
> In writing, subordinate clauses are very common.

OTHER SENTENCE MODIFIERS

A number of other kinds of sentence modifiers occur but mostly in speech or in the writing of dialogue. We shall notice them briefly. Names used to address people are set off with commas:

> George, we're waiting for you.
> We're waiting for you, George.

The words *say, look, listen* constitute a small structure group for which there is no traditional name. We might call them "attention-getting signals." They are set off in the writing of dialogue:

Say, here comes Andy now.

Listen, I've just had a good idea.

The words *oh, now, why, well* constitute another structure group. They signal that the utterance which follows is a response to a previous utterance. They are set off:

Oh, I don't think so.

Why, I didn't mean anything of the kind.

The words *yes* and *no,* another structure group, are set off, as are *okay* and *all right,* still another group:

No, he didn't come at all.

Okay, we'll do it your way.

EXERCISE 39

Make two columns on your paper and number from 1 to 40. Most of the following sentences contain a sentence modifier. Some do not. If the sentence has a sentence modifier, indicate the kind of modifier in the first column, using the following symbols: subordinate clause (**SC**), verb cluster (**VC**), noun cluster (**NC**), adjective cluster (**AC**), adverb (**Adv**), prepositional phrase (**Prep**). If there is no sentence modifier, leave the space blank.

Punctuate the sentences according to the directions in Chapter 23. Write the punctuation mark and the preceding word in the second column. If no mark is needed, leave a blank.

EXAMPLE: A. Realizing that he needed a haircut Sam entered the barbershop.

            VC   *haircut,*

1. When the rainy season began he bought an umbrella.
2. There was no one in the house.
3. Hoping for the best Murchison entered the principal's office.
4. Furious at having been deceived he determined never to speak to Carmen again.

5. Outside the house needed a coat of paint.
6. By pushing a button on his desk he was able to release the latch on the door.
7. The reason for his sudden disappearance has never been satisfactorily explained.
8. Reaching for another banana Kumwelt dislocated his shoulder.
9. Since neither of us had a watch we had not the slightest notion of what time it was.
10. To emphasize my point I jabbed him vigorously in the chest.
11. Knowing that he would never get another chance he climbed aboard.
12. A hard fellow to best in an argument Johanson usually had his own way.
13. To know India is not to know Asia.
14. To the great surprise of everyone who was present Frank turned out to have a beautiful tenor voice.
15. Unquestionably he should have been dismissed long ago.
16. Confronted with the evidence he made a full confession.
17. Though he was not exactly truthful Clarence seldom told a downright lie.
18. Flattering him about his beautiful eyebrows won't get you anywhere.
19. The day being a beautiful one we decided to drive to Lyonesse.
20. Driving through Lyonesse we stopped to picnic on the banks of the river.
21. If we had only remembered to bring some food the picnic might have been a great success.
22. Aware that his client did not have a very good case Sir Tolbert decided to bribe the jury.
23. The fact that bribing jurors is against the law simply did not occur to him.
24. If you need anything just press the button beside your bed.
25. True to his principles Blackwell flatly refused to take part.
26. Surprisingly enough no plans had been drawn up at all.
27. Not wanting to anger him we pretended to agree.
28. Because food was his only real interest he settled down in Paris.
29. In the interests of those who had been unable to attend it was decided to postpone the vote.

30. Those who understand the problem best are most pessimistic.
31. Whoever comes in last should lock the door.
32. Stopping off for a day in New York Tipton bought a bauble for his fiancée.
33. Whenever he made a little extra money Rick popped it into his savings account.
34. The last bus having gone we had to walk all the way home.
35. With the firm intention of asking Angela to marry him Martin took a tranquilizing pill and set out.
36. By practicing every day for two years Henry got his bowling average up to eighty-five.
37. Stunned at the news she simply took to her bed and stayed there.
38. To keep from being biased he usually reviewed books before he read them.
39. The people who moved in upstairs said that they were from Sioux Falls, South Dakota.
40. By working double shifts they got the job done in three months.

24 DANGLING MODIFIERS

Some sentence modifiers present a problem in sentence construction, in addition to the problem of punctuation. Consider this sentence:

Scanning the horizon, Williams sighted a ship.

The immediate constituents are as we have indicated elsewhere:

Scanning the horizon   /   Williams sighted a ship.

The whole meaning of the verb cluster *scanning the horizon* applies to the whole meaning of the sentence pattern *Williams sighted a ship*. We cannot say that the verb cluster modifies *Williams*, for then we would have the construction *scanning the horizon Williams*, which is obviously not a possible grammatical construction.

However, there is a connection between the verb cluster and the subject of the sentence pattern, in this case the noun *Williams*. The connection is that the subject of the sentence pattern also names the performer of the action of the verb cluster. This connection is dictated by the derivation of the sentence from the basic patterns:

Source: Williams scanned the horizon.
Consumer: Williams sighted a ship.
Result: Scanning the horizon, Williams sighted a ship.

We can in similar fashion make sentence modifiers from any of the basic patterns, but we must be sure that the original subject-predicate relationship is not lost:

Birds sing sweetly.
Singing sweetly, the birds gave us pleasure.

John saw Jane in the store.
Seeing Jane in the store, John spoke to her.

The event occurred in April.
Occurring in April, the event surprised everyone.

John was ill.
Being ill, John stayed home.

WHAT IS A DANGLING MODIFIER?

If the subject-predicate relationship of the basic pattern is not shown, we get the structural fault called a *dangling modifier*, as in this sentence:

Scanning the horizon, a ship was sighted.

The reader's knowledge of normal English construction would lead him at first glance to take *ship* as the performer of the action of scanning, as if the cluster derived from this basic sentence:

The ship scanned the horizon.

Of course, knowing that ships do not scan, he quickly corrects himself; he does not actually get a wrong meaning. But he has been momentarily led astray by an ungrammatical sentence.

Here are some further examples of dangling modifiers:

> Running into the room, her engagement was announced.
> Corrected: Running into the room, she announced her engagement.

> Feeling a little under the weather, a visit to the doctor seemed indicated.
> Corrected: Feeling a little under the weather, he thought he'd better see a doctor.

> Seeing Mirabelle for the first time, her personality repelled us.
> Corrected: When we first saw Mirabelle, her personality repelled us.

AVOIDING DANGLING MODIFIERS

You might notice that some modifiers dangle because a passive is used in place of the active construction in the sentence pattern: *a ship was sighted* in place of *he sighted a ship*. This is no reason to avoid passives; one must just be a little careful in their use. Sometimes the passive is what is required. "Seen for the first time, Mirabelle was often thought repulsive."

Not all words ending in *-ing* must be followed by words which name the performer of the action. Some *-ing* words are conventionally used in an impersonal sense, as in this example:

> Assuming that he knows his business, it might work out all right.

It clearly does not name the assumer. Nevertheless, *assuming* is taken to mean "if one assumes," and the sentence is not ungrammatical. Other *-ing* words commonly used in this impersonal way are *considering, supposing, admitting*.

Verb clusters in which the verb is a past participle also dangle sometimes:

> Caught red-handed with the stolen watch, his guilt seemed obvious.

This is written as if the cluster derived from the sentence "His guilt was caught red-handed with the stolen watch." The sentence should go something like this:

> Caught red-handed with the stolen watch, he seemed obviously guilty.

Similarly:

> Arrested and put in prison, his mother's heart was broken.
> Corrected: His arrest and imprisonment broke his mother's heart.

> Sneered at by all the other children, life didn't seem worth living.
> Corrected: Sneered at by all the other children, she sometimes felt that life wasn't worth living.

Notice that it is not enough that the performer or undergoer of the action of the verb be named somewhere in the sentence pattern that follows. It must be named as the *subject* of the pattern. The following is a dangling modifier:

> Caught red-handed with the stolen watch, the policeman was forced to arrest Herbert.

If, as seems probable, it was Herbert and not the policeman who was caught with the watch, then the modifier dangles, because the structure would lead us to believe that it was the subject, the policeman, who was the thief. We correct it by making Herbert the subject:

> Caught red-handed with the stolen watch, Herbert was arrested by the policeman.

Observe that in this sentence we corrected the fault simply by making *Herbert* the subject of the main pattern. We might want, however, to give prominence to the policeman by making him the subject. In that case, we can use a subordinate clause instead of a verb cluster as the sentence modifier:

> Since Herbert had been caught red-handed with the stolen watch, the policeman was forced to arrest him.

Verb clusters with *to* sometimes dangle:

> To understand Asia, India must be studied first.

It would be more grammatical to write:

> To understand Asia, one must begin by studying India.

This gives us the subject *one*, an impersonal but plausible understander of Asia. However, the subject-predicate relationship is not so rigorously maintained with the *to* form as with the *–ing* and *–en* forms. Sentences beginning "To do this, it is necessary . . ." are not uncommon in professional writing, whatever the verb.

An adjective cluster sometimes occurs as a dangling modifier:

> Furious at the delay, a riot nearly broke out.

This is written as if the cluster were derivable from "The riot seemed furious." Of course, the cluster is not so derived, and one should write instead:

> Furious at the delay, the customers nearly started a riot.

Prepositional phrases do not cause trouble as dangling modifiers unless the object of the preposition is a verb or verb cluster. Then the same rule must be observed: the subject of the main pattern must indicate the performer of the action of the verb. Otherwise the phrase dangles:

> By racing through town at high speed, many lives were endangered.

We need to know the racer:

> By racing through town at high speed, Simkins endangered many lives.

Other prepositional phrases never dangle. Neither do subordinate clauses; indeed, some of the dangling modifiers in the examples above were corrected by the substitution of subordinate clauses for the verb clusters. Noun clusters of the nominative absolute type do not dangle either:

> Herbert having been caught with the goods, the policeman arrested him.

Here the person caught is named by the headword of the cluster, *Herbert*.

EXERCISE 40

For each sentence below, write the sentence pattern from which the sentence modifier derives. Its subject will be the subject of the sentence pattern that follows the modifier, and the modifier itself will provide the predicate. If the result is a sensible and grammatical sentence, write **G** at the right of your answer. If not, write **D** for dangling modifier.

EXAMPLES: A. Cheering wildly, the spectators encouraged the team.
             The spectators cheered wildly.   **G**
           B. Cheering wildly, the game was won.
             The game cheered wildly.   **D**

1. Running into Sam in town, a question popped into my mind.
2. Switching on the light, a mouse scurried across the room.
3. Calling on his last reserves of energy, Gilbaugh set a new meet record for the distance.
4. Stupefied by the implications of the remark, Georgia was unable to answer.
5. Having resided all her life in the country, Chicago seemed a bit terrifying at first.

6. Tormented by what he had done, a full confession seemed the only answer.

7. Peering at the congregation, Reverend Gordon wished he had chosen another profession.

8. By loosening his tie and unbuttoning his collar, a little relief was gained.

9. By taking a nap before dinner, he was able to stay awake through the whole opera.

10. In applying for the job, Darlingbrooks remarked that he spoke Swahili fluently.

11. Having been twice to the South Col of Everest, the best plan seemed to be to ask Sluter to join the expedition.

12. Drab and dirty by day, the city seems truly beautiful at night.

13. Returning to Lyonesse thirty years later, everything was just the same.

14. In reaching for a second helping, his shoulder was dislocated.

15. Tired of being a waiter, Andrews dumped the soup on the customer's head and walked out.

16. Resentful at being passed over again, a plan for revenge began to grow in his mind.

17. Bursting splendidly in the night sky, Johanson marveled at the fireworks.

18. Stepping back to view the picture, Milton's face wore a smile of satisfaction.

19. Sneaking into the locker room at night, seven basketballs were stolen.

20. Winding its way down the valley, the stream finally empties into the Wannakoochee.

EXERCISE 41

Number from 1 to 30. Some of the following sentences contain dangling modifiers; some do not. If the sentence has a dangling modifier, put a **D** beside the corresponding number on your paper. If it does not, leave the space blank.

1. Not wishing to hurt her feelings, he said he thought the dress very pretty.
2. Unable to agree on where to put the city hall, the whole building project came to a halt.
3. When he finally summoned enough courage to knock, no one answered the door.
4. Irritated at his frequent absences, the custodian was asked to resign.
5. Smiling quietly at the jury, Sir Tolbert said that he would call one more witness.
6. To become a first class Scout, several difficult tests must be passed.
7. After leaving us, he apparently went straight to his office.
8. Having spent seven years in the third grade, the other boys were much smaller than Murchison.
9. His mother having been an actress, he knew the theater very well.
10. Strolling down the main street of Los Angeles, South Bend seemed a million miles away.
11. To understand what has been accomplished, we must compare these figures with those of 1956.
12. Being a hopeless old drunk, nobody would have anything to do with him.
13. The gate being locked, she rang for the porter.
14. Happy to have her with us again, Angela was kissed by everyone present.
15. Crushed by the unexpected criticism, a tear rolled down her cheek.
16. Not having been caught early enough, the infection spread dangerously.
17. Feeling hot and thirsty, the glass of sarsaparilla tasted very good indeed.
18. Having very little money, college was quite out of the question.
19. Taken quite aback by the enthusiasm of the class, Miss Driscoll's lower lip trembled slightly.
20. Unwilling to move the high school, another route was chosen for the freeway.
21. Just to get a loaf of bread or a bottle of milk, he had to walk fifteen miles.
22. Since he carried no insurance, nothing could be done about it.

23. Inching carefully down the embankment, the rescuers managed to get within hailing distance.

24. Mindful of what had happened the time before, no invitation was sent to Clarabelle.

25. Having had too much sun and too little water, the lawn was in pretty bad shape.

26. Running down the steps to greet us, Clifford's hearty welcome warmed our hearts.

27. Refused flatly by Uncle Alfred, there was still a chance of getting something out of Aunt Cindy.

28. Already terrified by the darkness and the storm, the appearance of the bear set them screaming.

29. Roaring to a halt at the gas tank, the Ferrari was the most beautiful automobile I had ever seen.

30. To save a little more money, his lunch consisted of a small handful of barley.

EXERCISE 42

Each of the following sentences contains a dangling modifier. Revise each one, in whatever way seems best, to remove the fault.

1. Approaching us at eighty miles an hour, a collision seemed inevitable.

2. Walking along Fifth Avenue one day, a bauble caught Tipton's eye.

3. Having been convicted twice previously, a stiff sentence was to be expected.

4. Suddenly realizing what we would be expected to do, it seemed best to withdraw our application.

5. Not wishing to alarm the populace, the story was at first withheld from the newspapers.

6. Noticing that his teeth were falling out, the teacher sent Alonzo to the school nurse.

7. Angry at having been called a liar, his refusal to speak to her was to be expected.

8. Uncertain about the reception it would have, the new plan was temporarily shelved.

9. Bedridden for twenty years, television was a great solace to Mr. Daugherty.
10. In writing up the report, some very serious errors had been made.
11. By searching diligently the next day, most of the beads were recovered.
12. To appreciate the full significance of the proposal, a little background information may be necessary.

25 INTONATION

The unseasoned student, confronted with the rules of punctuation, is likely to consider them an impenetrable mystery. One studies them, if one is conscientious, one memorizes as many of them as possible, but one does not try to understand them. In truth, some rules of punctuation *are* arbitrary and meaningless; we do it in such and such a way simply because it is conventional or fashionable to do it in that way.

However, to a rather large extent, punctuation carries meaning. The letters that we use in writing symbolize, however imperfectly, the vowels and consonants that we produce when we talk. The punctuation of writing symbolizes, though also imperfectly, the intonation, or tone of voice, of speech. In order to understand punctuation, we need to understand something about intonation.

Intonation, or tone of voice, is made up of three features called *stress*, *pitch*, and *juncture*. Stress is a matter of the loudness or softness with which syllables are uttered. Pitch is melody. When the air that makes speech sounds comes through the throat, it passes through an apparatus called the vocal cords or vocal folds. These may be tense or relaxed. If they are tense, the air is made to vibrate. If it vibrates rapidly, we have high pitch; if it vibrates slowly, we have low pitch. Juncture is the breaking off or interrupting of the speech according to the structure of the sentence. It is closely related to pitch and somewhat less closely to stress.

We shall not have leisure here to examine intonation with any thoroughness. It is a complicated subject and in some ways difficult to study. Though we react constantly and accurately to subtle distinctions in intonation, to become consciously aware of just what they are takes time and practice. We shall confine ourselves to some of the more obvious distinctions, and particularly to those that relate to punctuation.

STRESS

Consider the word *anticipate*. This is made up of four syllables: *an-tic-i-pate*. They are not, however, uttered with equal loudness. The second syllable — *tic* — is the loudest of the four. In marking the stress of this word, we put the sign ´ over *tic* and say that this syllable has *primary* stress: *antícipate*. The weakest syllable is the following *i*. We mark this ˘ and call it *weak* stress: *antícĭpate*. The remaining two syllables — *an* and *pate* — are both louder than the *i* but softer than the *tic*. However, the *pate* is louder than the *an*. We say that *pate* has secondary stress and mark it with the symbol ^: *antícipâte*. The *an* has tertiary stress, which is marked with the symbol `: *àntícĭpâte*.

This word *anticipate*, pronounced by itself, illustrates the four stress contrasts of English. In any utterance of sufficient length, these four stresses will appear. Each syllable will be either primary or secondary or tertiary or weak. The stress system is part of what we learn when we learn English, and it is an important part of English. If you don't get the stresses right, your English sounds at best foreign and at worst unintelligible. Foreign speakers, for example, frequently say *anticipáte*, confusing the verb stress pattern with that of the noun *anticipátion*. We who speak English natively,

however, learned early to separate in a regular way the verbs of this
class from the corresponding nouns:

antícipate   anticipátion
séparate   separátion
óperate   operátion
eláborate   elborátion

Stress is used all through the grammar to make distinctions of
one kind or another. You may remember that earlier we said that
the phrase *the orderly room* is ambiguous: it could mean a room
that is neat, or it could mean a room for orderlies. But if we indicate
the stress, the ambiguity disappears:

the orderly róom (a room that is neat)
the órderly room (a room for orderlies)

When an adjective modifies a noun, the primary stress is on the
noun; when a noun modifies another noun, the primary stress is
commonly on the first noun. Thus if we hear the stress, we can tell
immediately which meaning is intended.

Any sentence or phrase has a normal stress pattern which depends on the make-up of the sentence. For instance, in uttering the
sentence "He needs some money" we normally put the primary
stress on the first syllable in *money:*

He needs some móney.

However, we can instead shift the stress to any of the other words
to indicate a contrast:

Hé needs some money. (but I don't)
He néeds some money. (but he won't get it)
He needs sóme money. (but not a great deal)

These are called contrastive stresses, and they show another way

in which stress can carry meaning. In writing we might indicate
these meanings by underlining (in print, italicizing) the word with
primary stress:

> *He* needs some money.
> He *needs* some money.
> He needs *some* money.

PITCH

As there are, in English, four stress contrasts, so there are four
pitch contrasts. These are given numbers, rather than names: low
pitch — 1; next to low — 2; next to high — 3; high — 4. We use 1,
2, and 3 all the time. We use 4 mostly when we get excited.

For example, the normal way of uttering the sentence "He needs
some money" is to begin on the second pitch level, to stay on it
until the syllable with primary stress is reached, then to rise to the
third level, and somewhere between there and the end of the
sentence to fall to the lowest level. We can mark the pitch thus:

$$^{2}\text{He needs some }^{3}\text{money}^{1}.$$

Like stress, pitch carries meaning. For example, in this sentence
if, instead of falling to the lowest pitch, we stay on three, we get a
question instead of a statement.

$$^{2}\text{He needs some }^{3}\text{money}^{3}?$$

There are other possibilities. We can put excitement or anguish
into it by rising to the highest pitch instead of three:

$$^{2}\text{He needs some }^{4}\text{money}^{1}.$$

Or by falling to two instead of one, we can add a note of pleading
or apology:

$$\overset{2}{\text{He}} \text{ needs some } \overset{3}{\text{money}} \overset{2}{.}$$

It is sometimes said that the voice rises on questions and falls on statements. This isn't quite true. It generally rises on questions that can be answered *yes* or *no:*

$$\overset{2}{\text{Does}} \text{ he need the } \overset{3}{\text{money}} \overset{3}{?}$$

But on questions introduced by interrogatives, like *who, what, when, why,* the normal pitch pattern is like that on statements:

$$\overset{2}{\text{Who}} \text{ needs the } \overset{3}{\text{money}} \overset{1}{?}$$

Both types, however, can take other pitch patterns with changes in meaning easily caught by the native speaker of English.

What this has to do with punctuation we shall see in the next chapter.

EXERCISE 43

Copy the following items on a separate sheet of paper and mark (´) the syllable on which the primary stress falls. Assume that each item has only one primary stress and that the stress is normal, not contrastive.

EXAMPLES: A. antícipate
            B. He needs the móney.

1. relate
2. brother
3. happy
4. insist
5. talker
6. movement
7. quickly
8. because
9. president
10. accidental
11. refugee
12. possibility

13. inescapable
14. arbitrary
15. resentfully
16. adaptation
17. incontrovertible
18. indignation
19. indignant
20. indubitably
21. at home
22. in the house
23. in a flash
24. an old hat

25. a tomcat
26. a streetcar
27. walked away
28. Dig it up.
29. went to the store
30. He went to the store.
31. a high school principal
32. a high school teacher
33. He just went by.
34. He just walked away.
35. He's looking better.

EXERCISE 44

Follow the instructions for Exercise 43 on page 171.

1. He bought a car.
2. He left it outside.
3. He's a college president.
4. He's a college professor.
5. There's no one here.
6. There's no one in the house.
7. Why did you do it?
8. Has anyone seen him?
9. Keep your shirt on.
10. Put your shirt away.
11. He hung up the gloves.
12. He was a good friend.
13. He was a candy salesman.
14. He's an airline pilot.
15. He's a small-town crook.
16. He's a friend of mine.
17. They'll never finish it.
18. She lost her physics book.
19. Someone must have stolen it.

20. Was anyone with her?
21. The barometer was falling.
22. Turn it over slowly.
23. What did he do with it?
24. Keep your chin up.
25. We'd better clean the place up.
26. You don't understand it.
27. You don't understand it at all.
28. Whatever happened to Beaumont?
29. No one expected anything like that.
30. They kept the planes flying.
31. We thought her rather foolish.
32. He finally thought better of it.

SUMMARY OF TERMS • CHAPTERS 22–25

Antecedent (p. 145)   The word or group of words to which a pronoun refers. Generally pronouns refer to nouns or other pronouns, though they sometimes refer to clauses or to something in the physical context. The types of pronouns that have antecedents are the third person personal pronouns (*he, she, it, they,* etc.) and the demonstratives (*this, that, these, those*). The possessive determiners (*his, her, its, their*) also have antecedents.

Dangling modifier (p. 159)   A construction in which a sentence modifier with a verb or *be* as headword is not followed in the main pattern by a word that can logically be the subject of the verb or *be*. "Opening the book, a pressed flower appeared" is an example of a dangling modifier. This would seem to derive from a sentence "A pressed flower opened the book." This is, of course, not the meaning intended. In the sentence "Opening the book, John discovered a pressed flower," there is no dangling modifier. This derives from "John opened the book," which is what is meant.

Intonation (p. 167)   The element of speech which, superimposed on vowels and consonants, gives meaning to sentences. Intonation is made up of three features: *stress, pitch,* and *juncture.*

Juncture (p. 167)   The mechanism by which sentences or parts of

sentences are ended. Juncture involves a lengthening out of a final syllable plus possible alterations to the pitch. English is generally said to have
three final junctures: *level juncture* (in which the pitch remains level);
rising juncture (in which the pitch rises a little); *falling juncture* (in which
the pitch falls a little).

Nominative absolute (p. 154)   A noun cluster in which a noun headword is modified by a verb cluster with *–ing*, the whole construction then
functioning as a sentence modifier: "The door being bolted, we climbed
in the window." "The chairman having failed to appear, it was decided
to adjourn."

Pitch (p. 167)   The melody with which sentences are spoken. Our
speech organs contain an apparatus, very like those used in musical
instruments, which alters the tone from high to low. These alterations
are used in many languages, including English, to give different meanings to sentences. Questions, for example, are sometimes distinguished
from statements by pitch alone. It is generally believed that English has
four contrasting levels of pitch: 4 (high), 3 (next to high), 2 (next to
low), 1 (low).

Stress (p. 167)   The relative prominence with which syllables are
spoken. Stress is generally thought of as being a matter of loudness or
softness, though other features, particularly length, no doubt play a part.
English is usually described as having four stress contrasts: primary
(loudest stress), secondary (next to loudest), tertiary (next to softest),
weak (softest). Another common term for stress is *accent*.

26 INTONATION AND PUNCTUATION

Let us now consider the sentence "The people who were here
went away." This might be spoken with various intonations and
with one or more primary stresses. If there is just one primary
stress, and if no contrast is intended, the primary stress will fall
on *away:*

The people who were here went awáy.

Spoken in this way, the sentence would have the following pitch pattern:

2   3   1
The people who were here went a way.

KINDS OF JUNCTURE

At the very end of the sentence, the voice not only falls to pitch level one but drops a bit below it, and the final sounds of the last word are lengthened out. This dropping off and lengthening out is what is called *falling juncture*.* It is a kind of punctuation mark of speech, showing that a certain kind of structure has been concluded.

Now if we speak the same words in the same order but speak them as a question, we have a 2 3 3 pitch pattern:

2   3   3
The people who were here went a way ?

That is, the voice does not fall to level one but stays on level three. However, at the very end there is again a lengthening out of the vowel and this time a slight rise of the pitch, in the direction of, but not as far as, level four. This lengthening out and rise of pitch is called *rising juncture*. It signals that another kind of structure, in this case a question, has been concluded.

Now suppose that we utter this sentence with not one primary stress but two. The added primary stress will fall on *here:*

The people who were hére went awáy.

Spoken as a statement, the sentence will have the following pitch pattern:

2   3   2 2   3   1
The people who were here   went a way.

---

* What are here called *falling juncture, rising juncture,* and *level juncture* are called in *Patterns of English* and some other books *doublecross, doublebar,* and *singlebar* junctures respectively.

That is, the voice rises to three on *here* and falls back to two; then, at the end of the word *here*, there will be a break — a slight pause and a lengthening out of the last sound in the word; the sentence then starts again on the same pitch level. This pause and lengthening out, the pitch neither rising nor falling, is called *level juncture*.

Whenever in an utterance we have two primary stresses, we always have a juncture of some kind — falling, rising, or level — between them. In general, the end of a sentence is marked by a falling or a rising juncture, depending on what kind of sentence it is. Junctures occurring within a sentence are usually either rising or level junctures. Rising junctures are usually symbolized in writing by a comma. Level junctures are usually not indicated by any punctuation mark.

We will use a level arrow (→) to mark level juncture, a rising arrow (↗) for rising juncture, and a falling arrow (↘) for falling juncture. Then we can mark our sentences in this way:

The people who were here went awáy ↘

The people who were hére → went awáy ↘

Note that the sentences do not differ in meaning. The second pronunciation is simply a little slower than the first. It is probably the more common way of saying the sentence. Students writing such a sentence often succumb to the temptation to put in a comma between the subject and the predicate, in this case after the word *here*. If challenged, they will say they pause there in speaking. What they call a pause is what we have described as level juncture. It does involve a short pause as well as a drawing out of the sound after the primary stress. But it is not generally symbolized in writing by any punctuation.

It would also be possible to speak this sentence with three primary stresses. The added one would then fall on the first syllable of *people*, and we would have another level juncture:

The péople → who were hére → went awáy ↘

This would be a very slow and deliberate, perhaps somewhat un-
natural, way of speaking the sentence. There would still be no
commas in writing.

OPTIONAL AND OBLIGATORY JUNCTURES

Now let us take the sentence "My father who was here went
away." This differs from the other one in that it *must* have three
primary stresses and therefore three junctures. "The people who
were here went away" *can* have one or two or three, but "My
father who was here went away" *must* have three. Furthermore,
the two junctures within the sentence will, for most speakers, be
rising rather than level junctures. The sentence therefore goes
like this:

My fáther ↗ who was hére ↗ went awáy ↘

The level junctures, then, of our first example, are optional: you
have them or not depending on the style with which you utter the
sentence. The rising junctures of the second example are obligatory;
you have to have them in a sentence of this type. These obligatory
rising junctures are symbolized by commas in writing:

My father, who was here, went away.

Here is another example of a sentence with optional level junctures in contrast with one with obligatory rising junctures:

An old man that we knew brought us some peaches.
Alexander, whom we had known for a long time, came to
visit us.

In the first sentence, you might have one primary stress — on
peaches — more likely two — on *peaches* and *knew* — possibly three
— on *peaches* and *knew* and *man*. You may or may not, therefore,
have a level juncture after *knew* or after *knew* and *man*. In any case,
these junctures would not be indicated by commas. In the second
sentence, there will necessarily be three primary stresses — on
Alexander, *time*, and *visit* — and necessarily junctures, usually ris-

ing, after *Alexander* and after *time*. These must be symbolized by commas.

Here are further examples:

Optional Level:	Those who saw the exhibit were very pleased with it.
Obligatory Rising:	Donald, who saw the exhibit, was very pleased with it.
Optional Level:	The houses which Emerson built were very comfortable.
Obligatory Rising:	Our house, which Emerson built, was very comfortable.

All the examples so far have illustrated structures containing relative clauses. Verb clusters can also occur in this position, either with optional level junctures and no commas or with obligatory rising junctures and commas:

Optional Level:	The man facing us looked scornful.
Obligatory Rising:	Albert, facing us, looked scornful.
Optional Level:	The boys arrested by the police denied everything.
Obligatory Rising:	My brother, arrested by the police, denied everything.

Noun clusters can occur here also:

Obligatory Rising:	My brother, a wild youth who was frequently in trouble, was arrested by the police.
Obligatory Rising:	Austin, the capital of Texas, is one of the prettiest towns in the United States.

Noun clusters used in this way are called *appositives*. They always have obligatory junctures before and after them and therefore are always set off by commas.

Obligatory rising junctures can occur in various other positions in the sentence:

Optional Level: We decided to ask someone who knew the Middle East.

Obligatory Rising: We decided to ask Arnold, who knew the Middle East very well.

You will notice that there are two ways of making this connection between intonation and punctuation. One is by learning to distinguish level juncture (a short pause and lengthening, the pitch continuing level across the break) from rising and falling junctures (a longer pause and greater lengthening, the pitch rising or falling at the break). The level junctures are optional and are not punctuated. The obligatory junctures within the sentence are rising for some people, falling for others. Whichever they are, they are marked by commas.

Some students have difficulty distinguishing the different junctures. If you do, you can achieve the same result by concentrating on the primary stresses. "The people who were here went away" will most likely have two primary stresses but might have one or three: no commas. "My father, who was here, went away" will necessarily have three: two commas.

EXERCISE 45

Say each of the following sentences aloud. Note the primary stresses. If the sentence *must have* more than one primary stress, with rising or falling junctures between them, a comma is needed. On a separate sheet of paper write the word that comes before and the word that follows each juncture point with a comma between them. If a sentence needs no comma, leave a blank after the corresponding number on your paper.

EXAMPLE: A. My father who was here went away.
father, who . . . here, went . . .

1. The man holding the baby is David.
2. David holding the baby felt suddenly ill.
3. Arnold who had never met Angela gasped in surprise.
4. She lived in Lyonesse a town on the banks of a river.
5. Those who have seen it like it very much.
6. All students who fail will be given another chance.
7. My mother who is terrified of mice let out a scream.
8. The sheriff a husky fellow in his early thirties grabbed Mortimer by the collar.
9. I never met a man who knew so much about pigeons.
10. Nobody who loves dogs could ever do such a thing.
11. He lived in a house which has since burned down.
12. He lived in the historic old Darlingbrooks house which has since burned down.
13. He lived in Chicago when he was young.
14. He lived in Chicago in the thirties when he was young.
15. Murchison who had heard the story many times yawned rudely.
16. Gertrude whom I intend to marry is a waitress at the Argonaut.
17. The Gertrude that I mean is a waitress at the Argonaut.
18. The tale that he told us seemed completely incredible.
19. Barnes a curriculum vice-principal at Davidson High was a rather droll chap.
20. All children who have two heads will be admitted free.
21. She gave his best suit which he had bought in London to the clothing drive.
22. The rooms that face the street are very noisy.
23. My room which faced the inner courtyard was very quiet.
24. Aunt Mary having foreseen what was coming left the room.
25. I confided in my brother a man whose judgment I greatly respected.
26. Tipton presented his gift a bauble that he had bought in New York.
27. Persons carrying identification cards were admitted at once.
28. Uncle Harry knocking the ashes out of his pipe set fire to the Pentagon.
29. Knocking the ashes out of his pipe Uncle Harry set fire to the Pentagon.
30. The lawyer for the defense Sir Tolbert Willoughby-Hughes had never lost a case.

31. The suit he was wearing had been gnawed by mice.
32. Waukegan a town situated on the shore of Lake Michigan is the birthplace of Edward Jorgenson.
33. Who is the youngster climbing the flagpole?
34. Danforth saluting smartly said he would like to volunteer.
35. Those who know their way around never volunteer for anything.
36. My sister furious at me for betraying the secret stormed out of the room.
37. Stung by his remark I hit him with a frying pan.
38. He had a few mannerisms which annoyed me.
39. It was already five which meant that we had to drive a hundred and fifty miles in two hours.
40. He showed us his violin which is one of the most valuable in the world.

27   RESTRICTIVE AND NONRESTRICTIVE

Look at these two sentences:

The ones wearing wool were very warm.
Josephine, wearing wool, was very warm.

We saw in Chapter 26 that such sentences have different kinds of intonation. The first sentence may be spoken with only one primary stress; if there are two or three primary stresses, the junctures between them will be level junctures. The second sentence will necessarily have three primary stresses, and the junctures will be rising or falling junctures. These contrasting intonation patterns signal differences in structure and differences in meaning.

The verb cluster *wearing wool* in the first sentence is what is traditionally called a *restrictive* modifier. That means that it restricts or limits the meaning of the preceding noun or pronoun. The sen-

tence means that the ones wearing wool were warm and implies
that others, not wearing wool, were not warm.

In the second sentence, *wearing wool* is a *nonrestrictive* modifier.
It does not limit the meaning of the noun *Josephine*. It does not
mean that a Josephine who wore wool was warm, whereas another
Josephine was not. It means rather that Josephine wore wool and
that Josephine was warm.

CUTTING TO DETERMINE THE KIND OF MODIFIER

We can perhaps see more clearly the structural differences here
if we approach the sentences from the point of view of immediate
constituents. The first sentence is cut between subject and verb:

The ones wearing wool   **/**   were very warm.

Wearing wool is thus seen to be a part of the noun cluster, modifying
and restricting *the ones*. But we cannot cut the second sentence in
that way, for then we would have as one part *Josephine, wearing
wool* which does not seem to be a unit in any structure.

Compare these sentences:

Wearing wool, Josephine was very warm.
Josephine, wearing wool, was very warm.

The first type we have already encountered in our discussion of
IC's. We saw that it must be cut after *wool:*

Wearing wool   **/**   Josephine was very warm.

The whole meaning of the verb cluster *wearing wool* applies to the
whole meaning of *Josephine was very warm*, and we say that it is a
sentence modifier, modifying the sentence pattern that follows.
In the second sentence, *wearing wool*, though its position has shifted,
is still a sentence modifier. There are again two IC's: *Josephine . . .
was very warm* and *wearing wool*. In other words, restrictive modifiers
are noun modifiers (or sometimes verb modifiers), whereas nonrestrictive modifiers are sentence modifiers.

PUNCTUATING NONRESTRICTIVE MODIFIERS

Now in any sentence such a modifier must be signaled as either a noun or verb modifier or as a sentence modifier. If we can't tell which it is, the sentence will be ambiguous. If the modifier comes at the beginning of the sentence, it is signaled by position as well as by intonation as a sentence modifier:

> Knowing what he had to do, Johnson didn't hesitate.

The verb cluster is signaled as a sentence modifier by intonation: a primary stress on *do*, followed by rising or falling juncture. But it is also signaled as a sentence modifier by position; in this position it couldn't be anything else. For this reason, though we usually put in a comma after sentence modifiers at the beginning of sentences, as a kind of extra signal, we sometimes omit the comma — for instance, with adverbs and prepositional phrases.

However, when the sentence modifier comes inside or at the end of a sentence pattern, the intonation of speech or the comma of writing may be the *only* signal that shows it is a sentence modifier. Compare these:

> The girls wearing wool were very warm.
> The girls, wearing wool, were very warm.

These do not mean the same thing. The first sentence implies that other girls were not wearing wool and were cool. The second means that all the girls wore wool and that all were very warm. In the first sentence *wearing wool* is a noun modifier, part of the noun cluster; it is restrictive. In the second sentence, *wearing wool* is a sentence modifier, not a part of a noun cluster; it is nonrestrictive.

Relative clauses can also be sentence modifiers and therefore nonrestrictive:

> The boys who knew the country best were dubious.
> The boys, who knew the country best, were dubious.

The first implies that other boys, not knowing the country very well, were not dubious. The second means that all the boys concerned knew the country better than, say, the girls, and that all the boys were dubious.

Appositives are usually sentence modifiers:

> Randolph Gentry, a history teacher from Springfield, was the next witness.

The IC's are these: *Randolph Gentry . . . was the next witness* and *a history teacher from Springfield.* The punctuation marks, or the junctures of speech, signal a break in the structure. The first one indicates that the main pattern is being interrupted by another idea; the second signals that the interruption is concluded and that the main pattern will be resumed.

Sentence modifiers can also come at the end of sentences:

> Sam introduced us to a woman smiling broadly.
> Sam introduced us to a woman, smiling broadly.

Here a large difference in meaning rests solely on the juncture or the comma. The IC's are these:

> Sam   /   introduced us to a woman smiling broadly.
> Sam introduced us to a woman   /   smiling broadly.

In the first, *smiling broadly* is part of the noun cluster *a woman smiling broadly;* it is the woman who smiles. In the second, *smiling broadly* is a sentence modifier; Sam smiles.

Sentence modifiers can also contrast with modifiers of verbs. That is, subordinate clauses can be sentence modifiers at the end of sentences as well as at the beginning. But at the end of sentences, position is no longer a sufficient signal that they are sentence modifiers:

> He came when he needed money.
> He came, although he didn't want to.

In the first, the subordinate clause modifies the verb:

    He   **/**   came when he needed the money.

In the second it modifies the whole sentence:

    He came   **/**   although he didn't want to.

The first sentence might be a response to a question involving the verb: "When did he come?" The second might be a response to something like "What did he do when he needed money?"

Sometimes the differences are subtle:

    I haven't seen him since he left.
    I haven't seen him, since he left.

In the first, the clause is a verb modifier, and the *since* has a time meaning. In the second, the clause is a sentence modifier, and the *since* means "because."

The differences might be subtler still:

    He left home because he was unhappy. (In response to "Why did he leave home?")
    He left home, because he was unhappy. (In response to "What did he do?")

Some subordinators most commonly introduce verb modifiers: *if, when, until, after, that.* Others most commonly introduce sentence modifiers: *although, whereas, provided.* But there is a good deal of shifting about. The only way to know whether a subordinate clause is a sentence modifier and nonrestrictive and needs punctuation is to listen for the juncture.

EXERCISE 46

    The members of each of the following pairs are exactly alike except in punctuation. Read each pair aloud, observing differences in intonation. Then prepare to state differences in structure and meaning.

1. The girls who were here went away.
   The girls, who were here, went away.

2. My sister who lives in Toledo visited us.
   My sister, who lives in Toledo, visited us.

3. The man peering in the window nodded his head.
   The man, peering in the window, nodded his head.

4. The question raised by the Chairman got immediate attention.
   The question, raised by the Chairman, got immediate attention.

5. He pointed to the dog looking at me hopefully.
   He pointed to the dog, looking at me hopefully.

6. The streets which were particularly dirty got hosed off.
   The streets, which were particularly dirty, got hosed off.

7. The freshmen who remained received a stiff lecture.
   The freshmen, who remained, received a stiff lecture.

8. He handed me a letter which surprised me.
   He handed me a letter, which surprised me.

9. The reporters traveling with the President knew exactly what was happening.
   The reporters, traveling with the President, knew exactly what was happening.

10. The sailor looked at the water standing near the rail.
    The sailor looked at the water, standing near the rail.

EXERCISE 47

Number from 1 to 35. None of the following sentences are actually ambiguous, but some contain nonrestrictive sentence modifiers and need punctuation to make the meaning quickly clear. If the sentence contains a nonrestrictive modifier, copy the sentence and insert the needed punctuation. If the sentence does not contain a nonrestrictive modifier, leave a blank after the corresponding number on your paper.

EXAMPLE: A. Josephine wearing wool was very warm.
Josephine, wearing wool, was very warm.

1. John who knew eastern Idaho very well shook his head.
2. Anyone needing further information should apply at the main office.
3. His Aunt Minnie having adopted him gave him all her attention.
4. His Aunt Minnie having adopted him he had no money problems.
5. Every soldier who needed spiritual advice was sent to the chaplain.
6. The part which had been torn out was most important.
7. His left arm which had been injured during the war still gave him some pain.
8. He introduced us to his uncle a colonel in the Air Force.
9. Having a slight headache Sue took an aspirin.
10. Sue having a slight headache took an aspirin.
11. Sue took an aspirin having a slight headache.
12. He always intended to return to Sioux Falls where he had spent his boyhood.
13. He didn't want to go where he wasn't wanted.
14. The elder thief smiling an ugly little smile drew a knife from his pocket.
15. Her physician who was supposed to be an eminent specialist told her she had nothing to worry about.
16. People who live in stone houses shouldn't throw glass.
17. The door being made of oak resisted all our efforts.
18. We suggested that he try soaking it in grape juice an idea which had not occurred to him.
19. I hadn't seen him since the previous winter.
20. I haven't seen him since I don't like him very much.
21. Renfrew afraid that it might rain decided not to go.
22. Irritated by Chamberlain's insolence Baker reported the incident to his den mother.
23. We enjoyed watching the children playing with their teddy bears.
24. He shook his head sadly knowing that there was no hope.
25. We entrusted the toasting of the marshmallows to Alice who had been a Campfire Girl.
26. I didn't own a watch which would keep good time.
27. Climbing out of the spaceship the men found themselves in a meadow through which ran a little brook.
28. McIntyre standing on the steps of the spaceship addressed the natives in French.

29. They have a cabin at Fallen Leaf a small lake near Tahoe.
30. The men who had crossed the river noticed that those who stayed behind were under heavy attack.
31. The river swollen with the recent rains proved a formidable obstacle.
32. The 29th of May his mother's birthday was only three days away.
33. He saw with dismay that all his papers the fruits of ten years of study had been burned in the fire.
34. The rabbit sleeping in the corner of the pen is a California Dutch.
35. The advance guard moving quietly through the trees took the enemy sentries completely by surprise.

EXERCISE 48

Write sentences in which the following constructions are used as sentence modifiers in the positions specified.

1. a relative clause in the middle of the sentence
2. a relative clause at the end of the sentence
3. a verb cluster at the beginning of the sentence
4. a verb cluster in the middle of the sentence
5. a verb cluster at the end of the sentence
6. an appositive in the middle of the sentence
7. an appositive at the end of the sentence
8. a subordinate clause at the beginning of the sentence
9. a subordinate clause at the end of the sentence
10. an adjective cluster in the middle of the sentence

28 COLONS AND OTHER MARKS

We have so far, in discussing punctuation, talked mainly about commas, and we have seen that commas are used (1) before conjunctions that connect sentence patterns, (2) after most sentence modifiers that come at the beginning of sentences, and (3) before or around all sentence modifiers that come at the end or in the middle of sentences. In this chapter, we shall consider the conventional use of certain other punctuation marks — colons, semicolons, dashes, parentheses, quotation marks.

THE COLON

Colons are used mostly to introduce lists or explanations of some kind. For example:

> Arnold had three major interests: baseball, stamps, and chamber music.
>
> Five men stepped forward to volunteer: Blackwell, Corelli, Haversmith, Grunenberk, and Stacy.
>
> The year 1853 saw the appearance of two of Verdi's best-loved operas: *Trovatore* and *Traviata*.
>
> He had a perfectly good reason for not running for Governor: his mother wouldn't let him.
>
> General Howells came up with another suggestion: that the first objective be to turn the enemy's left flank.

In ordinary expository writing, it is conventional to have a full sentence pattern before a colon, as in each of the five examples above. One would, for instance, avoid writing "Arnold's major interests were: baseball, stamps, and chamber music." Instead, one would either omit the colon or put a full sentence pattern before it:

> Arnold's major interests were baseball, stamps, and chamber music.
>
> Arnold's major interests were these: baseball, stamps, and chamber music.

The observant reader will have noticed that the writer of this book frequently breaks this rule. For instance, in the second paragraph of this chapter a colon occurs after the expression *for example*. The justification is that special kinds of writing, like the writing of textbooks, have their own special requirements. In any case, a writer should never hesitate to break rules when by doing so he can avoid awkwardness or achieve greater clarity.

THE SEMICOLON

One must not confuse the colon with the semicolon. As we saw in Chapter 17, the semicolon is used principally between sentence patterns, with or without a sentence connector like *however* or *therefore:*

> The night was cold, and snow seemed probable; however, we were determined to keep going.
>
> The night was cold, and snow seemed probable; we had no alternative but to turn back.

In either of these sentences, a period could be used in place of the semicolon. The semicolon indicates a closer relationship in meaning, causal or otherwise, than the period does. In neither sentence could a colon be substituted.

It is almost always true that semicolons have full, unsubordinated sentence patterns both before and after them. The exception would be something like the following:

> Several rather grave charges were brought against General Grapefield: that the night crossing of the river, in the course of which hundreds of men were drowned, was an error in judgment; that, through his negligence, the troops had not been supplied with ammunition; and finally, and most damaging of all, that he had attacked in the wrong direction.

Commas in place of the semicolons here would make the series of subordinate clauses hard to figure out. The semicolons mark off clearly the three main points.

THE DASH

Dashes are sometimes used where one might expect colons:

> Arnold had three major interests — baseball, stamps, and chamber music.
>
> He had a good reason for not running for Governor — his health was failing.

The dash is somewhat less formal here than the colon would be.

Dashes are sometimes used also, in place of commas, to set off sentence modifiers:

> We discovered — to our immense surprise — that he had already returned to Japan.
> Two privates — Hazeltine and Curtis — stepped forward.

Here the dashes emphasize and highlight the sentence modifiers. Sometimes they also prevent misreading. If the second sentence were written " Two privates, Hazeltine and Curtis, stepped forward," the reader might think that four people were involved: two privates, Corporal Hazeltine, and Sergeant Curtis. In neither of these examples could colons be used; colons are not used in pairs.

Sometimes a complete, unsubordinated sentence pattern occurs as a sentence modifier inside another sentence pattern. In such a construction, dashes (or parentheses) must be used rather than commas:

> A man of his age — he was ninety-eight in August of that year — should not have been encouraged to play handball.

PARENTHESES

Parentheses are always used in pairs. Where a pair of dashes occur, it is usually possible to substitute a pair of parentheses:

> We discovered (to our immense surprise) that he had already returned to Japan.

However, such usage gives the page a look of technicality better avoided in ordinary writing. There are some situations in which only parentheses can be used — for example, in marking off figures used to number a list, as in the first paragraph of this chapter.

QUOTATION MARKS

Quotation marks are used to mark off the exact words of a speaker, as opposed to a restatement of what he said:

> Jim said that he wanted to take a bath.
> Jim said, "I want to take a bath."

Note the comma that precedes the quotation. If the words "Jim said" come in the middle of the quotation, the punctuation goes like this:

> "I want," Jim said, "to take a bath."
> "I want to take a bath," Jim said. "I'm very dirty."

In the second example, a comma in place of the period would produce a run-on sentence.

Note that the quotation marks are placed outside adjacent commas or periods. If a question mark is involved, the quotation marks include it, if the quoted part is the question, otherwise not:

> Jim said, "Can I have a bath?"
> Did Jim say, "I want a bath"?

Quotation marks are also used to mark off words under discussion:

> The word "obloquy" is derived from Latin.

Alternatively, such words can be underlined or, in print, italicized.

Finally, quotation marks are used to mark off terms for which the writer does not want to take responsibility:

> We have here another example of the "unit teaching" so common in the high schools these days.

This suggests that the writer doesn't like the term *unit teaching* or doesn't like what it stands for.

Sometimes quotation marks are used to mark slang terms:

> He was a real "jerk."

This practice often gives a kind of mincing effect, however. Usually it is better to use the slang term without apology or to avoid it entirely.

EXERCISE 49

Some of the following sentences need colons, semicolons, dashes, or parentheses. On a separate sheet of paper, put down each mark that is needed together with the word preceding the mark. Do not use commas. Most sentences need one or two marks.

EXAMPLE: A. Two volunteers Smith and Jones appeared.
                volunteers —   *Jones* —

1. He had just one ambition to get out of the Army.
2. His experience in South America he had been fifteen years in the Amazon made him a natural choice for the appointment.
3. He packed only a few of the most necessary items socks, shoes, underwear.
4. We knew there was little hope of succeeding nevertheless we felt we had to try.
5. The girls chosen for the final judging were Laurabell, Eloise, and Mary.
6. Her father a grumpy, irascible type if there ever was one met him at the door.
7. Three animals a horse, a camel, and a bear were led across the stage.
8. The only explanation we could find to account for his behavior was that he had lost his mind.
9. Some lawyers Sir Tolbert Willoughby-Hughes, for example make a great deal of money.
10. He didn't really have anything more to say he just couldn't bring himself to say good-by.
11. One fact stood out with perfect clarity that Summerwell was the only real officer on the ship.
12. His only daughter Edna Bixby, a teacher of French at Franklin High School lived with him and kept house for him.
13. The continuing bad weather it had now been raining almost steadily for three weeks had made the roads virtually impassable.
14. He couldn't seem to get one thing through his head that he had no authority to change the curriculum.
15. The next day's journey was a long one therefore we decided to leave before dawn.

16. The only items in the suitcase were a bottle of catsup, a monkey wrench with a silver handle, and a dead cat.
17. There is of course one easy explanation for his behavior he was in love.
18. His closest cronies Loomis and Pierre were engaged in the lint trade.
19. I asked Nick to get me a few things at the store some rat poison, a very sharp knife, and a long rope.
20. Mr. Scrimmons asked only three things of his employees that they get to work every day, whatever the state of the weather that they give the firm their complete, unquestioning loyalty and that they never, under any circumstances, ask for a raise.

EXERCISE 50

Most of the punctuation has been omitted from the following passage. On a separate sheet of paper, supply such punctuation marks — commas, semicolons, colons, dashes, quotation marks — as are required. In each case, give the word that precedes the needed mark.

EXAMPLES: A. "I really don't know what to do about it Jim said.
it,"
B. "Having been away all summer I'm out of touch with everything.
summer, . . . everything."

1. Archie Sluter had one burning ambition to cross the Atlantic in a rowboat.
2. His friends tried to argue him out of it describing the undertaking as foolhardy nevertheless Sluter persisted.
3. "I know he would say "that the dangers are great but I am perfectly willing to risk my life in the interests of science."
4. When asked what scientific interests could be served by such a stunt Sluter would talk vaguely of phenomena he proposed to observe ocean currents, winds, marine life.
5. But actually as he himself knew perfectly well his real motivation was a simple one a boundless craving for adventure.

6. Sluter proposed to leave from Finley a small seaport near Derve.

7. Since he expected the voyage to last between a hundred and two hundred days depending on how fast he rowed he gave a great deal of thought to provisions.

8. He finally decided to depend mainly on three staples dried beef, raisins, and powdered milk.

9. Coffee which he liked very much was a luxury that he couldn't manage for he would have no way to heat it.

10. However, since he was very fond of sweets he did put in such items as chocolate bars and licorice sticks.

11. The citizens of Finley a town which had seen many adventurers go forth regarded Sluter's venture with interest and good humor.

12. One oldster in particular a sea captain whose career went back to the days of sailing ships gave Sluter a great deal of good advice.

13. "You'll want to have a good compass he remarked one day in order to tell which way you're going.

14. Sluter who hadn't thought of this thanked the Captain and put it down on his list.

15. Another time Cap'n Bob his real name was George but everyone called him Cap'n Bob asked whether Sluter had remembered to leave space for water kegs.

16. "I won't need water Sluter replied because I shall be drinking powdered milk."

17. "Yes said Cap'n Bob but you'll be needing water Mr. Sluter to put the milk into liquid form."

18. Sluter seeing the force of the argument put water on the list too.

19. At last the day of departure arrived and a large crowd estimated at five hundred people came down to the beach to see Sluter off.

20. Willing hands helped him get the boat through the breakers and everyone cheered when he broke out the oars and started to row.

21. Encouraged by this send-off Sluter rowed briskly for two hours.

22. Then he rested for a bit and had lunch dried beef, raisins, and powdered milk.

23. He was well through the surf though he could still see the people waving to him on the shore.

24. By nightfall he could still see them but he couldn't distinguish faces.

25. Sluter rowed much of the night and all the next day he was determined to get out of sight of the crowd which embarrassed him.

26. When on the second evening he could still see the well-wishers on the
beach he felt rather discouraged.

27. Exhausted from nearly thirty-six hours of rowing he fell asleep and
slept all night long.

28. Awakening he found that the sun was shining and that several
people were standing around the boat which had drifted ashore.

29. "Where you made your mistake Mr. Sluter said Cap'n Bob who
was among those present "was in starting from this side of the
ocean.

30. The winds and currents are all against you whereas they'd be helping
you if you were coming the other way.

31. Sluter feeling a little piqued that the Captain had not told him this
before nevertheless thanked him courteously.

32. However he proposed to rest a little before deciding whether to cross
the ocean and try again.

29 PARALLEL STRUCTURE

In Chapters 15 and 17 we discussed conjunctions, and particularly the words *and* and *or*. These words are used to produce what
are called *compounds*. We now want to look a little more closely at
the nature of compounding in language.

COMPOUNDING BASIC SENTENCE ELEMENTS

The general rule goes something like this: any two like elements
in the basic sentence patterns, or any two elements which are derived in a like way from the basic patterns, can be made into a
compound element by being joined with *and*.

The application of the rule will be obvious where simple constructions are involved. For example, two subjects can be compounded:

> The boys chased the cats.
> The girls chased the cats.
> The boys and the girls chased the cats.

Or two verbs:

> The boys chased the cats.
> The boys caught the cats.
> The boys chased and caught the cats.

Or two objects:

> The boys chased the cats.
> The boys chased the dogs.
> The boys chased the cats and the dogs.

Or two whole predicates:

> The boys chased the cats.
> The boys killed the pigeons.
> The boys chased the cats and killed the pigeons.

Predicates compounded need not be of the same basic pattern:

> John caught the pass.   (FOUR)
> John became a hero.   (THREE)
> John caught the pass and became a hero.

So long as both of the elements compounded are predicates and both are grammatical, the rule is satisfied. Similarly, two compounded objects or subjects may have different kinds of modifiers:

> John chased the Siamese cats.
> John chased the dogs that inhabited the alley.
> John chased the Siamese cats and the dogs that inhabited the alley.

Now let us consider a sentence that breaks the rule:

> The boys should and have gone home.

Here the compounded elements are not alike, even though they are both auxiliaries. *Should* is a modal and is followed by the simple form of the verb; *have* is followed by the *-en* form of the verb. The compound is constructed in this fashion:

> The boys should gone home.
> The boys have gone home.
> The boys should and have gone home.

But the first of the underlying sentences is ungrammatical, and therefore the compound is ungrammatical. The following would be grammatical:

> The boys should go home.
> The boys have gone home.
> The boys should go and have gone home.

COMPOUNDING DERIVED ELEMENTS

Derived elements can also be compounded, provided they have the same derivation. For example, relative clauses can be compounded:

> The man who was here left immediately.
> The man who asked for Father left immediately.
> The man who was here and who asked for Father left immediately.

But it would be ungrammatical to compound two structures of different derivation, say a prepositional phrase and a relative clause: "The man in the red coat and who left a message..." We would say instead "The man in the red coat who left a message," expressing the idea in an uncompounded noun cluster.

Similarly, it is ungrammatical to say, "He was an irritable man and who liked to have his own way." The elements joined are unlike; one is a noun cluster, an expansion of the predicate noun, and the other is a relative clause. We would either express the idea without compounding ("an irritable man who liked to have his own way") or compound two relative clauses ("a man who was irritable and who liked to have his own way") or else build it up from two PATTERN TEN predicates:

He was an irritable man.
He was one who liked to have his own way.
He was an irritable man and one who liked to have his own way.

Modifiers before a noun headword can also be compounded, always provided they have a like derivation:

an old man
a foolish man
an old and foolish man

Old and *foolish* both derive from PATTERN TWO ("He seemed old," "He seemed foolish") and so they can be compounded. But the following would be ungrammatical:

an old and city man

Old derives from PATTERN TWO, but *city* from PATTERN ONE ("lives in a city"). To compound them is therefore to break the rule.

ELEMENTS IN A SERIES

A somewhat different type of compounding occurs when elements are listed in a series of three or more:

The boys, the girls, and the dogs chased the cats.
The boys sighted, chased, and caught the cats.
The boys should, must, and will chase the cats.
The man who called, who left a message, and who departed immediately was George Scanlan.
an old, foolish, unhappy man

The same general rule applies for a series of three or more as for a compound of two: the elements must be alike or derived from like sources. The examples above all meet this requirement. The following do not:

He should, must, and has chased the cats.

He was contented, happy, and a wealthy man. (Corrected: He was contented, happy, and wealthy.)

He gave her a ring, a diamond bracelet, and kissed her. (Corrected: He gave her a ring, a diamond bracelet, and a kiss *or* He gave her a ring and a diamond bracelet and kissed her.)

Sometimes a sentence will be unparallel and hard to follow because of the dropping out of a structure word — a *the*, a *that*, a *to* — that would occur in the basic pattern:

She left the white hat, white dress, and the black shoes. (Insert *the* before *white dress*.)

He told me to shut up, mind my own business, and to leave him alone. (Insert *to* before *mind* or delete *to* before *leave*.)

Constructions involving correlative conjunctions — *either . . . or, neither . . . nor, both . . . and, not . . . but* — should also be parallel in form. The mechanism for building such constructions from simple patterns is the same as for *and*, and the same general rule applies:

Not Parallel: Either he should do it or let me do it.
Parallel: Either he should do it, or he should let me do it.
Parallel: He should either do it or let me do it.

Not Parallel: Not only was he handsome but wealthy too.
Parallel: He was not only handsome but wealthy too.

Not Parallel: She was both pretty and could cook.
Parallel: She was both a pretty girl and a good cook.

We have stated the rule flatly: the elements joined must be alike or derived in like fashion. This is not to say that users of the language always follow the rules. If student writers always did, there would be no red marks on papers. But sometimes writers deliberately depart from the rule. Thus Eliot writes "not with a bang but a whimper." The grammar of the language may be thought of as a center of expectation. Often we move from the center, for various reasons, deliberately or unaware. If we all move from the center and in the same direction, we get a different grammar describable by a different rule. Thus grammars change.

PUNCTUATING COMPOUND ELEMENTS

Constructions joined by conjunctions follow certain conventions of punctuation. If just two elements are joined by an *and* or an *or*, there is no comma preceding the conjunction unless the two elements are unsubordinated sentence patterns (see Chapter 17). When three elements appear in a series with a conjunction joining the last two, a comma regularly occurs between the first two items and usually before the conjunction:

> He was happy, healthy, and wealthy.
> He owned a nice home, rented a cabin at the beach, and was on the point of buying a new car.

The punctuation of a series, in other words, follows the pattern A, B, and C. However, there is some variation. A, B, and C is normal for books and magazines, but newspapers frequently omit the comma before the *and*, printing A, B and C.

Adjectives occurring in a series before a noun sometimes are separated in speech by rising juncture and sometimes are not. A rising juncture here is indicated by a comma. Compare these:

> a dilapidated old house
> an old, dilapidated house

The first would usually be spoken with just one primary stress — on *house*. The second would have a primary stress also on *old* and rising juncture after *old*.

In the general topic of parallelism we may note an error of a slightly different sort from those mentioned. This is what is sometimes called faulty comparison:

> Her smile is a lot more friendly than Jane.

This sentence implies the underlying patterns:

> Her smile is friendly.
> Jane is friendly.

But the intent is presumably not to compare a smile with a girl but a smile with a smile:

> Her smile is friendly.
> Jane's smile is friendly.
> Her smile is more friendly than Jane's.

Here are examples of similar faults:

Faulty:	He thought Mays better than any baseball player.
Corrected:	He thought Mays better than any other baseball player.
Corrected:	He thought Mays the best of all baseball players.
Faulty:	He was the tallest of all the other boys in the room.
Corrected:	He was the tallest of all the boys in the room.
Corrected:	He was the tallest boy in the room.

EXERCISE 51

Number from 1 to 35. Some of the following sentences contain faults in parallel structure. Some are all right. If the sentence is faulty, write **F** beside the corresponding number on your paper; if it is satisfactory, write **S**.

1. It was an interesting suggestion and which we promised to mull over.
2. He said that he would take just a cup of tea and a small doughnut.
3. In the evenings we would swim in the lake and dancing afterward.
4. He decided that he needed a larger car and with plenty of space in the trunk.

5. Daniel had visited Sioux Falls several times and fully intended to go again.

6. Being afraid of people in general and of women in particular, Stacy was not a great social success.

7. Murchison had spent seven years in the third grade and not much hope of ever graduating.

8. She was a conscientious girl and whose word could be completely relied on.

9. He had twice been nearly killed in racing accidents and was not very willing to risk another.

10. I suggested that he apply disinfectant to the cut, bandage it, and that he see a doctor as soon as possible.

11. Edward was very witty, liked to dance, and an exceptionally fine athlete.

12. He started the motor, backed the car out of the garage, and honked the horn.

13. They tried to humiliate him, and he responded with a grim and angry silence.

14. The house was old, needed paint badly, but in some ways a very good buy.

15. He was a gentle and sympathetic father and one who idolized his children.

16. Either he forgot about the party, or he didn't want to come.

17. It had been a long, hot, dreary summer but one that she would not soon forget.

18. He had been driving all day and almost too tired to look for a place to sleep.

19. Sir Tolbert stood up, adjusted his jacket, and with a contemptuous smile on his lips, walked toward the witness stand.

20. He just wanted to loaf a little, do a little fishing, and to try to regain his strength.

21. Angela was born in Toronto but had moved to Lyonesse with her parents when she was a little girl.

22. Not only was he thoughtless but also insolent.

23. Marvin was easily the best knot-tier in the Beaver Patrol.

24. He thought that Calvin Coolidge was greater than any President.

25. He played a good game of golf, excellent at bridge, and was much liked by everyone.

26. The Duke was getting old and garrulous and tended to confuse the present with the past.

27. When he thought of how little he had done and how much he had still to do, he felt rather discouraged.

28. He asked the waitress for a bowl of soup, a ham sandwich, and whether they had any ice cream.

29. His novels are not nearly so hardboiled as Ernest Hemingway.

30. He both helped in the kitchen and a good helper in the yard too.

31. He wanted to be one of the gang but didn't know how.

32. Either say what you have to say, or I wish you would please sit down.

33. He was keenly aware of the dangers and insistent that certain precautions be taken.

34. The report said that General Maxwell's division had attacked the enemy center, General Porter's the right flank, and that General Grapefield's didn't show up at all.

35. He was affable and easy to talk to, patient, when the situation called for patience, and yet, on certain occasions, as hard and unyielding as any stone.

EXERCISE 52

Some of the punctuation has been omitted from the following sentences. Decide where commas are needed. Write the commas and the words preceding them on a separate sheet of paper. If no comma is needed, leave a blank. Punctuate series on the pattern A, B, and C.

EXAMPLE: A. He was young rich and handsome.
            young,   rich,

1. He bought a ball of twine a jackknife and a bottle of olive oil.

2. John opened one eye looked owlishly about the room and decided to stay in bed.

3. The Macedonian peasants are very poor and gain a precarious living from long hours of toil.

4. Albert held the stake steady with his hands and his father swung the sledge hammer.

5. The doctor said that Albert would live and that they might be able to save his arm.

6. We were shocked at the ugly angry oaths that issued from her pretty little mouth.

7. It was perfectly true that the house was overrun by rats that the parents were seldom home and that the children were starving.

8. The country was bitterly cold in winter intolerably hot in summer and generally wet in spring and fall.

9. He started the motor put the car in reverse and crashed into his mother's convertible.

10. He gazed pensively into the fire and thought of that strange summer so many years ago.

11. Who he was where he came from and what he wanted are questions which may never be answered.

12. Randolph knew instinctively what he had to do and he did not hesitate to do it.

13. Lord Argyle remarked that there are just two kinds of people in the world: those that are kind to their servants and those that are not.

14. A beautiful little girl opened the door and curtsied gracefully.

15. Bertram always had a smile on his lips a song in his heart and a deck of marked cards in his pocket.

16. A strange unwholesome odor rose from the marshy lands below.

17. We needed a man who was fearless who would follow orders exactly and who had no relatives.

18. Rick spent every Sunday washing polishing and lubricating his new garbage truck.

19. Milton came to the party as a pirate Pierre as a man from Mars and Nick as a glass of ginger ale.

20. His father made him promise three things: to save a tenth of whatever he earned to attend church on Sundays and never to marry a redheaded woman.

21. The tickets cost ten dollars apiece but we felt they were well worth it.

22. Coach Blisterwell sent Honeywell Rocco and Stevens into the game and told Murphy to take a shower.
23. It was an old car but one that seemed to have had very good care.
24. A fierce unearthly light burned constantly in his pale blue eyes.
25. He gloved her hands and tied her shoes and kissed her ruby lips.

EXERCISE 53

All of the following sentences are faulty in construction. Rewrite them, improving the structure.

1. It was a gloomy day and which made us all depressed.
2. Banners were affixed to the doors, the walls, and an especially large one over the bed.
3. The place was quiet, empty, and almost a ghost town.
4. The message said that we were to leave the house immediately, proceed to the corner of Durant and Telegraph, and that then we would receive further instructions.
5. He liked nothing better than a book of poetry, to find a quiet bench, and an hour or so of relaxation.
6. He bought a piano, an instruction book, and started to learn how to play.
7. In some ways Sioux Falls, South Dakota, is more interesting than any town in America.
8. Being a fearful man and who distrusted everyone, he was watchful, wary, and took elaborate precautions.
9. Maxwell watched the sea in an absent way and unaware that something in the sea was watching him.
10. He told us that he refused to leave the house, would fight if we tried to get him out, and why didn't we mind our own business.
11. She pulled into the gas station, demanded a map, and which was the shortest way to Stanhope Corners.
12. He liked a round of golf in the afternoon, to relax in the evening, and always early to bed.

30 PREDICATION

Most errors in writing occur not in basic sentence patterns but in complicated structures derived from basic patterns. We have already had a variety of examples. No one would write "Some boys is here," but students not uncommonly miss the agreement in the *there* construction derived from that sentence and write "There is some boys here." No one would write "He should gone home," but this error is possible in the compound derivative: "He should and has gone home."

Errors of this type — in fact, nearly all errors in sentence structure — can be eliminated only if the writer looks through the complicated structures to the basic patterns. What do our complicated sentences boil down to? What are the basic patterns? Are the underlying patterns grammatical? If they are not, the structures derived from them will not be grammatical either.

ERRORS IN PREDICATION

Errors in which the predicate of a sentence for some reason does not suit the subject are called errors in *predication*. Again, these errors are virtually uncommittable in the basic patterns. For example, we would never say "The reason feared something." Our knowledge of English grammar tells us that *reason* does not belong to the class of nouns which go with verbs like *feared*. But if the subject and predicate are expanded through modification, we can too easily lose track and write something like this:

> His chief reason for worry about his son feared that he would fail in school.

The intended idea here can be expressed grammatically in several ways. All of the following boil down to a grammatical kernel:

He was chiefly worried about his son's possible failure in
school. ("He was worried.")

His chief worry was that his son would fail in school. ("The
worry was this.")

His chief reason for worry was his fear that his son would fail
in school. ("The reason was the fear.")

Here is another example of faulty predication:

His intention to modify the school curriculum failed to take
into account the wishes of the teachers.

If we boil this down, we get a base something like this: "The intention took it into account." This is ungrammatical. An intention
cannot take something into account and consequently can't fail
to do so. Only a person can take something into account. Again
there are several possible revisions:

He intended to modify the school curriculum but failed to
take into account the wishes of the teachers.

Intending to modify the school curriculum, he failed to take
into account the wishes of the teachers.

His intention to modify the school curriculum was praiseworthy, but he failed to take into account the wishes of
the teachers.

All of these derive from grammatical basic sentences: "He modified
the curriculum," "He took them into account," "His intention was
praiseworthy," and so on. Often the predication error results, as
here, from the use of an abstract subject (*intention*) with a verb
that must have a human noun (*he, principal*) as subject.

The predication error is sometimes a little more subtle:

The plans for Homecoming Day were done by the Student
Affairs Committee.

The underlying sentence is "The plans were done," a passive from
"They did the plans." But this is not quite grammatical English.

We say not "They did the plans" but "They made the plans" or "They worked out the plans."

Here is another:

> His insistence on banning automobiles ignored the fact that many students had no other way to get to school

"Insistence ignored" is ungrammatical. We would say instead:

> In insisting on banning automobiles, he ignored the fact that many students had no other way to get to school.
>
> He insisted on banning automobiles, ignoring the fact that many students had no other way to get to school.

Sometimes predication errors occur when the predicate consists of two verb clusters joined by a conjunction. The subject may fit the first but not the second:

> The highhanded attitude of Mayor Scrofula annoyed many of the citizens of Pridewell and was easily beaten in the fall election.

This contains the passive "The attitude was beaten" from "Somebody beat the attitude," an ungrammatical sentence. You can beat a mayor but not an attitude. We would say,

> The highhanded attitude of the mayor annoyed many of the citizens of Pridewell, and he was easily beaten in the fall election.

A slightly different kind of predication error occurs in expansions of PATTERN TEN — **Noun   be   Noun**. The nouns must fit each other. In the following example they do not:

> His anger at the School Board was a feeling that his son had been badly treated.

What is meant is something like this:

> His anger at the School Board was a result of feeling that his son had been badly treated.

His anger at the School Board stemmed from a feeling that
his son had been badly treated.

He was angry because he felt that the School Board had
treated his son badly.

The last of these revisions, if it is what is meant, is probably the
best because it is the most economical and straightforward.

"THE REASON IS BECAUSE . . ."

Generally included in discussions of predication faults are variations of PATTERN EIGHT, in which the *be* is followed by certain
prepositional phrases and subordinate clauses that are felt to be
ungrammatical in this pattern:

His arrival was by means of a helicopter.

The reason for his anger was because he thought that his son
had been badly treated.

The funniest part of the performance was when the snake
charmer accidentally swallowed the snake.

These errors, if errors they be, are not on all fours with those
discussed previously. The earlier ones were clearly ungrammatical,
un-English in their underlying patterns. The sentences above, however, are normal in much English speech, though many people
object to them in writing.

The first is easily mended by expression of the "arrival" idea in
the verb, the sentence becoming a PATTERN ONE:

He arrived by means of a helicopter.

Most editors object to the construction "the reason was because,"
preferring "the reason was that . . ." Often such a sentence can be
better revised in other ways:

He was angry because he thought his son had been badly
treated.

The construction "is when" probably occurs more often in print than "is because." However, more graceful alternatives are often available:

> The funniest part of the performance was the snake charmer's accidental swallowing of the snake.

EXERCISE 54

Number from 1 to 20. Some of the following sentences contain an error in predication. If the sentence is faulty, write the ungrammatical *basic* sentence on your paper. If the sentence is satisfactory, just write **S**.

EXAMPLES: A. His highhanded attitude offended the citizens and was beaten in the election.
Somebody beat the attitude.
B. His highhanded attitude offended the citizens and cost him the election.
S

1. Mrs. Oliver's warm sympathy for helpless things pitied the little boy sincerely.
2. The resistance of the civilian population contributed significantly to the winning of the war.
3. The final talks in preparation for the meeting at the summit were done in Geneva.
4. His idea of improving the football team forgot that certain Conference rules had to be obeyed.
5. Sir Tolbert's openly expressed contempt for the judge neglected his duty toward his client.
6. Gilbaugh's tremendous athletic ability assured another victory for Cleveland High.
7. The roaring of the animals frightened Jimmy half to death and wished that he hadn't come.
8. Our refusal to take part in the July 4th parade seemed unpatriotic to many people.
9. The disappearance of the fog revealed a small village directly ahead.

10. Sam's new explanation of what had happened wanted us to believe that he had had a lapse of memory.
11. His arrival at International Airport came by jet bomber.
12. One result of the charges made against him resulted in his losing his job at the gas works.
13. Her ability to make the most of such clothes as she had always looked very pretty.
14. The extent of the financial transactions in which he had been engaged surprised everyone who had known him.
15. The angry reply to the committee was perhaps justified but was done at the worst possible time.
16. His astonishing quickness at language learning acquired very good French in less than three months.
17. The ferocity with which he replied indicated how much Clara meant to him.
18. His chief feeling about school wished that the place would burn down.
19. His insistence on carrying so much insurance was a pathological fear of being destitute in his old age.
20. The knowledge that he was mortally ill was not widely known.

EXERCISE 55

Each of the following sentences is faulty in predication. Rewrite the sentences, improving them. Often the use of a personal subject (*he, she, Mr. Culver*) will yield the best results.

1. His anger about not being invited to the party determined not to invite us to his.
2. The result of the appointment of the Planning Commission in time produced a much more beautiful city.
3. The tendency to let more and more students enter college tends to make a college education less a mark of distinction.
4. The chairman's ideas for the spring dance had the notion of hiring a big band from San Francisco.
5. His way of getting to school was by taking a bus.

6. The rejection of his claims for damages refused to admit that the company was at fault.
7. One justification of the new traffic laws was when the number of traffic accidents decreased sharply.
8. His increase in wages was done when he threatened to look for another job.
9. Her resentment at not being appointed to the committee had the feeling that the omission was deliberate and spiteful.
10. In those days my ideas about the future dreamed of living quietly in a little fishing village in Greece.

31 SUBORDINATION

There is a curious discrepancy between the linguistic sophistication of a child — a grade-school child, say — and the simplicity of his writing. We have seen that by the age of five or six every normal child, no matter how dull he is, has built himself a grammar. He has figured out not only the basic sentence patterns but also the complicated machinery for transforming these patterns into derivations of infinite variety.

Yet when he writes in grade school, the child tends to use the basic patterns rather than the derivations. Whether the explanation is that the material given him to read is made up mostly of basic patterns or that, confronted with the difficult task of learning to write, he goes instinctively back to the kernel is hard to say. Whatever the reason, it is generally true that the writing patterns of a nine-year-old child are usually much less complex than the same child's speech patterns.

As he goes on in school, the child has the task of learning how to use on paper the structural complexity that he commands by virtue of being a speaker of the language. He must become at least as mature a writer as he is a speaker. Such maturity doesn't come chiefly from studying how to be mature. It comes from much reading of the work of mature writers and from much practice in putting into one's own work their turns of phrase and manipulation of structures. One can perhaps speed up the process, however, by becoming consciously aware of the resources of the language.

Let us begin with this string of sentences:

> Mary had a dog. It was a poodle. Mary liked it very much. It was mean. It bit the postman. It bit the milkman. Mary's father was angry. He would not let her keep the poodle. Mary cried.

Notice that almost all the sentences are basic, with very few derived forms. It could be reduced a little more — "Mary's father was angry," for example, to "Mary had a father," "The father was angry" — but it couldn't be reduced much more.

One way to make this essay more sophisticated is to use conjunctions to connect the sentence patterns:

> Mary had a dog, and it was a poodle, and Mary liked it very much, but it was mean, and it bit the postman, and it bit the milkman, and Mary's father was angry, and he would not let her keep the poodle, so Mary cried.

This does not have much more sophistication, but it has some. The use of *but* expresses a contrast, and the *so* indicates a result. The *and*'s show additions. The writing is still very childish, but relationships begin to be indicated. Further improvement can be made by using conjunctions to collapse some of the patterns:

> Mary had a dog, and it was a poodle, and Mary liked it very much, but it was mean and bit the postman and the milkman, and Mary's father was angry and would not let her keep the poodle, so Mary cried.

This use of conjunctions reduces the nine main sentence patterns to six with some gain in readability.

THE USES OF SUBORDINATION

Further progress can be made only through *subordination* — that is, through the expression of certain ideas not as main patterns but as modifiers of other patterns or parts of patterns. There are no rules showing the right way to do it. The right way depends on the particular emphasis one is seeking. But, for example, one might express the second sentence as an appositive:

Mary had a dog, a poodle . . .

The third sentence might become a relative clause:

Mary had a dog, a poodle, that she liked very much . . .

The middle part might be reduced by expressing the "mean" idea as a noun and putting the rest into a prepositional phrase with a verb cluster as object:

. . . it displayed meanness by biting the postman and the mailman . . .

The last two sentences could be combined by turning one into a subordinate clause:

. . . Mary cried when her father would not let her keep the poodle.

We can get the third from the last in by expressing it as a simple adjective:

. . . Mary cried when her angry father would not let her keep it.

If we now put these three main patterns together we get this:

Mary had a dog, a poodle, that she liked very much, but it displayed meanness by biting the postman and the milkman, and Mary cried when her angry father would not let her keep it.

An almost infinite number of other possibilities present themselves, each carrying different kinds of emphasis — highlighting this, playing down that. For instance, we might write:

> Mary cried when her father made her get rid of her dearly
> loved poodle, which had displayed its meanness by biting the
> postman and the milkman.

This puts the greatest emphasis on Mary's crying, which is expressed as the subject and verb of the only main sentence pattern.
Everything else is expressed in some kind of subordinate structure.*
   We could highlight the father by giving him the main structure
and subordinating other matters:

> Though Mary cried, her father made her get rid of her dearly
> loved poodle, which had displayed its meanness by biting the
> postman and the milkman.

The structures of the language permit the achieving of virtually
any effect desired. Suppose that it is the writer's intention — con-
ceivable, though unlikely — to bring the postman and the milkman
into prominence. It can be done:

> The postman and the milkman, bitten by Mary's mean though
> much loved poodle, caused the angry father to get rid of the
> beast and thus unwittingly brought on the daughter's tears.

SUBORDINATION AND CO–ORDINATION

   It must not be supposed that subordination is always better than
co-ordination — that is, that it is always preferable to express a
string of ideas in one main pattern rather than in two or three. We
might very well wish to put two or more ideas on a level:

> Despite his daughter's tears, Mary's father made her get rid
> of her beloved poodle, for it had displayed its meanness by
> biting the postman and the milkman.

We now have two main patterns, with *father* the subject of one and

---

* It is of course not true that the most prominent idea in a sentence is always expressed
in the subject and verb of the main sentence pattern. In "I think your house is on
fire," the chief point is made in a subordinate clause. Expression in the main clause is,
however, one important way to give emphasis to ideas.

it the subject of the other. The conjunction *for* not only joins them but expresses a causal relationship between them.

Nor should one draw the conclusion that long sentences are always better than short ones. It's not necessarily so. A sentence that goes on too long may become tortuous and hard to follow, however skillful the writer, and excessive length may defeat the purpose of stressing what ought to be stressed. In overly complicated sentences, the ideas may get so entangled in one another that they lose their force.

What the writer should aim at is range. He should learn to control all the structures of the language, elaborate and simple, so that he will always have at hand the one that serves his immediate need.

EXERCISE 56

Express each of the following strings in one sentence with only one main sentence pattern, stressing the information in the italicized sentence and subordinating everything else.

EXAMPLE: A. Mary had a poodle. It bit the postman. *Her father wouldn't let her keep it.*
Because Mary's poodle bit the postman, her father wouldn't let her keep it.

1. The day was stormy. We had a long way to drive. *We started early.*
2. Nothing had been heard from Mortimer. *We thought he was dead.*
3. The mailman brought two letters. *One was from my sister.* The other one was a bill.
4. He leafed through the book. He found a twenty-dollar bill. *He was very much surprised.*
5. The restaurant was dirty. The service was slow. The food was bad. *We wished we hadn't come.*
6. He liked Hawthorne. He liked Poe. *He liked Henry James more than either of them.*
7. He looked up suddenly. The street had been empty. There were now

two people in it. One carried a gun. The other had a drawn sword. *He was alarmed.*

8. The day was hot. The class was dull. Sam wanted some excitement. There had been no excitement for a long time. *He set fire to the wastebasket.*

9. The car was an excellent buy. Johnson did not really need a car. He had a new Dauphine. *The salesman was persuasive.* Johnson decided to try it out.

10. Ted was not a good swimmer. The girl was crying for help. No one else was in sight. He hesitated a moment. *He dived in.*

11. General Grapefield had made some mistakes. These mistakes had seriously endangered the war effort. *No one was surprised at his early retirement.*

12. The boy called "wolf" again. *The villagers paid no attention.* They remembered too well the last time he had called for help.

13. His friends were all busy. There wasn't a movie in town that he wanted to see. *He decided to spend a quiet evening with his stamp collection.*

14. There was no one playing tennis on any of the courts. *The attendant insisted on checking his book of reservations.* Then he let us have one.

EXERCISE 57

In each of the following strings, one noun is italicized. Rewrite each string as one sentence with one main sentence pattern, using the italicized noun as the subject of the main pattern.

EXAMPLE: A. Don had a *car*. It was made in 1918. It needed a ring job. It was a Dort.
                Don's car, a 1918 Dort, needed a ring job.

1. Mary bought a *book*. It was written by Fanny Burney. It was published in the eighteenth century. She paid five dollars for it.

2. They came home by train. The *ride* took seven hours. They were very tired.

3. The white rat belonged to Steve. It got loose in the physics lab. It was not Steve's fault. The *teacher* was very angry.

4. The room had not been cleaned. The bed had not been made. *Mr. Culver* was disgusted. He moved to another hotel.

5. We were forty points behind. The team was dispirited. The *coach* called Gilbaugh. He sent him into the game. The rooting section cheered.

6. Sally met an *Indian*. He was sitting by the roadside. She asked for directions. He couldn't help her.

7. The bridge had been opened the day before. It had taken three years to build. It was threatened by the rising *waters*.

8. The painting was by *Avery Trimble*. It was called "High Noon." It won first prize.

9. Sievers had a new *job*. He put caps on soda bottles. It was tedious. It paid good money.

10. The newspaper had just arrived. *Rutherford* was reading it. He noticed a headline. It concerned a train wreck in Georgia.

11. Johnson Richards wrote a new *play*. He was a well-known dramatist. The play closed opening night. It closed because of rain.

12. Mrs. Trumbull had a spirited *stallion*. He was a champion show horse. He won the blue ribbon that was coveted by all.

13. The gas station was owned by a native of Brookville. His name was *Summerfield*. The station had not been very successful. He moved it to another part of the city.

14. Calder was an air-conditioner salesman. *October* brings cooler weather. This meant fewer sales for Calder.

15. Mrs. White was the bank's favorite customer. She kept the *manager* waiting until five o'clock. He usually left at three.

SUMMARY OF TERMS • CHAPTERS 26–31

Appositive (p. 178)   A noun or noun cluster used to rename or to identify a preceding noun or noun cluster. In the sentence, "John Weybrew, the president of the club, voted against the proposal," the noun cluster *the president of the club* is an appositive. Appositives are usually set off by commas.

Co-ordination (p. 216)   The expression of ideas on the same level, with grammatical elements joined by conjunctions or in series instead of some being subordinated to others.

Faulty comparison (p. 201)   The comparing of items in a sentence construction which are not logically comparable. "His eyes are bluer than John" is an example. Presumably the intent is to compare someone's eyes not with John but with John's eyes: "His eyes are bluer than John's."

Nonrestrictive (p. 182)   Not limiting the meaning of a sentence element but instead adding another idea. In "John, who was old enough, was allowed to go," the clause *who was old enough* does not restrict the meaning of *John* or of anything else. Instead it adds to the main idea "John was allowed to go" another idea, "John was old enough." Nonrestrictive modifiers are set off by commas. The terms *restrictive* and *nonrestrictive* apply particularly to such modifiers as relative clauses, subordinate clauses, verb clusters, and appositives.

Obligatory juncture (p. 177)   A juncture which is required by the grammatical structure and meaning of the sentence.

Optional juncture (p. 177)   A juncture which may or may not occur, depending on the style or speed with which a sentence is uttered. The occurrence or nonoccurrence of an optional juncture does not change the grammatical structure or the meaning.

Parallel structure (p. 196)   Sentence structures consisting of two or more sentence elements joined by conjunctions — most commonly by the conjunction *and*. The general rule is that elements so joined must be of the same general type — e.g., two nouns or noun clusters, two verbs, two prepositional phrases, two relative clauses. If unlike elements are joined — e.g., a noun and an adjective, an *-ing* verb (*singing*) and a *to* verb (*to play*), a noun and a relative clause — the sentence error called *faulty parallelism* occurs.

Predication (p. 207)   The meaning expressed in the predicate of a sentence, what is said about a subject. In the sentence "The boy went to the store" *went to the store* is the predication. Errors in predication occur when the predicate does not relate grammatically to the subject. "John angered the desire" is an error in predication, since *angered* is not the type of verb that can have *desire* as object and *John* as subject. A person cannot anger an abstraction. In writing, most errors in predication occur not in basic sentences but in transformations of basic sentences, in which the writer loses track of the development of the sentence and does not realize that an underlying basic sentence is ungrammatical.

Restrictive (p. 181)   Limiting the meaning of some part of the sentence. In "The boys that were old enough were allowed to go," the clause *that were old enough* is a restrictive modifier. It restricts or limits the meaning of *the boys,* making it mean not all the boys but just those who were old enough were allowed to go. Restrictive modifiers are not set off by commas.

Series construction (p. 199)   The expression of three or more like grammatical elements in a string: A, B, C, (*the man, the boy, the donkey*); A, B, and C (*the man, the boy, and the donkey*); A, B, C, and D (*the man, the boy, the donkey, and the zebra*). Some constructions, particularly adjectives, occur in series of two — A, B — with no conjunction between them: *a dull, foolish person.* The conventional punctuation of series is that shown.

Subordination (p. 215)   The expression of ideas not as basic sentence patterns but as modifiers of other patterns or of parts of patterns. All subordinate constructions derive ultimately from basic patterns. However, the elements from the basic patterns are modified through rules of transformation so as to express various relationships to other ideas and various degrees of emphasis.

32   QUESTIONS AND RELATED STRUCTURES

Nobody has to go to school to learn how to ask questions, as any mother of a four-year-old will gladly testify. Asking questions is so automatic to us and seems so normal, that we are likely to be unaware of the machinery involved. Yet there is machinery, altogether peculiar to English. Someone learning English as a second

language must expend considerable effort to master it. Though this
has very little bearing on writing problems, we will describe some
of this machinery here, as a further illustration of transformation
and of the essential nature of language.

APPROPRIATE TENSE FORM

In earlier chapters, we considered such sentences as "John drives"
or "John goes" or "They work" as being composed of a subject
plus a verb. However, the verb of such a sentence will be one of
three different forms. For *go*, it will be *go* or *goes* or *went*, depending
on the subject and the tense. To take into account the fact that we
must choose a tense form for the verb, we can write the formula
this way:

Subject	Tense	V	
John	present	go	→ John goes.
They	present	go	→ They go.
They	past	go	→ They went.

There is a reason for putting the tense before the verb rather than
after it. It is that if we add another element, a modal auxiliary for
instance, it is the modal (**M**), not the verb, that takes the tense
form. Whatever comes first in the predicate shows the tense:

Subject	Tense	M	V	
John	present	can	go	→ John can go.
John	past	can	go	→ John could go.

If we add *be* plus *–ing*, the *be* shows the tense, and the *–ing* goes
with the verb:

Subject	Tense	be	- ing	V	
John	present	be	- ing	go	→ John is going.
John	past	be	- ing	go	→ John was going.

If we add *have* plus *–en*, the *have* shows the tense, and the *–en* goes
with the verb:

Subject	Tense	have	- en	V		
John	present	have	- en	go	→	John has gone.
John	past	have	- en	go	→	John had gone.

Or we might make some combination:

Subject	Tense	have	- en	be	- ing	V	
John	past	have	- en	be	- ing	go	→

John had been going.

X-Y TRANSFORMATION

This shows all the elements of the sentence, but not in their proper order, for the tense goes after the *have*, the *–en* after the *be*, the *–ing* after the verb. In the sentences to the right of the arrows in the examples above, we switched these elements around and got them into the correct order. We can show exactly what we did in the following rule: call any *tense* or *–en* or *–ing* an **X**; call any modal or *have* or *be* or verb a **Y**; then whenever a sequence **X - Y** occurs, change it to **Y - X**. Thus:

	X	Y	X	Y	X	Y
Subject	Tense	have	- en	be	- ing	V
John	past	have	- en	be	- ing	drive
John	have	past	be	- en	drive	- ing

John had been driving.

Or:

	X	Y	Y	X	Y	X	Y
Subject	Tense	M	have	- en	be	- ing	V
John	past	can	have	- en	be	- ing	drive
John	can	past	have	be	- en	drive	- ing

John could have been driving.

QUESTION TRANSFORMATION

The transformation which produces questions applies *before* the transformation by which **X - Y** becomes **Y - X**. This is the rule:

Subject	Tense	M	V	→	Tense	M	Subject	V
Subject	Tense	have	V	→	Tense	have	Subject	V
Subject	Tense	be	V	→	Tense	be	Subject	V

Thus, in their final forms:

> John can work.   ⟶ Can John work?
> John had worked. → Had John worked?
> John is working.   → Is John working?

But if there is no modal, *have*, or *be*, this happens:

Subject	Tense	V	→	Tense	Subject	V

This produces what might be called a floating tense — that is, a tense with nothing to attach itself to. We then note the further rule that whenever we have a floating tense, we put in the word *do* to carry it. So:

Subject	Tense	V
John	past	work

becomes

past	John	work	(question transformation)

becomes

do	past	John	work	(*do* transformation)

becomes

Did John work?

It is worthwhile to observe the machinery in such detail because this machinery is used not only in questions of this type (questions that can be answered by *yes* or *no*) but also in many other structures. For example, we find the same thing in what are called *wh–* questions — questions introduced by such interrogative words as *where, when, what:*

> John can go home.   Where can John go?
> John has gone home.   Where has John gone?
> John is going home.   Where is John going?

But:

> John goes home.   Where does John go?

In the sentences with a modal, a *have,* or a *be,* the modal, *have,* or *be* plus the tense reverses with the subject. But when there is no modal, *have,* or *be,* only the tense reverses, and then a *do* is put in to carry it.

NEGATIVE TRANSFORMATION

The same apparatus is used with negatives:

Subject	Tense	M	V	Adv
John	past	can	go	home

To form a negative we add *not* (or *'t* or *n't*) after the modal:

| John | past | can | not | go | home |

The tense goes on the modal, producing "John couldn't go home." Similarly, with *have* or *be,* we would get "John hadn't gone home," "John wasn't going home." But if there is no modal, *can,* or *be,* we get this:

John	past	go	home
John	past	not	go	home

The tense now floats, so *do* is added:

| John | do | past | not | go | home |

John didn't go home.

EMPHATIC TRANSFORMATION

Sometimes we want to emphasize the verbal structure, as in "John *can* go home," in which we pronounce the *can* with extra loud stress. Let **E** stand for emphatic stress on a preceding word. Then:

| John | past | can | E | go | home |

John *could* go home.

And similarly:

John *is* going home.
John *has* gone home.

If there is no modal, *have*, or *be*, the **E** separates the tense and the verb:

> **John   past   go   home**
> **John   past   E   go   home**

Do is added to carry the floating tense, and the *do* receives the emphasis:

> John *did* go home.

But notice that *do* occurs in affirmative statements *only* when it is pronounced with emphatic stress, never when it is pronounced with weak stress. That is, English contains no sentences like

> John did go *home*.
> John did *go* home.

We have by no means exhausted the use of this particular apparatus. Here are some more examples:

> Has John gone home?   Yes, he has.   No, he hasn't.
> Is John going home?   Yes, he is.   No, he isn't.
> Did John go home?   Yes, he did.   No, he didn't.

Or:

> Never   could   the man work.
> Never   had   the man worked.
> Never   was   the man working.
> Never   did   the man work.*

---

* In Chapter 9 we noted that whereas *be* is just a *be*, *have* is both a *have* and a verb. Here we can observe a result of this description. Consider this basic sentence: "John has a car." If we write it in formula fashion, it becomes

> **John   present   have   a   car**

According to the rule, we reverse the subject with *present-have* to get

> **present   have   John   a   car**
> Has John a car?

But since *have* is not only a *have* but also a verb, the sentence "John has a car?" is also an instance of this:

We see the *do* transformation everywhere in English structure. Once we notice it, our description of English becomes much simpler, because we see all these structures — questions, negatives, short answers, etc. — as related structures, variations on a central theme. What is important is that we begin to get an idea of what it is in language that makes language learnable. When the English-learning child once grasps the *do* transformation, however he grasps it, then his learning goes with a rush. He finds it popping up all over the language, and he is therefore immediately in control of a great deal of English that he did not control before.

EXERCISE 58

It is difficult to understand such material as that presented in Chapter 32 by simply reading an explanation, just as it is difficult to understand an algebra or geometry explanation without working problems. One learns by taking a pencil and going through the process step by step.

Below you are given a series of basic patterns. For each, you are to choose words that fit the symbols, then, on successive lines, to make the changes called for by the transformations indicated on the left. If you do it correctly, you will come out each time with a grammatical English sentence. The first one is worked for you.

John	**present**	**V**	**a**	**car**

This becomes, by rule,

present	**John**	**V**	**a**	**car**	
do	**present**	**John**	**have**	**a**	**car** *(do* transformation)

Does John have a car?

We say that *have* is both a *have* and a verb because both "Has John a car?" and "Does John have a car?" are grammatical sentences (as are also "John hadn't a car" and "John didn't have a car" and so on). But *be* is only a *be*. "Did John be here?" and "John didn't be here" are ungrammatical.

Here is a summary of the essential terms:

do transformation — add *do* to any tense not immediately followed by a modal, *have, be,* or verb

emphatic transformation — add **E** (for emphatic stress on preceding word) after (1) tense plus modal, (2) tense plus *have,* (3) tense plus *be,* (4) tense alone if it is not followed by a modal, a *be,* or a *have*

modal — can, may, will, shall

negative transformation — add *not* after (1) tense plus modal, (2) tense plus *have,* (3) tense plus *be,* (4) tense alone if it is not followed by a modal, a *be,* or a *have*

question transformation — reverse the positions of the subject and (1) tense plus modal, (2) tense plus *have,* (3) tense plus *be,* (4) tense alone if it is not followed by a modal, a *be,* or a *have*

tense — past or present

X — any tense or *–en* or *–ing*

X - Y transformation — change any sequence of **X - Y** to **Y - X**

Y — any modal or *have* or *be* or verb

yes - no question — a question that can be answered by *yes* or *no* (or various other things, like *maybe*); "Did he go?" is a *yes – no* question, but "Where did he go?" is not

1.		Subject	Tense	M		have	- en	V
		the man	past	shall		have	–en	go
	Question tr.:	past	shall	the man		have	–en	go
	X–Y tr.:	shall	past	the man		have	go	–en
	Result:	Should the man have gone?						

2.		Subject	Tense	be	- ing	V
	Question tr.:					
	X–Y tr.:					
	Result:					

3.		Subject	Tense	have	- en	be	- ing	V
	Question tr.:							
	X–Y tr.:							
	Result:							

4.   **Subject   Tense   V**
     Question tr.:
     do tr.:
     Result:

5.   **Subject   Tense   M   be   - ing   V**
     Negative tr.:
     X–Y tr.:
     Result:

6.   **Subject   Tense   have   - en   be   - ing   V**
     Negative tr.:
     X–Y tr.:
     Result:

7.   **Subject   Tense   V**
     Negative tr.:
     do tr.:
     Result:

8.   **Subject   Tense   be   - ing   V**
     Emphatic tr.:
     X–Y tr.:
     Result:

9.   **Subject   Tense   M   have   - en   be   - ing   V**
     Emphatic tr.:
     X–Y tr.:
     Result:

10.   **Subject   Tense   V**
     Emphatic tr.:
     do tr.:
     Result:

11.   **Subject   Tense   M   V**
     Question tr.:
     Negative tr.:
     X–Y tr.:
     Result:

33 THE DICTIONARY

It is important that every student have, or have access to, a good dictionary. By "good" we mean not a many-volumed or an "unabridged" dictionary, but a desk dictionary with something between eighty thousand and a hundred and forty thousand main entries. Such a dictionary will cost between four and seven dollars and be worth it. Dictionaries can be bought for a dollar or less, but such dictionaries are of little value except as guides to spelling.

It is important also that the student understand what kind of book the dictionary is. Too often he thinks it divinely inspired, like the Bible. He supposes that language questions can be decided only by looking words up in the dictionary, and he doesn't ask himself how the maker of the dictionary knows what is right. Does he have a special dictionary of his own in which he looks up words? Then who made that dictionary, and how did *he* know?

AN OBJECTIVE REPORT ON USAGE

Actually dictionaries are — or are supposed to be — objective reports on how people use language. Dictionary makers spend much time and money gathering facts about how language is used and then simply publish their findings. They indicate not how words should be spelled but how writers and editors spell them. They put down not what they think words ought to mean but what speakers and writers of the language use them to mean. They tell us not which expressions are elegant and which are inelegant but which are used in elegant circles and which are not.

The dictionary is an extremely useful book, but it is not really central to the process of language learning. We do not, for example, learn the meaning of words mostly by looking them up in the dictionary. We build our vocabularies by hearing or seeing words in context. Every time we read a book we add words to our vocabularies, whether we use the dictionary or not. If there is plenty of familiar context — that is, if not too many new words come at once — we may understand everything perfectly without dictionary help. Similarly, we learn to spell largely by noticing how words are spelled. We learn to pronounce words by hearing other people pronounce them. We learn good usage by listening to the usage of the people we admire and look up to and wish to emulate.

It is perhaps not putting it too strongly to say that we use the dictionary as a last resort. Whenever the language problem falls within our experience, we are guided by our experience; when the problem lies outside our experience, we ask someone who knows or we consult the dictionary. If we are writing and we want to use a word whose spelling escapes us, we look it up in the dictionary. If in our reading we keep meeting a strange word whose meaning is not made clear by the context, we use the dictionary. If we have never heard anyone pronounce the word *schism* and become curious about its pronunciation, we open the dictionary.

KINDS OF INFORMATION IN DICTIONARIES

A good dictionary contains many different kinds of information about words. For any word it gives the spelling or spellings, the pronunciation or pronunciations, the meaning or meanings, and the etymology — that is, the history of the word. The dictionary will also tell us if there is something special about the word, whether it is used only in certain professions or by certain social groups or in certain areas; this information can be summed up as the *status designation*. For some words the dictionary will give what are called *synonymies* — lists of synonyms together with an explanation of the slight differences between them.

The spellings are the simplest part of the information in the dictionary, in the sense that there can be little argument about them. English spelling has now been stable for nearly three hundred years, and the great majority of words are spelled in only one way. Where alternative forms occur — *adviser* and *advisor*, for example — the dictionary will give both, listing the most common form first.

Most words have more than one meaning. Dictionaries try to separate the different senses of the word and to list them all. Usually the different meanings will be numbered, as many as thirty or forty meanings being listed for some words. Dictionaries differ on the order in which the meanings are listed. Some try to arrange the meanings in the order of frequency of occurrence — the most common meaning first and the rarest last. Others use a historical order — the earliest meaning first and the most recent last. Whatever the order used by your dictionary, you usually have to hunt around to get the meaning you want. If you are looking up a word encountered in your reading, you have to check the different meanings against the passage in which you found the word, selecting the meaning that fits, or most nearly fits, the context. Ultimately it is always the context that indicates what the word means.

Your dictionary will also tell you how words are pronounced, employing for this purpose a semiphonetic alphabet with various special marks above some of the letters. The value of the symbols is indicated in key words listed in the front or back of the dictionary and sometimes at the bottom of each page. Some systems are more complicated than they need be, but a little practice will render them easy to understand. Pronunciation differs widely over the English-speaking world. The correct pronunciation of Boston is not the same as that of Dallas, Minneapolis, or London. One learns how words are pronounced by listening to the pronunciation of one's parents or friends or teachers and looks to the dictionary chiefly for those words which one has not heard. The dictionary intends to give the pronunciation of educated people, but in the area of pronunciation the dictionary is often incomplete and sometimes wrong. One should certainly not assume that one's elders are in error because they pronounce a word one way and the dictionary indicates another.

It is rewarding to get in the habit of noticing the etymology when one looks up a word. The etymology is the history of the word. It tells where the word comes from, what language it is borrowed from if it is borrowed, what its earlier meanings were, something of the changes of form that it has undergone. Most people find etymologies of great interest, and they are often valuable in fixing the word in one's memory.

If you look up a word like *pride,* you will probably find not only its meanings but also a list of its synonyms — words of similar meaning like *arrogance, haughtiness,* etc. — together with a discussion of the shades of meaning that differentiate the synonyms. A study of synonymies is a way of developing vocabulary and attaining a greater precision in using words. Sometimes you will be directed to a synonymy by a cross reference; for example, in the entry for *arrogance,* you may find the direction "Syn. see *pride.*" This means that the synonyms for *arrogance* are given under the word *pride.*

USAGE LABELS

If a word is in general unrestricted use, no status designation is given. But if there is something special about the use of the word, the dictionary tells us what the restriction is. The word, or one of its meanings, may be restricted, for example, to a certain profession or trade — law, medicine, music, printing, football, etc. Such a restriction will be indicated, often by an abbreviation — *med., mus.* Sometimes the restriction will be geographical, and we will find status designations like *Brit., Chiefly U.S., N.Eng.,* for words or meanings found in Britain, chiefly in the United States, or in New England, respectively. Sometimes the restriction is social; the word may be used only in slang or in informal conversation, or it may be dialectal or found only in the speech of uneducated people. For such words we will find labels like *slang, colloq.* (colloquial), *dial.* (dialectal), *vulg.* (vulgate).

In designating status, the dictionary is reasonably reliable but not infallible. Here, as elsewhere, one depends principally on one's own experience and goes to the dictionary when one's experience is wanting.

EXERCISE 59

Using your dictionary, answer the following questions.

1. When is Empire Day?
2. What does F.L.B. stand for?
3. What is the population of Danbury, Connecticut?
4. What is anthropophagy?
5. Where are mastabas found?
6. Which is the more common spelling, *adviser* or *advisor?*
7. Give a word that rhymes with *Flaubert.*
8. What does U.S.S.R. stand for?
9. What does *alma mater* mean in Latin?
10. From what language was the word *bungalow* borrowed?
11. Where are the Cinque Ports?
12. What status designation does your dictionary give for *jalopy?*
13. What is meant by *v.t.?*
14. When did Johann Gutenberg die?
15. On what syllable is the word *dilatant* stressed?
16. Under what name is Iosif Dzhugashvili better known?
17. What does the abbreviation ME stand for?
18. What did the name *Claribel* mean in Latin?
19. List five synonyms for the adjective *brave.*
20. What was the nationality of the inventor of *braille?*
21. Give an English word with which *Dzungaria* would alliterate.
22. Where is Dzungaria?
23. What is the status designation of the noun *bobby?*
24. Give a word rhyming with *putsch.*
25. What did the word *lady* mean literally in Old English?
26. Give four synonyms for the word *law.*

27. List six professions, trades, or sports in which the word *lead* has a special meaning.

28. In what country is the term *memsahib* used?

29. Give four synonyms for the word *model*.

30. How many slang meanings does your dictionary give for the verb *plug?*

EXERCISE 60

Write out the etymologies given in your dictionary for the following words. Do not use abbreviations.

EXAMPLE: A. ferret   Middle English *feret* or *foret*, from Old French *furet*, a diminutive of *furon*, from Late Latin *furo*, a ferret, from Latin *fur*, a thief.

1. fetish   6. slogan
2. mitigate   7. lumber
3. rankle   8. buckaroo
4. rival   9. bishop
5. admiral   10. glamour

EXERCISE 61

Many words borrowed from Latin and Greek can be translated literally into native English words. For example, *propose* means literally "put" (*pose*) "forward" (*pro*); *avert* means "turn away"; *dendrophile* means "lover of trees" (*dendro* — "tree;" *phile* — "lover"). Use your dictionary to find the literal meaning of the following:

1. revert   9. provide
2. intervene   10. dissent
3. predict   11. revoke
4. transcribe   12. erupt
5. interject   13. euphony
6. infer   14. polygyny
7. preclude   15. apathy
8. fratricide   16. microcephalic

17. geophagous   22. hypodermic
18. protozoa   23. endemic
19. acrophobia   24. Eugene
20. patronym   25. plutocracy
21. monopoly

34 PRONOUN AND VERB FORMS

In the second chapter we made a distinction between what we called Grammar 1 and Grammar 2:

> 1. Henry brought his mother some flowers.
> 2. Henry brung his mother some flowers.

Roughly speaking, Grammar 1 is the grammar of educated people, and Grammar 2 is the grammar of uneducated people. Naturally, English isn't simply one or the other. There are infinitely many varieties of English connoting all sorts of differences to be found among English-speaking people — differences in age, sex, temperament, geography, as well as differences in amount and kind of education. We have no leisure to inspect all of these variations. We limit our discussion to certain obvious expressions, expressions which, if used among educated people, are likely to cause the user embarrassment or worse.

Let us note again that the speech forms used by uneducated people are not bad in themselves. "He did it" is not intrinsically superior to "He done it." It is merely an accident of history that educated people say "He did it" and eschew "He done it." The important thing is that this *is* the practice of educated people. We describe here — or try to — not what ought to be but what is.

Most of the expressions obviously denoting lack of education involve pronoun forms or verb forms. In its earlier stages, English

— like its relatives, Latin and Greek — had numerous *case* forms for nouns and pronouns. That is, each noun and pronoun had a list of distinct forms which correlated with the use of the noun or pronoun in a sentence. For instance, one used one form if the word was a subject, another if it was an object, another if it was an indirect object, others after certain prepositions, and so on.

CASE FORMS IN MODERN ENGLISH

Little of this variety remains in present-day English. English nouns have now just two case forms: common case (*John, boy, boys*) and possessive case (*John's, boy's, boys'*). English pronoun forms have been reduced, too, but five of them still have one extra form. These are the pronouns *I, we, he, she,* and *they,* which have the corresponding forms *me, us, him, her,* and *them.* In addition, the relative *who* has the corresponding form *whom.*

We shall call *I, we, he, she,* and *they* the subject forms and *me, us, him, her,* and *them* the object forms. The subject form is used when the word is subject and — usually — when it is in the predicate noun position of PATTERN TEN. The object form is used in all other positions.

Most of this usage is automatic for everyone, whether educated or not. Nobody, for example, says "Me did it," except Indians on television. Nobody says "He saw I" or "He gave I the money." The object forms seem to be used, among uneducated people, mostly when the subject is compound: "Me and Harry did it," "Him and me did it." The educated usage is of course "Harry and I did it," "He and I did it."

There is a considerable tendency to use the object forms in the PATTERN TEN predicates: "It's me," "It was them," "Nobody knew that the winner was her." However, no one could call these usages uneducated, since they will be heard from many educated speakers too. Others prefer "It is I," "It is they." *Me* and *us* are more commonly used by the educated in this pattern than are *him, her,* and *them.*

After prepositions the object forms are normal: *to me, with them, for Jim and her, between you and me.* One often hears expressions like *between you and I.* These are likely to result from too great a zeal for correctness. Most likely the user has been corrected for using *me* in the subject position and has made the incorrect inference that *me* is suspect everywhere.

In many dialects the pronoun *them* is used as a demonstrative in place of *those:* "Them people did it." This is of course not educated usage.

IRREGULAR VERBS

Trouble with verbs mostly involves the *–ed* (past tense) and *–en* (past participle) forms of irregular verbs: *done* for *did, seen* for *saw, throwed* for *threw* or *thrown.* The *–ing* forms give no trouble, because they are constructed the same way for all verbs. There are a few irregular *–s* forms: *has, does, says* (irregular in sound, though not in spelling). These cause no difficulty. Perhaps all that need be mentioned here is the use of *don't* in place of *doesn't.* Educated usage prefers *doesn't* with singular subjects: *he doesn't, my brother doesn't* in place of *he don't, my brother don't.*

We list here the *–ed* and *–en* forms of the more important irregular verbs. Remember that the *–ed* form is the past tense; the *–en* form is the form used after *have* (*have seen it*) or in modification. Verbs with similar patterns are grouped together. Forms in parentheses and marked with an asterisk are those heard in nonstandard dialects.

Simple	- ed	- en
arise	arose	arisen
drive	drove	driven (*drove)
ride	rode	ridden (*rode)
rise	rose	risen
smite	smote	smitten
throw	threw (*throwed)	thrown (*throwed)
grow	grew (*growed)	grown (*growed)
know	knew (*knowed)	known (*knowed)

Simple	- ed	- en
fly	flew (*flied)	flown (*flied)
break	broke	broken (*broke)
choose	chose	chosen (*chose)
freeze	froze	frozen (*froze)
steal	stole	stolen (*stole)
weave	wove (*weaved)	woven (*weaved)
bid	bade	bidden
bite	bit	bitten (*bit)
draw	drew (*drawed)	drawn (*drawed)
eat	ate	eaten (*ate)
fall	fell	fallen (*fell)
forget	forgot	forgotten (*forgot)
forbid	forbade	forbidden
give	gave (*give)	given (*give)
lie	lay (*laid)	lain (*laid)
see	saw (*seen)	seen
begin	began (*begun)	begun
drink	drank (*drunk)	drunk
ring	rang (*rung)	rung
shrink	shrank (*shrunk)	shrunk
sing	sang (*sung)	sung
sink	sank (*sunk)	sunk
spring	sprang (*sprung)	sprung
stink	stank (*stunk)	stunk
swim	swam (*swum)	swum
bind	bound	bound
find	found	found
grind	ground (*grinded)	ground (*grinded)
wind	wound (*winded)	wound (*winded)
cling	clung (*clinged)	clung (*clinged)
dig	dug	dug
fling	flung	flung
sling	slung	slung

Simple	- ed	- en
slink	slunk	slunk
spin	spun	spun
stick	stuck	stuck
sting	stung	stung
swing	swung (*swang)	swung
win	won	won
wring	wrung (*wringed)	wrung (*wringed)
fight	fought	fought
get	got	got
hold	held	held
shine	shone (*shined)	shone (*shined)
sit	sat (*set)	sat (*set)
slide	slid (*slided)	slid (*slided)
stand	stood	stood
come	came (*come)	come
run	ran (*run)	run
do	did (*done)	done
go	went	gone (*went)

Some of the forms in parentheses occur in educated usage. There is a verb *set*, for example, but it is not the past tense form of *sit* for educated people. There is a wide difference in the effect of the parenthesized forms. One might, for example, say "It shined on me" in polite circles without anyone's thinking it odd. But occurrence of "He had went," "They run away," "We seen it," "Who throwed it?" would probably cause the hostess to revise the guest list.

EXERCISE 62

On a separate sheet of paper, write the *–ed* or *–en* form of the verb that would be appropriate in educated speech.

EXAMPLE: A. do   He _____ it.
              did

1. see   Nobody _____ Harry.
2. come   He _____ home at five.
3. eat   He had not _____ for two days.
4. give   We _____ him his answer.
5. throw   He had been _____ out.
6. shrink   He _____ from telling the truth.
7. run   He _____ all the way from the station.
8. cling   She _____ to him.
9. sing   She _____ rather well.
10. blow   He _____ on the coals.
11. break   The pump had _____ down.
12. grind   He _____ his own coffee.
13. know   I had _____ what would happen.
14. sling   He _____ it over his shoulder.
15. sit   She _____ on the porch and rocked.
16. freeze   During the night the pond had _____.
17. slink   She _____ into the room.
18. speak   No one had _____ to him.
19. swim   He _____ across the pool.
20. rise   He had _____ at six o'clock.
21. swear   He had _____ to be true.
22. spin   He _____ around quickly.
23. stink   I thought the garbage _____.
24. forget   He had _____ to bring it.
25. bear   She had _____ him a son.
26. fly   He _____ his own plane.
27. wind   The stream _____ through the valley.
28. wring   She _____ her hands.
29. spring   He _____ to his feet.
30. sink   He _____ into a coma.
31. forbid   I _____ him to do it.
32. steal   Someone had _____ it.
33. lie   He _____ quietly on the sofa.
34. grow   He had _____ it himself.
35. choose   Which one has been _____?
36. ring   Somebody _____ the bell.

35 CHOICE OF WORDS

Correct writing might be defined as the kind of writing that the reader expects. Expectations vary, obviously, from reader to reader. Educated speakers expect certain forms, and their expectations, taken together, constitute what we call standard English. In the last chapter, we considered these expectations as they relate to pronoun and verb forms. In this chapter, we shall consider some other matters.

We repeat that correctness has very little to do with logic. We can, for example, give no logical reason why *himself* is standard English and *hisself* is substandard. *Hisself* expresses the same meaning as *himself* and, if one is used to it, just as clearly. Further, we say *myself* rather than *meself*, so why not *hisself* rather than *himself?* It is nothing but a historical accident that educated speakers in the United States and Britain say *himself*, whereas *hisself* occurs only among groups of uneducated people. Those who say *hisself* do not do so because they are lazy or stupid or perverse. They say *hisself* simply because that is the form taught them as children by their parents and their playmates.

But logical or not, it is a fact that in many circles it can be socially or economically ruinous to say *hisself* or *yourn* or *he brung it* or *I ain't got none* or *nowheres* or *it don't matter*. The student speaking a dialect in which such forms occur does not necessarily have to stop speaking it when he goes to college or enters the business world; but he must certainly learn to speak the English of the educated too and must use this English when he moves in educated circles. For such a student the acquiring of standard English is similar to, though not nearly so difficult as, the acquiring of a second language.

Probably relatively few students entering college face a dialect problem of this sort. Most students either don't say *he done good* or, if they do, have learned long since that when they write, they must use *he did well*. Rather more a problem is that illustrated by the expression "He took me for granite." This difficulty is likely to be a result of acquiring vocabulary orally — for example, from radio or television — rather than through books. It happens that the words *granted* and *granite*, though spelled quite differently, sound very much alike, particularly in rapid speech. Never seeing the expression, the student may say and write "Take me for granite" or "Take it for granite" a long time before someone calls the error to his attention.

Similar blunders are *might of* for *might have*, *use to* for *used to*, *condensation* for *condescension*. Many such difficulties are really errors in spelling: *effect* for *affect* and *affect* for *effect*. These errors are hard to eliminate, because of course if one knew he were making them he wouldn't make them. Some will be pointed out by teachers or friends. Others can be corrected through reading. When one is doubtful whether an expression is correct or not, he of course consults the dictionary.

COLLOQUIAL ENGLISH

Somewhat more subtle are the differences between colloquial English and what is sometimes called edited English. Colloquial English is the language that educated people use in speech or in informal letters. Edited English is the kind of English that is printed in books, magazines, and newspapers. In general, English classes aim at the writing of edited English.

There is some tendency in this century to blur the distinction between colloquial and edited English, to make even serious writing more conversational than it was fifty years ago. Still, some distinctions remain. In printed writing, the distinctions between *who* and *whom*, for instance, are generally observed, though many people no longer bother about them in speech. Such expressions as "He was mad at Jones," "He was enthused about it," "like he said," "a bunch of girls," "different than me," "lots of times," "a real nice girl," would probably be rejected by most editors and replaced with more formal alternatives.

However, many points of usage, formerly much belabored, are ceasing to be objects of concern. Probably few copy editors nowadays are bothered by such distinctions as *shall/will, further/farther, provided/providing.* Few object on principle to prepositions at the end of sentences. Some eliminate split infinitives (*to even look*); others don't mind or don't notice.

SLANG

Slang might be considered a subdivision of colloquial language. Slang is also prominent and even necessary in conversation and generally to be avoided in writing. Slang differs from other colloquialisms in that it carries a sense of fun and of group identification. You show that you belong to a group by using the slang of the group. Most slang terms, though not all, are short-lived. They tend to be overused and to lose their savor.

TRITE EXPRESSIONS

One would not ordinarily in serious writing use such expressions as *prof* for *professor, math* for *mathematics, cop* for *policeman, dough* for *money, bucket* for *jail.* Students sometimes think to make a slang term acceptable by putting quotation marks around it: "He was a 'cop' in Des Moines." This practice should generally be avoided. It is better either to use the slang term without apology or to avoid it altogether.

One reason for not using slang expressions in writing is that they are likely to be trite: too frequently used, they have lost their force. In general, trite expressions are certainly to be avoided, but triteness is one of the hardest of all writing defects to recognize and avoid. Most trite expressions are old metaphors, and the young writer is likely to be attracted to them as metaphors without realizing that they are old. He hears someone say, for example, "Her head was always in the clouds." This strikes him as an arresting picture, and he uses the expression, perhaps unaware that so many others have used it too that to an experienced reader it conveys nothing except that the person mentioned was impractical and that the writer is not very inventive.

Trite phrases are only too easily illustrated: "worked like a horse," "like walking on eggs," "gone to the dogs," "a forest of masts," "from where I sit," "for all practical intents and purposes," "stand up and be counted," "with bated breath," "on pins and needles," "in righteous indignation," "in the very nick of time," "without a shadow of a doubt," "grasping at a straw." It is really very hard to escape phrases like these. They are so handy and easy and they save us so much thinking that they slip into our writing without our being aware of it. Even the professional writer succumbs too often to the lure of the cliché, the trite expression. But every conscientious writer knows that triteness is a vice to be shunned if possible. We should learn to distrust the arresting phrase that comes quickly to mind; most likely it has come just as quickly to ten thousand other minds before us.

Similarly handy, similarly tempting, and similarly bad are the words of very general meaning which save us the trouble of searching for the words that will express our thought precisely. In ordinary conversation, for example, we use the word *nice* as a general term to cover such various meanings as *handsome, pretty, interesting, balmy, warm, witty, agreeable, well-constructed*, and many others. The general word may be just what we want, but in writing it is usually better to hunt for the more precise term.

The student wishing to get a little more sparkle out of his writing will do well to become suspicious of words and phrases like *thing, condition, case, circumstance, factor, contact, proposition, feature, striking, in terms of*. These may be sometimes the very words we need and ought to use. More often they are just a substitute for thought and make our prose go all gluey.

EXERCISE 63

Each of the following sentences contains a word or phrase for which a more formal word or a word more appropriate to edited or educated English might be substituted. Identify this word or phrase on a separate sheet of paper and write a more appropriate substitute after it on the same line. Most of the items involved have not been mentioned specifically in Chapter 35. If the answer is not immediately obvious to you, you will of course have to use your dictionary. Pick out the word or words in the sentence that seem suspect and see what the dictionary will tell you about them.

EXAMPLES: **A.** He took me for granite.
             granite   granted
             B. He was a cop in Des Moines.
             cop   policeman

1. We couldn't find it nowheres.
2. The policeman shot him in the abdomen, and he croaked.
3. They should of reached the house by eight thirty.
4. He determined to make the attempt, irregardless of the difficulty.
5. Being as we had plenty of time, we decided to visit the zoo.
6. I wanted very much to attend the wedding reception, but I didn't get an invite.
7. Most everybody who heard Abercrombie's speech praised it very highly.
8. He refused to start the construction without he got some money in advance.
9. Few lawyers could play on a jury's emotions like Sir Tolbert could.
10. Melissa was always enthused about some new friendship she had made.
11. The evidence was perfectly plain, but we couldn't hardly believe it.
12. Grandma was content to set all afternoon on the porch, quietly rocking.
13. The governor was mighty sorry that he could not attend the opening game.
14. The Jaguar and the Volkswagen belonged to Sweeney and Carruthers respectfully.

15. His parents located in Portland, Oregon, when he was a little boy.
16. What he said inferred that he thought himself better than the rest of us.
17. We knew that his mother would be kind of upset when she heard about it.
18. According to the dictionary, the word *nice* formally meant *foolish*.
19. When we heard what he proposed to do, we were simply incredible.
20. Though reluctant to campaign, Bronson agreed to except the nomination.
21. The announcement throwed the whole committee into confusion.
22. Obviously Williams hadn't ought to have broken the photographer's camera.
23. There is undoubtably something to be said for his point of view.
24. He liked nothing better than to lay on the lawn and watch the clouds moving overhead.
25. Stinson couldn't make the football team, but he was exceptionably good at soccer.
26. Senator Quigley's greatest weakness was a tendency to get mad when opposed.
27. She wasn't really pretty, but she always dressed very neat.
28. Despite the grave warning he had received, Dockmeyer proceeded unrelentlessly on his way.
29. Her mother would not even leave him enter the house.
30. We knew him to be one of the most imminent professors of speech education in northern South Dakota.

EXERCISE 64

Each of the following sentences contains a trite expression. Rewrite each sentence, expressing the same idea in a less hackneyed way. Your revision need not necessarily be metaphorical.

EXAMPLE: A. It was like walking on eggs.
It was like juggling hand grenades.
or:
It was a very delicate situation.

1. She waited with bated breath for Montrose to continue.
2. A mantle of snow covered the yard.
3. Fred Finklehoff is a man who, I am sure, needs no introduction.
4. When I saw Stuart's new car, I was green with envy.
5. I had the time of my life in Denver this summer.
6. I had to work like a Trojan to finish in time.
7. She worked her fingers to the bone to put her son through college.
8. In the twinkling of an eye the meal appeared before us.
9. She looked for all the world like something the cat dragged in.
10. I was sure that there was some method in her madness.
11. A sea of faces looked up at us.
12. This is something that must certainly be nipped in the bud.
13. She sat in the corner just as quiet as a mouse.
14. She was as white as a sheet, but her brother was as brown as a berry.
15. You will find the encyclopedia a veritable mine of information.

36 PHONEMES

Before moving on to the complicated and vexing problem of English spelling, we shall take a short look at English sounds. English spelling, as everyone knows, is fearfully mixed up and capricious, but it does have a relation to English sounds. In so far as the letters of our alphabet stand for anything, they stand for the sounds that come out of our mouths when we talk. Many spelling errors result from the student's missing the connection between sound and symbol. Some students are therefore helped by a little attention to the sounds themselves. At any rate, the subject is an interesting one to all of us.

DEFINITION OF A PHONEME

English has a total of forty-five sound units called *phonemes*. A phoneme is not exactly a single sound. It is rather a collection of similar sounds which are likely to sound identical to the speaker of the language. For example, English has a phoneme /p/, which occurs in the words *pin, nip, spin, appear, upper*. All these "p" sounds are different. /p/ is not the same at the beginning of a word as at the end, not the same before a stressed syllable as after one, and so on. Yet these differences are not significant for English, and we who speak English have learned to ignore them.

In some languages these differences *are* significant. A speaker of Hindi or Korean, for example, would feel that the "p" in *pin* and the "p" in *spin* are not the same sound at all, for in these languages these sounds belong to separate phonemes. Such a person learning English would have to train himself to overlook this difference. On the other hand, we, if we were to learn Hindi or Korean, would have to train ourselves to recognize the difference and to react to it.

Languages differ widely in the number of phonemes they have. English, as we have said, has forty-five. Other languages have as few as eighteen or twenty or as many as seventy or eighty.

VOWELS AND CONSONANTS

Of our forty-five English phonemes, twelve are intonation phonemes — units of stress, pitch, and juncture. Most of these we have already discussed in Chapter 25, and we shall say nothing further about them here. The other thirty-three are vowels and consonants — twenty-four consonants and nine vowels. This is for the language as a whole. Many individual speakers, however, have only seven or eight vowels.

We shall not try here to describe the mechanism by which the sounds are produced but shall instead focus our attention on the result. The key given below relates principally to the author's California speech. This key will serve well enough to indicate the consonants occurring the country over; in the vowels there is more variation, and some readers will probably use quite different vowels in some of the words given.

Here, then, is the key. Note that when we write phonemes, we put them in diagonal lines to distinguish them from letters of the ordinary alphabet.

/p/   The first sound in *pin*, second in *spin*, last in *nip*.

/t/   The first sound in *tick*, second in *stick*, last in *kit*.

/k/   The first sound in *cat*, second in *scat*, last (ck) in *tack*.

/b/   The first sound in *ban*, last in *nab*.

/d/   The first and last sounds in *dad*.

/g/   The first and last sounds in *gag*.

/c/   The first sound (ch) in *chin*, last (tch) in *watch*.

/j/   The first sound in *Jim* or *gin*, last (dge) in *fudge*.

/f/   The first sound in *fall*, last (gh) in *laugh*.

/θ/   The first sound (th) in *thick*, last (th) in *breath*.

/s/   The first sound in *sin*, last in *hiss*.

/š/   The first sound (sh) in *shake*, last (sh) in *smash*.

/v/   The first sound in *vine*, last (ve) in *give*.

/δ/   The first sound (th) in *then*, last (the) in *breathe*.

/z/   The first sound in *zeal*, last in *his*.

/ž/   The last sound (ge) in *rouge*, as most people say it; the middle consonant in *vision* or *measure*.

/m/   The first and last sounds in *mum*.

/n/   The first and last sounds in *Nan*.

/η/   The last sound (ng) in *sing, hang, tongue*.

/l/   The first sound in *law*, last (ll) in *fall*.

/r/   The first and last sounds in *roar*. (But many speakers do not pronounce a final /r/ in *roar*.)

/y/   The first sound in *you*.

/w/   The first sound in *woo*.

/h/   The first sound in *his, hike, who*.

/i/   The vowel sound in *pit, bin, ship, tick, knit, fill, sing, pish, his, hiss*.

/e/   The vowel sound in *hep, beck, dead, beg, breath, flesh, strength*.

/æ/   The vowel sound in *nap, sack, bag, last, razz, rang, pal*.

/ɨ/   For many speakers the first vowel in *sugar* or *children*. Some speakers do not have this vowel except in syllables with weak stress, where it is very common, or before /r/, as in *sir, girl, fur*.

/ə/   The vowel sound in *but, dug, flood, tough, tongue*.

/a/   For the author, the vowel sound in *hot, cot, bomb, balm, rob, shock*. Many speakers have /ɔ/ in some of these words.

/u/   The vowel sound in *put, could, foot, pull, rook, stood*.

/o/   This does not occur except as part of a diphthong in most American speech. Some New Englanders have it in *home* or *whole*.

/ɔ/   For the author, the vowel sound in *law, wash, fought, caught, hog*. Some speakers have /a/ in some of these words.

DIPHTHONGS

In addition to these simple sounds, English has a variety of diphthongs, consisting of one of the simple vowels plus a gliding sound. We represent the glide with /y/ or /w/, depending on what sort of glide it is. Here are some common diphthongs:

/iy/   The vowel sound in *he, heat, field, beam, beat, sneak, queen, clean*.

/ey/   The vowel sound in *way, rain, Spain, plain, blame, stay, scale, steak, snare*.

/ay/   The vowel sound in *my, sky, write, kind, style, mice*.

/ɔy/   The vowel sound in *boy, boil, coin, Troy, point*.

/aw/   The vowel sound in *out, bout, round, mouse, cow*.

/ow/   The vowel sound in *go, snow, rode, moan, drove*.

/uw/   The vowel sound in *who, moo, rude, tomb, cool, few*.

Many other diphthongs occur in the various dialects of English. You may have others in addition to or in place of these.

Now here are examples of words written in phonemic transcription. Some people might pronounce some of them differently. The pronunciations given are common, though not universal, in the Central and Western United States.

pick	/pik/	train	/treyn/	rough	/rəf/
rib	/rib/	laugh	/læf/	cuff	/kəf/
drive	/drayv/	dream	/driym/	bent	/bent/
hung	/həŋ/	pink	/piŋk/	scream	/skriym/
out	/awt/	toes	/towz/	boil	/bɔyl/
food	/fuwd/	sir	/sɨr/	quick	/kwik/
should	/šud/	suds	/sədz/	talked	/tɔkt/
gross	/grows/	full	/ful/	sticks	/stiks/
grows	/growz/	zone	/zown/	bags	/bægz/
maimed	/meymd/	veiled	/veyld/	hopes	/howps/
rouge	/ruwž/	judged	/jəjd/	chips	/cips/
nudge	/nəj/	youth	/yuwθ/	these	/ðiyz/
vines	/vaynz/	thick	/θik/	then	/ðen/
wants	/wants/	thin	/θin/	crashed	/kræšt/

In words of more than one syllable, syllables with weak stress are likely to have the vowel /ɨ/. The vowel /ə/ often occurs under weak stress at the beginning and end of words. Other possibilities are

father	/fáðɨr/	chicken	/cíkɨn/	measure	/méžɨr/
woman	/wúmɨn/	about	/əbáwt/	ended	/éndɨd/
women	/wímɨn/	event	/əvént/	whether	/hwéðɨr/
vision	/vížɨn/	sugar	/šúgɨr/	pretty	/prítiy/
meager	/míygɨr/	shambles	/šǽmbɨlz/	drowning	/dráwniŋ/
singing	/síŋiŋ/	reproach	/rɨprówc/	sofa	/sówfə/

EXERCISE 65

Checking as much as necessary with the key on pages 250–51, write the following words in standard spelling.

1. /pik/	7. /sɨr/	13. /lɔ/
2. /big/	8. /fut/	14. /nat/
3. /dæd/	9. /ðen/	15. /hænd/
4. /təf/	10. /θin/	16. /bæŋ/
5. /rən/	11. /nek/	17. /riŋ/
6. /giv/	12. /hæŋ/	18. /niyt/

19. /heyt/
20. /drowv/
21. /bɔyl/
22. /suwn/
23. /θiyf/
24. /vayn/
25. /swiyt/
26. /hɨrd/
27. /šawt/
28. /ruwž/
29. /cip/
30. /ciyp/
31. /jəg/
32. /yuwθ/
33. /breθ/
34. /briyð/
35. /šeym/
36. /wɔkt/
37. /liynd/
38. /skræc/
39. /leŋkθ/
40. /piyld/
41. /rəbd/
42. /huwt/
43. /huw/
44. /zip/
45. /mæš/
46. /yɨrn/

47. /kweynt/
48. /bɔy/
49. /zown/
50. /jownz/
51. /jayb/
52. /gowt/
53. /frawn/
54. /sayz/
55. /ðowz/
56. /mawnd/
57. /vawc/
58. /kud/
59. /əbáwt/
60. /fáðɨr/
61. /méžɨr/
62. /trə́bɨl/
63. /əpíyl/
64. /tókɨr/
65. /ánɨst/
66. /hǽpiy/
67. /sówfə/
68. /jóyful/
69. /tírkiy/
70. /wéytiŋ/
71. /bríyzɨz/
72. /əbjékt/
73. /æbjékt/
74. /kɨnsíyd/

75. /sépɨreyt/
76. /fíymeyl/
77. /kwíkliy/
78. /ǽθliyt/
79. /rícɨrd/
80. /ǽlbɨrt/
81. /wílyɨm/
82. /šérɨn/
83. /sǽliy/
84. /márjɨriy/
85. /dánə/
86. /kyúwbɨkɨl/
87. /pírkɨleyt/
88. /ríyzɨnɨbɨl/
89. /mæθɨmǽtiks/
90. /riyzémbɨl/
91. /kwáyɨtliy/
92. /fowníymiks/
93. /rícuwɨl/
94. /esθétiks/
95. /ínfɨntayl/
96. /régyuwleyt/
97. /prínsɨpɨl/
98. /bayálɨjiy/
99. /simpɨθétik/
100. /kámyɨnizm/

EXERCISE 66

Checking as much as necessary with the key on pages 250–51, write the following words in phonemic spelling. You will have most trouble with the vowels. The best way to determine whether vowel sounds are like or unlike is to test for rhymes. For example, *hook* rhymes with *rook*, so it should be written /u/.

1. sick	18. wait	35. tribe
2. dig	19. grow	36. these
3. fad	20. toil	37. Ruth
4. hive	21. brief	38. Sam
5. rough	22. room	39. Sue
6. shun	23. sheet	40. George
7. girl	24. vine	41. Al
8. thick	25. drive	42. Ed
9. this	26. rest	43. Rick
10. beck	27. tooth	44. Jean
11. rang	28. cat	45. Bob
12. saw	29. sail	46. Jill
13. hot	30. crutch	47. Steve
14. stand	31. brick	48. Nan
15. would	32. love	49. Tom
16. book	33. shout	50. Gay
17. bomb	34. child	

EXERCISE 67

Follow instructions for Exercise 66 on page 253.

1. cheat	14. cads	27. says
2. wretch	15. picks	28. gives
3. which	16. pigs	29. hates
4. wild	17. wreaths	30. robs
5. ouch	18. laughs	31. talked
6. brain	19. times	32. robbed
7. zip	20. rakes	33. sagged
8. match	21. pails	34. popped
9. sign	22. toes	35. dreamed
10. wood	23. walks	36. banged
11. trees	24. writes	37. laughed
12. rats	25. drives	38. raced
13. caps	26. thinks	39. razed

40. rushed	44. waned	48. whom
41. missed	45. thrived	49. when
42. mist	46. quick	50. phone
43. slapped	47. queen	

EXERCISE 68

Write the following words in phonemic spelling. Mark the primary stress (there will be only one) on each item. Most of the unstressed vowels will be /i/.

1. travel	18. bubble	35. Thomas
2. happy	19. monkey	36. Ethel
3. sicken	20. announce	37. Edith
4. mother	21. between	38. Martin
5. stiffly	22. around	39. Sally
6. reject	23. away	40. Ellen
7. window	24. cougher	41. watches
8. teacher	25. coffer	42. admires
9. above	26. select	43. smashes
10. insist	27. arrange	44. catches
11. dopey	28. anxious	45. passes
12. woman	29. whither	46. bulges
13. women	30. salad	47. razors
14. bashful	31. Mabel	48. acquires
15. neatly	32. David	49. babies
16. sadden	33. Mary	50. judges
17. stable	34. Robert	

EXERCISE 69

Follow instructions for Exercise 68 above.

1. ended	4. started	7. insistent
2. baited	5. studded	8. mischievous
3. pouted	6. indulges	9. studying

10. radical	24. occasion	38. activity
11. effective	25. underwear	39. intonation
12. location	26. telephone	40. differential
13. adhesive	27. syncopate	41. significant
14. arrangement	28. allowance	42. symbolism
15. addiction	29. fabulous	43. alphabetical
16. refugee	30. popular	44. availability
17. Eleanor	31. emancipate	45. authorization
18. theater	32. occupation	46. inaudibility
19. manikin	33. psychology	47. unexceptional
20. attractive	34. analytic	48. dendrophilism
21. communist	35. destination	49. anachronistic
22. publisher	36. excitable	50. predestination
23. satisfy	37. satisfaction	

37 SPELLING

The misspelled word is the error that hits every reader in the eye. Your reader may not notice or may notice only vaguely your dangling modifiers, your comma faults, your bad diction. But write *recieve* or *studing* and he concludes instantly that you're a dimwit. The conclusion may be unjust: all dimwits are bad spellers, but not all bad spellers are dimwits. Some very bright people spell badly. Nevertheless, the conclusion is drawn.

Spelling comes much easier to some people than to others. Nobody knows just why. Some people apparently have a greater power of visualization and retention. The words they see take shape in their minds and stay there and are available when they need to be written. But probably nearly all students capable of going to college, even those who have no natural gift for spelling, can learn to spell passably well if they go at it with some care and diligence.

SPELLING AND PRONUNCIATION

The reason that English is hard to spell is that a large gap has grown between writing and pronunciation. Our spelling indicates the pronunciation of the fifteenth, sixteenth, and seventeenth centuries. In many words the sound has changed, but the spelling has not, and all sorts of confusions have resulted: silent letters (de*b*t, si*g*n, give, wa*l*ked); two or more letters indicating a single sound (*th*is, ki*ck*, *ch*ip, wa*tch*, sma*sh*); two letters indicating the same sound (*a*ny, B*e*nny — bl*oo*d, m*u*d — *c*at, *k*it); the same letter indicating different sounds (m*ea*t, st*ea*k — *th*in, *th*en — n*o*t, n*o*te — *c*ent, *c*an't). And so on.

One must not conclude, however, that there is no connection between English sounds and English spelling. There is a connection, a system, though it is complicated and has many exceptions. Many spelling errors can be avoided if we pay some attention to the pronunciation of the words we are trying to spell.

For instance, the silent letter *e* in words like *hope, note, cape, same, bide, fine* does have a meaning; it indicates that the word is pronounced with a diphthong and not with a single vowel. Compare these:

not	/nat/	note	/nowt/	hop	/hap/	hope	/howp/
cap	/kæp/	cape	/keyp/	bid	/bid/	bide	/bayd/
Sam	/sæm/	same	/seym/	fin	/fin/	fine	/fayn/

Attention to this sound-symbol contrast will eliminate numerous serious spelling errors.

Similarly, a doubled consonant in words ending in *-ing, -ed, -able*, and other suffixes beginning with a vowel indicates a preceding simple vowel; an undoubled consonant indicates a diphthong:

knotted	/natɨd/	noted	/nowtɨd/
capper	/kæpɨr/	caper	/keypɨr/
sinned	/sind/	signed	/saynd/
dinner	/dinɨr/	diner	/daynɨr/
hopped	/hapt/	hoped	/howpt/

scrammed	/skræmd/	screamed	/skriymd/
written	/ritɨn/	writing	/raytɨŋ/
cappable	/kæpɨbɨl/	capable	/keypɨbɨl/

Even where neat patterns of this sort do not exist, many spelling errors can be avoided if one pays some attention to pronunciation. *Studying*, for example, is a three-syllable word: /stɔ́diyɨŋ/. Those who misspell it "studing" are treating it as if it had two syllables: /stɔdiŋ/. Those who misspell *persuade* as "presuade" should note that it begins /pɨr/ not /priy/ — that is, vowel-r, not r-vowel. *Similar* is pronounced /sɨ́mɨlɨr/; the misspelling "similiar" suggests /sɨ́mɨlyɨr/. *Pronunciation* is pronounced /prɨnənsiyéyšɨn/. The spelling "pronounciation" would suggest /prɨnawnsiyéyšɨn/. A careful sounding of words of whose spelling one is in doubt will solve many problems.

Only too frequently, of course, pronunciation is not a guide. Suffixes are particularly difficult, because sound changes have eliminated pronunciation distinctions in pairs like *–ible/–able*, *–ence/–ance*, *–ant/–ent*. Even here, however, attention to sounds can help. The ending of *different*, for example, can be inferred from the related *differential*. The ending of *capable* can be inferred from *capacity*.

The student who misspells *height* as "heighth" may have a somewhat different problem. More than likely he pronounces it /haytθ/ instead of /hayt/, which is more common in educated circles. He has then either to remember that he can't spell this word as he pronounces it or else change his pronunciation. Other words for which variant pronunciations often lead to misspellings include *athletics, library, whether, tremendous, particular, surprise, suppress, disastrous*.

MORPHOLOGY

Some spelling errors can be avoided if one notices the morphology of the word — that is, the parts of which it is made. For example, *disappoint* is clearly composed of the verb *appoint* plus the common prefix *dis*. Awareness of this should keep one from spelling *disappoint* with two *s*'s. On the other hand, *dissimilar* is made of *dis* plus *similar* and therefore has two *s*'s.

Many spelling errors result from a confusion of words containing an apostrophe and words spelled in *–s* with no apostrophe. The apostrophe has two meanings: it can indicate that something has been left out, that the form has been shortened, as in *can't, shouldn't, let's, they're;* or it can indicate the possessive form of nouns: *boy's, boys', man's, men's.* We write *'s* for the possessive singular of nouns and *s'* for the possessive plural of regular nouns. The ordinary plural is just *s* with no apostrophe: "The boys are sick," "The boy's dog is sick," "The boys' dog is sick."

Pronouns do not have an apostrophe in the possessive: *his, ours, theirs, yours, its. It's* is a contraction of *it is.*

In speech, regular noun plurals are formed by the addition of an /s/ sound (*cat, cats* /kæts/), a /z/ sound (*pig, pigs* /pigz/), or an /ɪz/ sound (*witch, witches* /wicɪz/). In writing, the /s/ and /z/ are normally both indicated by the letter *s* and the /ɪz/ by *es*. Some common words ending in *–o* add *es* to form the plural: *heroes, potatoes.* Words in *–o* that have come into the language recently, however, simply add *s: cameos, folios.*

When all the generalizations that can be made have been made, we are still left with a good many words for which only memory will serve. It need not be brute memory, however. Various tricks, or *mnemonic devices*, as they are called, can be enlisted to help. Perhaps the most famous of these is the rhyme used to straighten out words with *ie* or *ei*. The version the author learned as a child went *"i* before *e* except after *c* or when sounded like *ay* as in *neighbor* and *weigh."* This is a useful rule to which there are only an average number of exceptions: *either, neither, weird, inveigle, seize, leisure.*

MNEMONIC DEVICES

Mnemonic devices can be easily invented for any words one wishes to remember. The trick is to make an association, find a peg on which to hang what one wants to remember. This is the way all memory experts work. Suppose one can't remember whether to spell *separate* with *er* or *ar*. One says, "There's a rat in separate." Similarly a villain lives in a villa, the principal of the school is my pal (whereas a princip*le* is a ru*le*), *all right* is like *all wrong*.

The association doesn't have to be clever or even true. Imagine someone named Tim and think of him as optimistic. Think of the iron in *environment,* part of science in *conscientious.* One simply finds the point in the word at which one is going wrong and then finds some association to help fix the correct spelling in one's mind.

EXERCISE 70

Write the following words from dictation.

A. Words in which the problem is whether or not to double a final consonant.

1. dined	11. transferred	21. quizzes
2. occurrence	12. proved	22. exhibited
3. permitted	13. dinned	23. happening
4. stated	14. dropped	24. divided
5. write	15. bidding	25. biding
6. bitten	16. groping	26. sloppy
7. roping	17. plotted	27. hating
8. doped	18. planned	28. planed
9. appearance	19. knitting	29. refined
10. preference	20. governing	30. flaked

B. Words in which the problem is *ie* or *ei.*

1. receive	8. niece	15. siege
2. weight	9. neither	16. thief
3. ceiling	10. height	17. conceive
4. weird	11. foreign	18. fiend
5. yield	12. believe	19. friend
6. mischievous	13. deceive	20. relief
7. neighbor	14. chief	

C. Words in which variations in pronunciation may cause the trouble.

1. mischievous	6. hindrance	11. genius
2. athletics	7. wondrous	12. height
3. surprise	8. sophomore	13. strength
4. tremendous	9. nowadays	14. privilege
5. evidently	10. auxiliary	15. incidentally

D. Words that sound alike and others commonly confused.

1. affect	16. angel	31. your
2. effect	17. angle	32. principal
3. its	18. alter	33. principle
4. it's	19. altar	34. prophecy
5. there	20. bridal	35. prophesy
6. they're	21. bridle	36. stationary
7. their	22. formerly	37. stationery
8. forty	23. formally	38. hoard
9. fourth	24. choose	39. horde
10. compliment	25. chose	40. mantel
11. complement	26. decent	41. mantle
12. all right	27. descent	42. feint
13. already	28. whose	43. faint
14. council	29. who's	44. ingenious
15. counsel	30. you're	45. ingenuous

E. Words in which attention to the prefixes and suffixes is helpful.

1. disappoint	6. co-operate	11. coolly
2. hurriedly	7. dissatisfied	12. extraordinary
3. recommend	8. disease	13. handkerchief
4. government	9. definite	14. immediately
5. competition	10. drunkenness	15. irreligious

F. Miscellaneous difficulties.

1. absence	6. accompanying	11. acquaintance
2. accessible	7. accumulate	12. across
3. accidentally	8. ache	13. aggravate
4. accommodate	9. achievement	14. aisle
5. accompanist	10. acknowledge	15. alcohol

16. alley
17. always
18. amateur
19. among
20. analogous
21. answer
22. apiece
23. apparatus
24. apparent
25. appetite
26. arctic
27. arithmetic
28. around
29. arrangement
30. arrival
31. article
32. assistance
33. attacked
34. awkward
35. becoming
36. beggar
37. beneficial
38. bicycle
39. boundary
40. brilliant
41. bureau
42. business
43. busy
44. calendar
45. captain
46. cemetery
47. certain
48. changeable
49. characteristic
50. clothes
51. collar

52. colonel
53. comparative
54. compatible
55. competition
56. concede
57. confident
58. conquer
59. conscience
60. conscientious
61. conspicuous
62. correspondence
63. courageous
64. courteous
65. criticism
66. crowd
67. curiosity
68. curtain
69. dealt
70. deceased
71. decision
72. defendant
73. dependent
74. desirable
75. despair
76. desperate
77. destroyed
78. diary
79. dictionary
80. difference
81. dilapidated
82. diphthong
83. disastrous
84. discipline
85. dissipate
86. disturbance
87. doctor

88. dominant
89. drudgery
90. duly
91. during
92. earnest
93. ecstasy
94. eighth
95. embarrassed
96. eminent
97. emphasize
98. enthusiasm
99. environment
100. especially
101. etc.
102. exaggerate
103. exceed
104. excel
105. excellent
106. exercise
107. exhaust
108. exhilarate
109. existence
110. extremely
111. familiar
112. fascinating
113. feasible
114. February
115. fiery
116. finally
117. forcible
118. forehead
119. fourteen
120. fundamental
121. generally
122. ghost
123. grammar

124. grievous
125. guarantee
126. guidance
127. height
128. heroes
129. holy
130. horizontal
131. hypocrisy
132. hysterical
133. illiterate
134. imaginary
135. imminent
136. implement
137. incessantly
138. incidentally
139. incredulous
140. independence
141. indispensable
142. inevitable
143. inheritance
144. initiative
145. innocence
146. intelligence
147. intercede
148. interesting
149. irrelevant
150. irresistible
151. isthmus
152. knowledge
153. laboratory
154. ladies
155. legitimate
156. leisure
157. library
158. lieutenant
159. lightning

160. likelihood
161. literature
162. loneliness
163. loyalty
164. lying
165. magazine
166. maintenance
167. marriage
168. meant
169. medieval
170. Mediterranean
171. misspelled
172. mortgage
173. mountainous
174. murder
175. mysterious
176. naturally
177. necessarily
178. nevertheless
179. nickel
180. ninety
181. ninth
182. noticeable
183. obeyed
184. obstacle
185. occasion
186. o'clock
187. official
188. omission
189. opinion
190. opportunity
191. optimist
192. organization
193. origin
194. outrageous
195. paid

196. parallel
197. paraphernalia
198. parliament
199. participle
200. particularly
201. partner
202. pastime
203. perform
204. perhaps
205. permanent
206. permissible
207. perseverance
208. persistent
209. personally
210. personnel
211. perspiration
212. persuasion
213. phenomenon
214. physical
215. physician
216. platitude
217. playwright
218. potatoes
219. prairie
220. precede
221. preference
222. prejudice
223. procedure
224. proceed
225. professor
226. pronounce
227. pronunciation
228. psychology
229. publicly
230. pursue
231. really

232. recede
233. recognize
234. reference
235. regard
236. reign
237. reminisce
238. renaissance
239. rendezvous
240. repetition
241. requirement
242. reservoir
243. resistance
244. respectfully
245. restaurant
246. rhetoric
247. rhythm
248. ridiculous
249. sacrilegious
250. safety
251. scene
252. schedule
253. secede
254. secretary

255. sensible
256. separate
257. sequel
258. sergeant
259. severely
260. significance
261. similar
262. specimen
263. sponsor
264. statue
265. strength
266. superfluous
267. superintendent
268. supersede
269. syllable
270. synonym
271. temperament
272. tendency
273. thorough
274. tragedy
275. treacherous
276. trouble
277. twelfth

278. tyranny
279. undoubtedly
280. unnecessary
281. until
282. usage
283. usually
284. vacuum
285. valuable
286. vegetable
287. vengeance
288. vertical
289. village
290. villain
291. visibility
292. volume
293. warrior
294. weather
295. Wednesday
296. wholly
297. women
298. writer
299. wrought
300. yacht

APPENDIX: PRÉCIS WRITING

Obviously, improvement in writing — like improvement in singing or golf — comes mainly from practice. Instruction, analysis, correction — these are helpful and sometimes can be of crucial importance. But they won't make you a good writer. You can have the most expert and powerful instruction, you can analyze sentences and paragraphs until the cows come home, but unless you practice, you are like the would-be golfer who has read all the books on the stance, the grip, and the backswing but who has never picked up a club. If you want to be a good writer, the most important thing is to put three or four million words on paper.

So long as you write a lot, *what* you write doesn't make very much difference. You can keep a journal, or write letters or newspaper copy or a novel. But obviously more improvement can be expected from hard exercises than from easy ones. A kind of exercise useful for people going on to college is the writing of what is called the *précis*. A précis is simply a summary of a passage, perhaps a quarter or a third as long as the original. This is a practical kind of exercise because it is similar to the sort of writing demanded in general college work — taking notes, for example, or preparing reports or writing term papers. It calls for greater discipline and toughness and precision of thought and syntax than the personal or descriptive or narrative essay. If you can learn to write a good précis, you shouldn't have any trouble with simpler assignments, like "What I Did on My Vacation" or "What I Think About Fraternities."

A good précis must have several characteristics:

1. *It must be accurate.* Précis writing is practice in reading as well as in writing. You must read the passage to be summarized carefully, so that you know exactly what the author is saying. Clearly, the précis will be poor if it misses the point of the original. It will also be poor if it misses the emphasis of the original — if it subordinates or eliminates a chief point or if it overplays a minor item.

The general organization and levels of emphasis of the original passage should be carried in miniature into the summary.

2. *It must be economical.* The student's task is to shorten what may already be a tight piece of prose to, say, a third of its original length. There is no room for verbosity. One must search always for the most direct, most thrifty way of making the point. In all writing, economy of expression is a virtue, and précis writing is good practice because it forces economy. Some shortening can be achieved simply by omission of illustrative material of the original. Usually, however, some illustration must be retained or the point will not be clearly made.

3. *It must be originally phrased.* The opposite of original phrasing is plagiarism. This means setting forth as one's own writing what is somebody else's. Obviously in writing a summary, one must use much of the vocabulary of the original. But one must be careful not to appropriate the metaphors, the turns of phrase, the tricks of style which the author might reasonably consider his own creation. You must not only report accurately the essence of the passage, but you must report it in your own words. A summary which is just a patching together of lines and phrases from the original passage deserves a failing grade.

4. *It must be grammatical.* You will find that précis writing has many more grammatical traps than, say, simple narrative. The necessity for economical statement of sometimes difficult subjects invites one to make errors in predication, parallel structure, and in other matters discussed earlier in this book. You must expend some effort to be sure that all your structures are derived from grammatical basic patterns. You will find that even such mechanical matters as spelling and punctuation become a greater problem as the subject grows more difficult. This is another reason why précis writing is good practice.

For examples of good and bad and mediocre précis writing, here is a passage followed by four summaries of it, with comments on each of the summaries. It would be a good exercise to summarize the passage yourself before looking at the summaries, then to compare your own précis with them.

No picture of the time can be complete with its leading characters left out. The very centre and pivot of mediaeval society was the baronage. For the support of these men three-quarters of the nation laboured with toil and sweat; by their personal prowess the country's battles were decided; through their act kings' crowns were lost or won. Nor did their power rest solely upon the privilege of birth. A man of great character and grit was the successful baron, and the qualities he needed were little different from those which went to the making of a successful king. He had extensive lands and manors to administer; quarrels and disputes of all sorts to decide; soldiers to train and to command. As wealth was counted, he was wealthy, not in money, indeed, but in farms and stock and horses, in castles and instruments of war; for in those times a large landowner was as powerful as a millionaire, and a suit of mail armour was almost equivalent in value to a motor-car to-day. Luxury, however, was not among the baron's failings: his was no soft or idle life, the castle, or, as was now more usual, the stone-built manor house, in which he lived was comfortless and draughty, without glass in the windows or carpets on the floors. Privacy there was none, for the entire household lived, ate, and often slept in the single castle hall. Culture was rare, for outside the monasteries books were scarce and few but monks had either ability or taste to read them. The baron's energies (and they were boundless) found vent in other ways. Outdoor sport was his favourite occupation, and he was never happier than when flying his falcons or following the stag. And, did he crave more perilous excitements, he could take his fill in war. Adventure was the ruling passion of his life, and the biographies of many barons read less like sober history than like fairy-tales.* (326 words)

First summary:

The barons were the leading characters of the Middle Ages. They toiled and sweated to support the nation. In some ways the barons were more important than the kings. Being a baron did

* From *England: A History of British Progress from the Early Ages to the Present Day* by Cyril E. Robertson. Revised edition copyrighted 1939 by Thomas Y. Crowell Company, Publishers.

not depend on birth. Anybody could be a baron if he were strong
enough and had the necessary characteristics. These were great
character and grit. The baron was wealthy, though not as wealthy
as people are today. He usually could not afford glass in his windows or carpets on his floors, and he just had one room for the
entire family. Anyway he spent most of his time outdoors. Barons
liked to hunt and fish more than reading. They liked war best of
all. (118 words)

This is a poor summary chiefly because it is inaccurate. It gives
no clear idea of the original, and there are several plain misstate-
ments. It betrays poor reading — the reading of words rather than
sentences. For example, the idea that the barons toiled and sweated
to defend the nation — whether true or not — is not what the
author said. The part on the baron's wealth is largely confused.
Nothing is said in the original about fishing. Note the juvenile style
of the summary and the poor structure of the next to the last
sentence.

Second summary:

The baronage was the very center and pivot of medieval society. Their prowess decided the country's battles and
crowned the kings. Their power did not rest solely upon the privilege of birth. It rested on great character and grit. He had lands
and manors to administer and soldiers to train. As wealth counted,
he was wealthy, though not in money. Luxury was not the baron's
failing, for his was no soft and idle life. His castle was uncomfortable. Privacy there was none. Culture was rare, and the baron's
boundless energies found vent in other ways. He was never happier
than when falcon hunting or following the stag. Adventure was the
great passion of his life. (115 words)

The great and obvious fault of this summary is plagiarism. It is
but a piecing together of sentences and phrases of the original. The
changing of a few structure words, the substitution of an adjective
here and there, does not make it any less plagiarism. The tissue is
still the original author's, and it has been stolen from him. If one
cannot find any other way to express something important in the

original, then one must put the phrase or sentence in quotation marks. Though more accurate than the first summary, this one is less acceptable and deserves a failing grade. Note the errors in pronoun-antecedent agreement that have crept in.

Third summary:

The barons were among the most important person-ages of the Middle Ages, and certainly the most picturesque. They lived a life of great adventure and peril. Their wealth, though very great for those times and certainly the equivalent of a modern millionaire, nevertheless was no luxurious life. The baron's castle was very uncomfortable by modern standards. He didn't usually mind, however, because he spent all his time outdoors anyway, flying his falcons and hunting deer. When he wasn't doing that, he was usually engaged in war. One gets the impression that what barons liked most was adventure and in general having a good time. (104 words)

Though better than the first two, this summary is still not very good. It is more accurate than the first, and it is not plagiarized like the second, but it gives a somewhat false impression of the original paragraph. Dwelling more than the original does on the baron's love of adventure and play, it does not show sufficiently his serious sub-stance and importance. The last sentence is out of place. It is a comment on the original passage, not part of the summary. There are many faults in sentence structure, as in the third sentence.

Fourth summary:

The barons were the most important people of the Middle Ages. They personally fought the battles and often crowned the kings. It took more than birth to be a baron; he had also to be a man of courage, skill, and administrative ability. The baron was wealthy, as wealth of his time was measured, though he lived very miserably by modern standards, with little privacy and few house-hold comforts. The baron couldn't read or write, and most of his activities took place out of doors — flying falcons and hunting deer. If this didn't satisfy his adventurous spirit, he could always find more excitement in war. The lives of many barons "read less like sober history than like fairy tales." (117 words)

Though not flawless, this summary is clearly the best of the four. There are a few inaccuracies. The author did not actually say, for example, that barons couldn't read or write. But in general the summary is true to the original, reflecting its proportions and emphases as well as particular points. The style is reasonably mature, and considerable use is made of subordination devices. Note that the writer, unable to find a suitable paraphrase of the conclusion, properly included it in quotation marks.

Following the suggestions and directions above, write summaries of the following exercises as assigned by your teacher.

1. The pictorial weakness of the Elizabethan stage placed an added burden on the dramatist, and with it offered a literary opportunity. When the curtain rises in our theaters we *see* whether we are in Orsino's palace or on the Illyrian seashore and whether the hour is noon or midnight. Shakespeare had to set his stage with the words his actors spoke; and that allowed him glowing descriptive passages which are out of place in the theater where the carpenter, scene-painter, and electrician replace the poet. Carl Sandburg once declared, "Don't ask me how I write my poetry! I just take words and lay down a barrage hoping to create a mirage!" When Shakespeare wants to create a scenic mirage that is exactly what he does:

> Light thickens, and the crow
> Makes wing to th' rooky wood.
> Good things of day begin to droop and drowse,
> Whiles night's black agents to their preys do rouse.

No reliance on scenic materials can recapture that ominous crow. Shakespeare's plays reek with atmosphere. He uses it dramatically. We do not see it, but we feel it — which is the essential thing. In a modern play the electrician throws his switches, but never so effectively as when Horatio turns on the dawn in *Hamlet* at the end of a short scene that begins at midnight:

> But look, the morn, in russet mantle clad,
> Walks o'er the dew of yon high eastward hill.

Often, however, there is no need of specifying a scene's location or hour. It is needful for two characters to converse; it makes no difference where they talk — upstairs, downstairs, or in my lady's chamber, or in her garden, or on a city square. In such scenes the painstaking tags of the editors are really an impertinence. Few of the scenes are definitely placed by headings in the original texts. Many are deftly fixed by allusions in the dialogue, but some should be frankly tagged in modern editions "unlocated." When Shakespeare wants to give us an impression of time and place, he drops a hint or two into the speeches. He is writing a score for the players, and his control of the audience's impression is masterly and economical. He addresses it chiefly to ears, not eyes. Since his medium is, then, essentially sound, the modern reader should read him aloud; and the modern producer should cut away all the scenic lumber he dares, and stake the success of the play, as Shakespeare staked it, on well-spoken words.* (414 words)

2. The Presidency is the greatest constitutional office the world has known, a splendid chieftainship sought eagerly by just about every first-rate political figure in the nation, not to mention a horde of second-raters. The Vice-Presidency is a hollow shell of an office, an uncomfortable heir-apparency sought by practically no one we should like to see as President. It has perked up noticeably in the past eight years, but fundamentally it remains a disappointment in the American constitutional system.

The Vice-Presidency is one of our oldest problems. Some of the more astute members of the Convention of 1787 doubted that there was any need for a Vice-President, and Hamilton was forced to refute numerous criticisms of the office in *The Federalist*. There were apparently three reasons for creating the Vice-Presidency: to establish a constitutional heir for the President, to facilitate the selection of "continental characters" under the original electoral system, and to provide a presiding officer for the Senate not immediately devoted to the interests of any particular state. The framers also recognized the advantage of a moderator for this body with a deciding vote in the event of a tie. In general, they expected the office to be filled by the nation's number two political figure, the man who had polled the second highest number of votes in the presidential election.

* From *The Art and Life of William Shakespeare*, copyright 1940, by Hazelton Spencer. Reprinted by permission of Harcourt, Brace & World, Inc.

However cogent the reasons of the framers, and however high their expectations, the Vice-Presidency was a failure, and was recognized as such, almost from the outset. John Adams, the first to hold it, lamented that "my country has in its wisdom contrived for me the most insignificant office that ever the invention of man contrived or his imagination conceived." Thomas Jefferson, his successor, said something more meaningful than he realized when he described the "second office of government" as "honorable and easy," "the first" as "but a splendid misery." And several early statesmen referred to the Vice-President as "His Superfluous Excellency." The rise of the Federalist and Republican parties, the near disaster of the Jefferson-Burr election of 1800–1801, the consequent adoption of the Twelfth Amendment, and the establishment of the "Virginia Succession" all contributed to the decline of the office. The first two Vice-Presidents may have been John Adams and Thomas Jefferson, but the fifth and sixth were Elbridge Gerry and Daniel D. Tompkins; the seventh, John C. Calhoun, resigned to enter the Senate. And somewhere along the line there was a Vice-President named Throttlebottom — and a good one, too. Public men then, like public men today, apparently preferred misery with power to ease without it.* (427 words)

3. The Mexican insurgents would have been strangely unlike their kind if they had not coveted the mission lands. The California insurgents, who in turn declared themselves free of Mexico, were largely stirred by the same animating purpose; but they were late in the field. Both parties had a perfectly good and reasonable case to present to the world. The Indians were to be released from bondage. A modicum of land, with the necessary equipment, was to be assigned to each and all. They were to raise their own crops, live their own lives, and be free and self-respecting citizens. Here and there churches were to be open for their service. Something — very vaguely stated — was to be done for the maintenance of such friars as remained at their posts; perhaps a field or so reserved for their use (nine acres, for example, out of two thousand at San Carlos); but the livestock, the stored grain, the mills, the warehouses, everything that was remunerative outside the church walls was sold to fill the yawning pockets of patriots.

---

* From *The American Presidency*, © 1956, by Clinton Rossiter. Reprinted by permission of Harcourt, Brace & World, Inc.

What happened was inevitable; but it came to pass more quickly than even the least sanguine observer had anticipated. Perhaps the missionaries' system was ill adapted to the training of citizens. Perhaps nobody really expected that the Indians would respond to the incentive of independence, and become industrious, sober, and frugal. Idleness was in their blood; irresponsibility had been fostered by their training. The Franciscans, while enforcing systematic labor, had been careful never to overwork their wards and to give them recreation and holidays. Now it became imperative for them to extract a living out of their land, and to do this with one wife apiece, which was manifestly absurd. Their forefathers had had all the land they wanted, and wives enough to do the necessary work; they themselves had always been sure of their dinners; but in this comfortless freedom, which they had never sought or desired, nothing was secure.

Then came the discovery that liberty was more than a name. They were free to sell their few acres for a few dollars. . . .Those few dollars yielded a brief delight, followed by the direst want. The friars had no place to shelter them, no food to give them. Other friends they had none. The amazing thing is the speed with which they died. They had always been a delicate race. That toughness of fibre which made the five Iroquois tribes a lasting wonder to the French *habitants* had no counterpart among the California Indians. Even in the missions the death rate was high, which accounts for the crowded churchyards. Under the new conditions they wandered away or fell by the roadside, and no one mourned their going. Of the thirty thousand natives, sober, temperate, and reasonably industrious, who filled the missions in 1810, hardly three thousand were left by the middle of the century. The survivors were the least fortunate of their race.* (504 words)

4. The Greeks understood philosophy to be an organized system of all man's knowledge of the world. There were subdivisions in it, of course. There were philosophies of nature, of ethics, of politics, of logic, of the "soul," of the heavenly bodies, and indeed of medicine. Moreover, a single man, if he had sufficient opportunity for study, could hope to speak authoritatively on all these subjects. Plato, for example, seems at least twice to have condensed

---

* From *Junipero Serra* by Agnes Repplier. Copyright 1933 by Agnes Repplier. Reprinted by permission of Doubleday & Company, Inc.

within the limits of one work his entire range of knowledge and conjecture. Aristotle's collected works are a kind of one-man encyclopedia.

Such glories are no longer possible, for there is much too much to be known. Nowadays, a biologist, for example, not only does not know all of science, but he does not even know all of biology. He knows only his own "field" — botany, perhaps, or parasitology or genetics — and possibly but a section of that. It looks like a deliberate narrowing of range. The converse, however, is true: it is not that the scientist's individual range is narrowed, but that the total range of knowledge has grown inconceivably vast. The scientist's mind is still stretched to capacity, but he just can't get all of science into it. The bottle which once held all man's knowledge of the world is now as a pint to an ocean.

I know that it is fashionable to cry down specialization and to cry up the merit of "broad views," to depreciate analysis and excessively appreciate synthesis. But, unless I am much mistaken, the loudest admirers of broad views possess views which are broad but empty, and the most zealous advocates of synthesis have (in the absence of analysis) nothing which they can synthesize. A scientist, being forced to specialize if he is to know anything in detail, can surrender his specialty only on pain of surrendering also all the knowledge he has, together with the further knowledge he may get.

The fact of specialization indicates triumph, not defeat. It proves the immensity of man's knowledge, not the poverty of it. And just as I think we cannot regret this fact when it holds for individual men, so I think we cannot regret it when it holds for individual disciplines. The long centuries during which philosophy embraced all the knowledge there was (and there wasn't much) gave way to a time when the young sciences, leaving the ancestral home, took what they needed and left the rest to philosophers. Thus "natural philosophy" became physics, chemistry, astronomy, and so forth; "political philosophy" became sociology; and "mental philosophy" became psychology. This last occurred as recently as forty years ago, amid the most horrid clamor of threats and imprecations and a free distribution of wounds, which are even yet not altogether healed.

Historically speaking, the content of philosophy is what is left over after the sciences departed. Nobody took ethics, not even the sociologists; nobody took logic; nobody took esthetics; nobody took (for who would want?) metaphysics. These subjects, therefore, remain part of philosophy's content, despite the fact that the mathematicians eye logic covetously and the gentlemen of the fine arts would like to ravish esthetics. The subjects themselves, I am happy to report, have thus far resisted all blandishments.* (540 words)

5. It will be well here to consider the manner in which languages and the teaching of languages were generally viewed during the centuries preceding the rise of comparative linguistics. The chief language taught was Latin; the first and in many cases the only grammar with which scholars came into contact was Latin grammar. No wonder therefore that grammar and Latin grammar came in the minds of most people to be synonyms. Latin grammar played an enormous role in the schools, to the exclusion of many subjects (the pupil's own native language, science, history, etc.) which we are now beginning to think more essential for the education of the young. The traditional term for "secondary school" was in England "grammar school" and in Denmark *latinskole*, and the reason for both expressions was obviously the same. Here, however, we are concerned with this privileged position of Latin grammar only in so far as it has influenced the treatment of languages in general. It did so in more ways than one.

Latin was a language with a wealth of flexional forms, and in describing other languages the same categories as were found in Latin were applied as a matter of course, even where there was nothing in these other languages which really corresponded to what was found in Latin. In English and Danish grammars paradigms of noun declension were given with such cases as accusative, dative, and ablative, in spite of the fact that no separate forms for these cases had existed for centuries. All languages were indiscriminately saddled with the elaborate Latin system of tenses and moods in the verbs, and by means of such Procrustean methods the actual facts of many languages were distorted and misrepresented. Discriminations which had no foundation in reality were nevertheless insisted on, while discriminations which happened to be nonexistent in Latin were apt to be overlooked. The mischief conse-

* From *Man Against Myth*, by Barrows Dunham. Copyright 1947, Little, Brown & Company. Reprinted by permission of Barrows Dunham.

quent on this unfortunate method of measuring all grammar after the pattern of Latin grammar has not even yet completely disappeared, and it is even now difficult to find a single grammar of any language that is not here and there influenced by the Latin bias.

Latin was chiefly taught as a written language (witness the totally different manner in which Latin was pronounced in the different countries, the consequence being that as early as the sixteenth century French and English scholars were unable to understand each other's spoken Latin). This led to the almost exclusive occupation with letters instead of sounds. The fact that all language is primarily spoken and only secondarily written down, that the real life of language is in the mouth and ear and not in the pen and eye, was overlooked, to the detriment of a real understanding of the essence of language and linguistic development; and very often where the spoken form of a language was accessible scholars contented themselves with a reading knowledge. In spite of many efforts, some of which go back to the sixteenth century, but which did not become really powerful till the rise of modern phonetics in the nineteenth century, the fundamental significance of spoken as opposed to written language has not yet been fully appreciated by all linguists. There are still too many writers on philological questions who have evidently never tried to think in sounds instead of thinking in letters and symbols, and who would probably be sorely puzzled if they were to pronounce all the forms that come so glibly to their pens.* (579 words)

   6. What really troubles [the European critic of America] is something which he is not able to put into words and which the American has never felt any need to analyze because it is not, in his own experience, a paradox. That something is simply this: materialism and stinginess, thinks the European, inevitably go together — and in his experience they usually have. But generosity and materialism are not at all incompatible — as the whole panorama of the American temperament abundantly demonstrates. We are not materialists in the sense that we love money for its own sake. We are not misers. We are spendthrifts who lavish wealth on ourselves, on our families, on our fellow citizens, and nowadays on the inhabitants of the four quarters of the globe. But we are ma-

* From *Language,* by Otto Jesperson. Used by permission of The Macmillan Company, and George Allen & Unwin, Ltd.

terialists — generous materialists — in the very simple sense that we believe everything worth having can be had if we are willing to spend enough money to get it.

Nearly everything which makes American life both richer and poorer, both better and worse, than life in any other civilized community ever has been before goes back to the virtues and limitations of this generous materialism. We believe, for example, in education — more passionately and more uncritically than any nation ever believed in it before. We believe in it so thoroughly that we are willing to spend prodigious amounts of public funds. In nearly every American community, citizens vote to tax themselves at higher and higher rates to pay for the education of other people's children. But there are few to whom it ever occurs that putting more money into schools is not a sure way of getting more education, or that any deficiencies which happen to become manifest will not be remedied by putting more into school buildings. Being convinced that you cannot have what you refuse to pay for makes us generous; believing that you will get what you pay for, or at least that if you don't there is no other way of getting it, constitutes materialism.

Your true American never misses an opportunity to make money. He assumes that no one else does either. Perhaps, therefore, we actually are more devoted to the pursuit of the dollar than most other nations are to their pounds, francs, or marks. But we are not particularly anxious to hold on to it when we catch it. Acquisitiveness, not miserliness, is our vice. We are very ready to forgive a man for doing whatever is necessary to make a profit. We are quite resigned, to take small examples, to having the symphony concert interrupted by a commercial or the highway disfigured by billboards. We do not expect anyone to forgo a profit even if making it annoys everybody else. But we expect the profiteer to give generously to charity and to vote for public improvements which will cost him much more than he personally will ever get out of them.

The American is not being hypocritical when he tells you that he is frantically making money because he wants his children to "have all the advantages." He does. And he will spend freely the money he has made to buy these advantages; even, not seldom, to buy some of them for other people's children as well. He is not a materialist in the sense of being one who believes that education, travel, fun, even "culture" are foolish frills. But he is a materialist in the sense that he is quite sure no child can have "advantages" without having money to pay for them, and almost as sure that if he does have money to pay he will get the "advantages." Thoreau thought money not required to buy one necessary of the soul. The typical American believes that no necessary of the soul is free, and that there are few, if any, which cannot be bought.* (647 words)

7. You need not be a spy-story addict nowadays to know that there are experts skilled in breaking down cryptograms without already having the key. How can they ever be sure they have the right answer? If they build up for themselves a kind of skeleton key, how do they know it fits? After all, with ordinary physical locks and keys, there is a click, and the hinges swing open. But in a cipher there are no clicks and no hinges.

Nevertheless, there are ways of knowing whether one has found the solution. The experienced cryptologist looks for two things, and they are equally important. First, the plain-text solution must make sense, in whatever language it is supposed to have been written; it must be grammatical ("Hearts green slow mud" would not do) and it must mean something ("Pain is a brown Sunday" would not do either). It does not matter whether what the solution says is true or not; it may be a pack of lies, but that is not the cryptologist's business. The important thing is that it must say something, and say it intelligibly.

This is perhaps obvious; the second demand the cryptologist makes is less so. Not only does the answer have to obey the rules of grammar and the laws of logic; the cipher system and the specific key also have to obey certain rules. We have already mentioned a few of the basic requirements of cipher systems, and we are still discussing cipher systems, so they still apply. Without reassuring himself that the system he has been using is a valid one, the cryptanalyst cannot be sure he has found the right answer. Without checking that the key or sequence of keys he has reconstructed can be used reasonably, precisely, and without ambiguity, there is still room for doubt.

But if there is rhyme and reason about the way he has reached the solution, if the system really is a rational and consistent sys-

---

* From *Human Nature and the Human Condition*, by Joseph Wood Krutch. © Copyright 1959 by Joseph Wood Krutch. Reprinted by permission of Random House, Inc.

tem, the keys really keys, and if when they are rigorously applied they produce a plain text which is really a text, he can begin to take himself seriously. The point must be reached where he begins to feel that the whole thing did not and could not happen by accident. But it is not simply a matter of his *feeling* this; the assessment can be far more rigorous. The mathematical theory of probability can be applied, and the chances calculated exactly. If the cryptanalyst finds a certain key, and (on the basis of the way it is built up) he calculates that the chances of its appearing by accident are one in one thousand million, his confidence in the solution will be more than justified. On the other hand, if he thinks he has found a key, and then works out that it can turn up by accident fifty times in a hundred, his confidence ought to be shaken. For then he can no longer be sure that the key was put there by anybody at all; it is just as likely to have happened by chance.

Getting a correct solution is not a matter of the cryptanalyst's thinking he has done the trick; it is not a question of opinion, but a question of proof. No solution can be taken as valid simply because the cryptanalyst says it is; he must in addition be able to show others that it is the right one. His demonstration must be unbiased, systematic, and logically sound; it must be free from appeals to insight, clear of guesswork, and should avoid imponderables like the plague; in a word, it must be scientific.* (694 words)

8. Not everyone realizes how much death rates have been reduced in recent times. Two hundred years ago a newborn child could look forward on the average to only thirty-five or forty years of life, even in the countries where conditions of health were most favorable. Estimates for former times, including calculations of the life expectancy in medieval Europe, ancient Greece and Egypt, and in prehistoric times, show a still more dismal picture of early death. At present the expectation of life in many countries exceeds sixty-five years and all over the world it is being lengthened, thanks mainly to a great reduction in the number of children who die in infancy. This progress of death control is one of the most important achievements of the modern age. It is without any precedent in the past, and it has a powerful effect on the population trend.

Major reductions of death rates were first recorded in the vital

---

* From *The Shakespearean Ciphers Examined*, by William F. and Elizabeth Friedman, copyright, 1957. Reprinted by permission of Cambridge University Press.

statistics of various countries in northwestern Europe early in the nineteenth century. There were probably substantial reductions during the eighteenth century also, before the national systems of birth and death registration were established in most of the countries concerned. The trend was quickly communicated to the more prosperous areas of European settlement overseas, and subsequently, to the countries of southern and eastern Europe. With minor interruptions, it has continued ever since; the average death rate today for European countries — around 10 deaths annually per 1,000 population — is less than one third of what it was in the early nineteenth century.

The initial effect on the population of Europe was a veritable mushrooming. The birth rates at first remained almost unchanged while the death rates fell. It has been estimated that between 1750 and 1900 the population of Europe and its emigrant offshoots overseas multiplied nearly fourfold.

The phase of rapid growth in the European population was finally brought to an end by falling birth rates. By 1900 the small-family idea was well established in the leading industrial countries of western, northern, and central Europe, and also in the United States, Canada, Australia, and New Zealand. Thirty years later the number of births in many of these countries was no longer sufficient to replace the population permanently, and their governments were beginning to consider the need for vigorous measures to avoid the threat of depopulation. That threat has now disappeared, at least for the time being, thanks to a revival of birth rates. But Europe still appears on the world map as a region of low human fertility, and its rate of population growth is now only about one half the world rate. The United States, Canada, Australia, New Zealand, and the Soviet Union have somewhat higher birth rates; their rate of increase is about the same as the world average, or slightly higher.

Any slackening of world population which might have been caused by lower birth rates in Europe was more than offset by falling death rates in other parts of the world, where birth rates were still high. The progress of death control in Latin America, Asia, and Africa has been most remarkable during the last few decades. Latin America as a whole now has a death rate not much higher than the average for Europe. The effect of this combined with the high birth rate of the Latin American peoples is to make

Latin America the fastest-growing region of the world today. Most countries in that region have recently been adding to their population rates between 2 and 3 per cent per annum, that is, about twice the world average. The same is true of many countries in Asia and Africa: Egypt, Turkey, Ceylon, and the Philippines, for example.

In other Asian and African countries, the population is growing more slowly at present, not because they have lower birth rates than the countries above, but because they have higher death rates. Consider India as an example. The death rate in that country at present is two or three times as high as in the United States. Even with a birth rate far above the world average, the population of India grows at a comparatively modest rate — somewhere between 1 per cent and $1\frac{1}{2}$ per cent per year.* (703 words)

9. Perhaps, however, the intellectual work most characteristic of Restoration England is to be sought not so much in literature as in science. English science, in fact, may properly be said to date from the epoch of the civil wars. The great discoveries of the previous century, made under the first impulse of Renaissance learning, had for the most part been the work of foreign thinkers, such as the two astronomers, Galileo of Pisa and Kepler the German. With the Stuarts, however, Englishmen too began to join the quest for truth. Chemistry became a fashionable hobby. Raleigh and Prince Rupert dabbled in it. Even Charles II was touched by the craze; and it was he who, in 1662, presented its original charter to the so-called Royal Society, a club formed "for the promotion of psycho-mathematical experimental learning." Among its members was numbered the great genius Sir Isaac Newton, whose studies first revealed the Law of Gravitation and the threefold composition of white light. Natural laws, which earlier theorists had but guessed at, were now tested and applied by practical experiment. The circulation of the blood, first announced by Harvey in King James' reign, was now examined microscopically and the blood-vessels detected. Aided by such research as this, medical science forged ahead. Careful collection of botanical and zoological specimens were made. The tides, the theory of magnetism, and the motion of comets were investigated by Halley and others. In 1675 Green-

---

* From *Population and World Politics*, by Philip M. Hauser, copyright, 1958. Reprinted by permission of The Free Press of Glencoe, Illinois.

wich Observatory was built; and thus in a hundred ways the foundations of modern scientific progress were laid down.

Nor was the spread of this scientific spirit without its influence on everyday affairs. Merchants began to organise their business on more systematic lines. Finance was studied more intelligently, and methods of banking were copied from the Dutch. Agriculture, too, began to benefit by the invention of new implements and new manures. We seem, in fact, to be passing into an atmosphere more closely resembling the age of modern civilization. Newspapers become more numerous and more ambitious, though indeed their news, still printed upon a single sheet, would scarcely fill a column of "The Times". Material comforts rapidly increase. Houses are planned with a keener eye to domestic conveniences; and the man of moderate means now learns to build himself a dwelling far snugger and more practical than the spacious and unhomelike mansions of the great. Furniture-making becomes an art which considers usefulness rather than mere necessity or show. Instead of the cumbersome and uncomfortable chairs of Elizabethan and Cromwellian times, we find chairs with slender legs and nicely rounded backs. Increasing trade brings useful commodities from overseas; and mahogany will soon oust oak as the favourite material of the upholsterer. Tea becomes a fashionable beverage, and "coffee-houses" are the regular rendezvous of the idle and the "wits," and though the fastidious man of taste is partial to peppering his nose with snuff, many prefer to smoke the tobacco from Virginia. We even find Mr. Samuel Pepys, Clerk to His Majesty's Board of the Admiralty, noting in a private diary the extravagant and burdensome expenditure of his wife upon new hats. Most assuredly we are approaching to the modern age.

Yet we must not imagine that Restoration England led an altogether secure and comfortable life. Man's mastery over nature was still very far from complete. Travelling, for instance, was at best a very tedious, and at worst a perilous, adventure. The roads were vile. Their central track of supposedly firm ground was often bordered by a quagmire of churned mud some feet in depth, and woe betide the unskilful driver who got bogged in it. A coach which set out with a team of less than six was flying in the face of Providence; and even so there were other and worse risks to be run than mud. Bridges were none too numerous; and after rain the fords were frequently impassable. Tragedies of vehicles engulfed and passengers drowned in their seats were far from rare. Then, too, the dreary wastes of unpoliced and unpopulated moorland through which the unhappy traveller needs must pass afforded a golden opportunity for crime. Highwaymen held up coaches even in broad daylight, stripped the "fares" of their belongings, and so success-fully evaded the weak arm of the law that whole districts continued for years to lie at the mercy of their depredations. Even in the Capital itself the man who ventured in the streets by night was seldom safe. Footpads and ruffian soldiers lurked in dark corners to waylay passers-by. The city watchmen, though increased, were still inadequate. Till 1684 street lamps were unknown; and only the rich could afford the luxury of an attendant "linksman" to light the passage of their sedan-chair through the ill-laid and un-illuminated streets.* (790 words)

---

* From *England: A History of British Progress from the Early Ages to the Present Day* by Cyril E. Robertson. Revised edition copyrighted 1939 by Thomas Y. Crowell Company, Publishers.

INDEX

Note to the student: Page references in boldface type indicate important discussions of a topic. References followed by **S** (for example, **99S**) indicate that a term is defined in the Summary of Terms on that page. Italicized references followed by an italic *n* (for example, *66n*) indicate that an entry is discussed in a footnote. Many incidental references to such words as sentence, grammar, language, etc., have been omitted from this Index.

C 2
D 3
E 4
F 5
G 6
H 7
I 8
J 9
K 0
L 1